BREAKING
the BONDAGE *of*
LEGALISM

NEIL T. ANDERSON
RICH MILLER
PAUL TRAVIS

HARVEST HOUSE™ PUBLISHERS

EUGENE, OREGON

Cover by Terry Dugan Design, Minneapolis, Minnesota

Cover photo © Craig van der Lende/Getty Images

BREAKING THE BONDAGE OF LEGALISM

Copyright © 2003 by Neil T. Anderson, Rich Miller, and Paul Travis
Published by Harvest House Publishers
Eugene, Oregon 97402
www.harvesthousepublishers.com

Library of Congress Cataloging-in-Publication Data

Anderson, Neil T., 1942-
  Breaking the bondage of legalism / Neil T. Anderson, Rich Miller, Paul Travis.
    p. cm.
  Includes bibliographical references (p.   ).
  ISBN 0-7369-1181-2
  1. Spiritual warfare. I. Miller, Rich, 1954-   II. Travis, Paul, 1933-   III. Title.
  BV4509.5.A5232 2003
  241.5—dc21   2003004364

*How can we ever give thanks enough
to our loving heavenly Father
for giving us the gift of our
wonderful wives—Joanne, Shirley, and Joyce?
In addition to all that they are and do every day,
they also stood with us steadfastly in prayer, love,
encouragement, and service as we researched
and wrote this book.
It was not easy for them.*

*It is a very small token of our great love for them,
but we dedicate this book to these three precious ladies,
to the praise of God's glorious grace in Christ Jesus.*

—Neil, Rich, and Paul

A Word from Author Steve McVey

Breaking the Bondage of Legalism is one of the best books on the characteristics and cure for legalism that I've read! It will challenge you to think about the way that legalistic influences have affected your life and will clearly lead you down the path to freedom. Now and then, a book comes along that covers all the bases—and this is one of them. It caused me to laugh at times, to repent at times and, all along the way through its pages, to thank my Father for the freedom He offers us from stale religion that focuses primarily on performance. Get this book. You won't be disappointed!

—Steve McVey
President of Grace Walk Ministries
and author of *Grace Walk, Grace Rules*
and *A Divine Invitation*

Acknowledgments

First, we want to thank our friends at Harvest House Publishers for their love for Jesus and for us. They have all been a great encouragement through the process of birthing this book. We want to especially thank Paul Gossard for his kindness, patience, and efficiency in editing. He is a true servant.

We also want to thank our dear friend Sally Jenkins for her special support and meaningful suggestions, most of which are included in this book.

We are also deeply grateful for David and Vickie Dort, who were waiting with a cup of cold water at each "mile marker" of this marathon project. Their encouragement and prayers gave us strength to keep going and to finish strong.

Finally, we want to say "thank you" to the many people who shared their journeys out of legalism with us. Though there was not room in the book for everyone's story, each one touched us personally. We trust that this book will shine light on your path as you continue moving from law into grace...from performance into freedom in Christ.

Contents

FROM RULES
TO RELATIONSHIP

The National Prisoner of War Museum located at the Andersonville (Georgia) National Historic Site is a monument to pain and suffering. My (Rich's) trip there was sobering. My friends and I mostly walked around in silence, reflecting on the nightmare of life and death in that place. Only this nightmare was real. Having watched the film *Andersonville*, I was somewhat acquainted with the horrors of this Civil War prison. But that had been in the safety of my living room. There was something deeply disturbing about being there in person.[1]

During the 14 months of its operation, the Andersonville military prison (which was designed for 10,000 men at a maximum) saw nearly 50,000 Union soldiers incarcerated there during the war. At one point, 33,000 were crammed into the 27-acre camp. As a result of poor medical care, malnutrition, lack of sanitation, overcrowding, and exposure to the elements, more than 13,000 men perished there.

A surgeon testifying at the postwar trial of camp commandant Henry Wirz said, "The haggard, distressed countenances of these miserable, complaining, dejected, living skeletons… formed a picture of helpless, hopeless misery which it would be impossible to portray by words or by brush."

The horrific conditions within the camp brought out both the best and the worst in the prisoners. Some reached out with love and mercy. But others betrayed one another, stealing from each other, even killing fellow soldiers.

After an hour or so of walking through the camp and reading the stories of what took place there, I started feeling physically ill (as did my companions). We got in our cars, prayed, and left quickly. Though our bodies felt better almost immediately, the memories have been much slower to fade.

As cruel and heartless as physical bondage can be, spiritual bondage is worse. And for that reason, in this book we want to throw open the doors of another kind of prisoner-of-war camp—one that is not so physically repulsive, but which is spiritually deadly. It is a "camp" where joy is stolen, faith is sometimes killed, and hope is often destroyed.

It is called *legalism*.

We have titled this book *Breaking the Bondage of Legalism* and have subtitled it *When Trying Harder Isn't Enough*. The meaning of the title may not be clear to you yet (we'll explore the meaning of the word "legalism" in chapter 1), but we are fairly certain the subtitle strikes a strong chord of recognition in your heart. It may very well be why you are reading this book. You've tried hard, harder, hardest to live the Christian life…and it simply hasn't worked for you.

This subtitle reminds us of the epitaph on the tombstone of a certain newspaper journalist: "I tried my best, but it wasn't good enough." And unfortunately, that could be the heart cry of countless believers in Christ across this nation—a silent heart cry that only God hears. Maybe that's the condition you find yourself in today. Perhaps it's a loved one of yours who is suffering. If so, we want to bring you hope. First of all, we want to tell you that you are not alone…not by a long shot. On the pages of this book you will read the stories of many different people who have suffered in a variety of ways from legalistic systems.

Our Shocking Findings

In preparation for the writing of this book, we contracted with the George Barna Research Group to conduct a nationwide survey of adults. We were trying to find out how widespread legalism is in the American church. This December 2002 survey, "Christian Beliefs about Spiritual Life and the Church," asked people to respond to six different statements (presented in random order) with "strongly agree," "somewhat agree," "somewhat disagree," "strongly disagree," or "don't know." Sadly, it verified statistically what we had already suspected: Christians in America are seriously infected with the spiritual disease of legalism.

Trying Hard...

One of the six survey statements was, *The Christian life is well summed-up as "trying hard to do what God commands."* How would you respond to that statement? Is that what the Christian life is all about—doing our best and trying hard to keep God's commandments? You may be vigorously nodding your head right now. If so, you would be in the majority, for 57 percent of respondents strongly agreed and 25 percent somewhat agreed (for a total of 82 percent in agreement).

There is only one problem with that statement's summary of the Christian life: *It is very wrong.*

Shocked? The Christian life is not, and never has been, a human effort to obey God's commands in the Bible. That deception, as you'll see from reading this book, is a very popular form of legalism—a performance-based Christianity that opposes the truth that apart from Christ we can do "nothing" (John 15:5).

The other serious misunderstanding this survey statement brings to the surface is this: For most believers, apparently, the Christian life is much more about *doing* than *being*. For them this life involves a striving to avoid sin and do right more than pursuing an intimate, personal relationship with God. And, sadly, only 16 percent of those who responded thought there was enough wrong with the first survey statement to say they disagreed. But would not the Christian life be much better summed up as *a personal faith-relationship with God the Father through abiding in His Son, Jesus Christ, and walking in loving obedience to His Word through the person and power of the Holy Spirit?* The Christian life is first and foremost a relationship, not rules!

...But Not Measuring Up

In light of the response we received from the first statement, it should not be surprising that a majority of respondents (58 percent) said they agreed (28 percent strongly, 30 percent somewhat) with the second statement we want to look at: *I feel like I don't measure up to God's expectations of me.*

If the Christian life is "trying hard to do what God commands" (as a majority believe), the results of the second statement show us that people don't feel like they're doing a very good job of it. But what would we expect? Just knowing what God expects us to do doesn't give us the power to do it. Certainly, the law makes clear the power of sin over us—but it provides us no power to overcome that sin (see Romans 7:8-11)!

It is obvious that many believers in Christ are living with some degree of guilt. Striving hard but not measuring up. Some are very likely struggling with their concept of God, believing that He is scrutinizing their every move with a constant scowl of disapproval and thinking, *When will they ever get their act together?*

Rigid Rules, Strict Standards

Where are believers in Christ getting this message that the Christian life is summarized by "trying hard to do what God commands"? Research reveals that the burden of responsibility lies primarily on the church. The third survey statement was, *Rigid rules and strict standards are an important part of the life and teaching of my church.*

We worded this one carefully, even using words that people normally shy away from—*rigid, strict*—in order to give congregations the benefit of the doubt. Still, despite that effort, 39 percent of those who responded said they strongly agreed with that statement, and 27 percent said they somewhat agreed. *We were stunned.*

This means that two-thirds of Christians surveyed (from a broad spectrum demographically and denominationally) view their churches as being heavily into rules and standards. That is not good news for modern man!

We recognize, of course, that many churches are doing well in communicating the gospel of grace, both to unbelievers and to believers. People in these congregations are generally healthy because they are being nurtured on God's grace and truth in Christ. But the evidence still stands. Either most churches are not truly preaching and teaching grace...or the people in the pews are just not getting it.

About this time you might be *really* nodding your head in agreement. Or maybe you are about to throw this book and these survey results in the fireplace. Before we tell you the second half of the survey results, which does have some good news, we want to assure you that the researchers' efforts to ascertain the truth were painstaking. The results are indeed valid. (If you'd like to know more on how the survey was conducted, see the information in the appendix.) One thing we would like to note here, however, is that the cooperation rate during the survey was 81 percent. This is unusually high (the industry norm is about 60 percent), so it significantly raises the confidence we may place in the resulting statistics.

Love and Acceptance

Now for some better news. The fourth survey statement we'd like to consider is, *People at my church are unconditionally loved and accepted regardless of how they look or what they do.* Seventy-seven percent gave their church high marks in this regard, and that is encouraging.* It should concern us though, that nearly one out of five (19 percent) who responded do not view their churches as doing a very good job of welcoming people who are different. Philip Yancey speaks to this in his autobiographical book, *Soul Survivor:*

> One church I attended during my formative years in Georgia of the 1960s presented a hermetically sealed view of the world. A sign out front proudly proclaimed our identity with words radiating from a many-pointed star: "New Testament, Blood-bought, Born-again, Premillenial, Dispensational, Fundamental..." Our little group of two hundred people had a corner on truth, God's truth, and everyone who disagreed with us was surely teetering on the edge of hell.[2]

Churches like this one (and they're still around today) are not just broadcasting what they believe—but they are stiff-arming the people in the rest of the world who believe differently. But Jesus said, "By this all men will know that you are My disciples, if you have love for one another" (John 13:35).

Years later, Yancey attended the "burial service" of that church (which was, ironically, selling its building to an African–American congregation):

> During the expanded service, a procession of people stood and testified how they had met God through this church. Listening to them, I imagined a procession of those not present, people like my brother, who had turned away from God in large part because of this church. I now viewed its contentious spirit with pity, whereas in adolescence it had pressed life and faith out of me. The

---

* According to the demographic data, those who have been divorced, older people (age 56 and up), Southerners, and weekly attenders were well-pleased with this aspect of their church life. Busters (age 18–36), nonwhites, and Midwesterners were not so favorably disposed.

church had now lost any power over me; its stinger held no more venom. But I kept reminding myself that I had nearly abandoned the Christian faith in reaction against this church, and I felt deep sympathy for those who had.[3]

Give Jesus One More Chance

We feel the same sympathy that Philip Yancey does. We earnestly desire to see those who have turned their backs on Christ and the church to glance over their shoulders just one more time...to believe somehow that the winsome Person found in the pages of the Gospels still lives on in His church today. In this book we will expose and diagnose the bondage of legalism, but our ultimate purpose is to point people caught in legalism to the Lord Jesus Christ, the One who came filled with grace and truth.

Our Lord and His apostle to the Gentiles, Paul, reserved their strongest, harshest indictments for the hypocrites who were perpetuating and proliferating religious legalistic systems. Jesus spoke, and Paul wrote passionately, to defend and rescue those who were ensnared by them.

In this book we have prayed and sought to be hard-hitting in revealing the spiritual wasteland of legalism. But conversely, we have prayed and sought to be gentle and caring toward those people wounded by legalistic systems. And most of all, we have sought to direct people to Christ.

This was a challenging book for us to write. While decrying the sin of self-righteousness, it is so easy to become self-righteous. And it is easy to cross the line and become judgmental while preaching against judgmentalism.

I (Rich) can be very quick to point out the sin in those around me. But when, for instance, I am angry at my children for being messy, am I as quick to recognize my own harsh and critical spirit with them?

After all, which is worse? Sinful behavior on the part of someone who may not even be a believer...or a proud, critical spirit on the part of someone who is? We so often love to wag a gnarly finger at sins we can see, but it is "sin under the skin" that is most repugnant to God. Not until we are willing to repent of our legalism and weep over another person's sinful condition are we ready to intercede for them in prayer.

That's why I'm so glad that Paul Travis, a "recovering fundamentalist" (Neil's term), has graciously allowed his testimony to pepper significant portions of this book. More than that, however, his heart for those trapped in legalism beats on every page. He genuinely hurts for even the staunchest legalists (even though he has been hurt *by* them), and his concern is genuine, his compassion real, his humility disarming.

Look for the Unshakable

As challenging as it was for us to write this book, it may be even more disturbing for you to *read* it. No, there's nothing harmful in here—this is a book about healing spiritual wounds. But if you have lived under the yoke of slavery to legalism, there will be some parts of this book you will find unsettling. And that can be a very good thing if it brings you to a new experience of freedom and grace in Christ.

The writer of Hebrews warned that in latter times "[God] has promised, saying, 'Yet once more I will shake not only the earth, but also the heaven.' This expression, 'Yet once more,' denotes the removing of those things which can be shaken, as of created things, so that those things which cannot be shaken may remain" (Hebrews 12:26-27). But by God's grace, once those "shaky" things are removed, what we're left with is unshakable—the kingdom of God (verse 28). And we trust God that, deep down, that is what you truly want.

Where We're Headed

The first half of this book, which we call "The Lies That Bind," is diagnostic. In it we are seeking to expose the lies of legalism so we can understand how they keep us from experiencing the joy of our salvation.

Chapter 1 opens with part of the life story of Paul Travis, using it as a launching point to define and describe what *legalism* is, so that we are all on the same page. We seriously doubt that many people would proudly proclaim, "I am a card-carrying legalist," but as we have seen already from the Barna survey, legalism is rampant in the church. You may be surprised at how subtle it can be!

In chapters 2 and 3 we talk about the twin issues of *guilt* and *shame*. Guilt is the sense that you have *done* something wrong. Shame is the sense that *you* are the something that is wrong. There is a place for guilt and shame, but all too often people wallow in false guilt and false shame that have been spawned by legalistic systems.

Chapters 4 and 5 take a close look at *fear* and *pride*—both of which, paradoxically, can be the fruit as well as the root of legalism. In chapter 6 we conclude the first part of the book by considering the *enemies of freedom*, both in the Bible and in twenty-first-century America.

Starting Out Toward Freedom

The second half of this book is reparative. Having diagnosed the illness and its symptoms and causes, how can we see the virus of legalism eradicated in our lives, families, and churches? We call part two "The Yoke That Frees."

Chapter 7 begins our journey into healing by looking at what Christ accomplished on the cross. This is good news— truly a *gospel of grace* that has freed us not only from legitimate guilt, but also from the law, attacks of false guilt, and the accusations of the evil one. We then call believers to rediscover the God who created pleasure and who wants us to enjoy it legitimately.

When shame is eating away at the very core of our being, our only hope for deliverance is a clear and unequivocal understanding of our new standing and *relationship with God through Christ*, which we explore in chapter 8. In Him, we are set free to walk in humility (not humiliation) and dignity (not dirt). As we gain a new realization of who we are—children of God, dwelling with Him in His house, His temple—we find that the shame that has acted as a "squatter" is served an eviction notice and beats a hasty exit!

Fear flees when faith grows, and chapter 9 provides the framework for a new walk of *dependence upon the Father*—the kind of dependence demonstrated in the life of the Lord Jesus. Found within that framework is a life of intimacy with God in prayer and new power in the Person of the Holy Spirit.

Chapter 10 explores one of the greatest wonders of God's operation (surgery!) in our lives...the phenomenon of *brokenness*. God opposes the proud (James 4:6), but a broken and contrite heart He will never despise (Psalm 51:17). Pride and control are not easily taken away from our hearts, but through brokenness the haughty spirit that energizes legalistic systems can truly be crushed.

The Steps to Freedom in Christ have been powerfully used by our Lord Jesus to help set captives free all over the world. In a similar fashion, chapter 11 will walk you through a process designed to help *break the bondage of legalism* in your life. As tempting as it might be to turn right to that chapter and try for a quick fix, we strongly urge you not to do that. Each of our chapters builds on the previous one, and you will find much benefit in going through the entire book before walking through that process.

Chapter 12 answers the crucial question, "How then do I live in the kingdom of God?" We will consider three components of life in this new kingdom: a *new commandment*, a *new covenant*, and a *new commission*. We will also look at the purpose of God's law and explain the difference between legalistic adherence to the law and new-covenant, Spirit-filled obedience. The difference is profound, and—as we saw in the first survey question—it is one that has largely been missed by the body of Christ.

The petition of our Lord Jesus in John 17—"that they may all be one"—remains a largely unanswered prayer to this day.

So we conclude the final chapter with a call to cease firing at one another, lay down our weapons, climb out of our doctrinal bunkers, and move toward true unity in Christ.

More About What Christians Actually Experience

At this point, you may be wondering what the final two Barna Research survey statements were. We'll use the consideration of these to wrap up our introduction and launch us into the main portion of the book.

Encouragement and Empowerment

The first of the remaining two statements said, *Attending church leaves me feeling encouraged and empowered to live the Christian life.* From some of the survey results we've already looked at, you might expect people to be down on their churches. But the exact opposite was true! More than 90 percent of those who responded gave their churches high marks on this one (with 71 percent strongly agreeing with the statement). Why is that? We would suggest several reasons.

One is that there are a significant number of churches that are conducting uplifting Sunday services. The Lord is blessing wonderfully! The worship is drawing people into the presence of God, the messages are edifying, the fellowship is encouraging. A lot of effort is going into making Sunday worship an enjoyable experience. And it is!

Some of these churches are truly preaching grace, and many of the believers inside are "getting it." But we cannot ignore the other results, which reveal that too many churches place a high premium on rigid rules and strict standards. Nor can we ignore the reality that somehow the excitement of Sunday morning is getting lost during the week, with people feeling like they're not measuring up.

What's the problem? A friend of mine who came out of a fundamental church offers this explanation:

> I identify with the phenomenon you mentioned. I recall leaving church feeling like I could and should be able to "do it." However, the way I felt on Monday morning was usually quite a different thing. (I wonder what results the poll would have gotten from a question about how people feel during the middle of the week.)

Indeed. We expect that many Christians, for the very reason that they feel spiritually deflated, dutifully troop off to midweek services in order to get pumped up again. Some of them, to be sure, are there because they *want* to be. But others are there because they feel they *have* to be.

The comment of another "recovering legalist" is insightful regarding this:

> Those survey results are indeed interesting, though they are not surprising. You are right about the meaning of the seemingly mixed results. Many church services are pep rallies, and pastors are cheerleaders. For one hour each week, we allow ourselves to again be convinced that we (simply by willing it so and bootstrapping ourselves up) can live a dynamic Christian life and perform kingdom exploits. Somehow we don't get taught how to depend on God.

The Question of Motivation

Our last statement brings another bittersweet revelation. It read, *I am motivated to serve God more out of a sense of guilt and obligation rather than joy and gratitude.* Most people (70 percent) disagreed with the statement (59 percent strongly), which ought to be very encouraging news to pastors and other Christian leaders.

The downside is that more than one-quarter of respondents agreed with it (15 percent strongly). That likely points to one of two things (and in some cases no doubt, both). Either people are serving God because they feel duty-bound to Him and are trying to gain His approval, or they are serving God because they are trying to please someone in the church (a pastor, a friend, a spouse, and so on). Either way, the motivation is wrong...and the blessing is gone.

Come to Him As He Really Is

Legalism is a killer, but grace is a healer. Legalism caused the apostle Paul to cry out, "Who has bewitched you?" to those who were trying to be perfected by the law (Galatians 3:1). And his pained words recorded in Galatians 4:15 are born out of a broken heart. In horror he asked, "What has happened to all your joy?" (NIV).

But grace proclaims loudly,

> In love He predestined us to adoption as sons through Jesus Christ to Himself, according to the kind intention of His will, to the praise of the glory of His grace, which He freely bestowed on us in the Beloved (Ephesians 1:4-6).

If we can accomplish this one thing through our writing and your reading of this book, we want it to be this: We want to see your joy return—the joy of your salvation.

We want to reacquaint you with Joy Himself. We want you to revel in worship in the presence of the God who created gentle snowfalls, taste buds, fall colors, warm sunshine, beaches, romantic love, and yes, even sex. We want you to go beyond just "living the Christian life" to *knowing Christ*, the One who longs for our presence, wooing us with the deepest, most holy, and most passionate love that mankind could ever experience...and that goes for us men, too!

Psalm 126 echoes our heart for you as we pray that the chains of legalism fall off and joy return:

> When the LORD brought back the captive ones of Zion, we were like those who dream. Then our mouth was filled with laughter and our tongue with joyful shouting; then they said among the nations, "The LORD has done great things for them." The LORD has done great things for us; we are glad.
>
> Restore our captivity, O LORD, as the streams in the South. Those who sow in tears shall reap with joyful shouting. He who goes to and fro weeping, carrying his bag of seed, shall indeed come again with a shout of joy, bringing his sheaves with him.

Philip Yancey echoes those words: "If I had to define my own theme, it would be that of a person who absorbed some of the worst the church has to offer, yet still landed in the loving arms of God. Yes, I went through a period of rejection of the church and God, a conversion experience in reverse that felt like liberation for a time. I ended up, however, not an atheist, a refugee from the church, but as one of its advocates."[4]

We believe there are many more "Philip Yanceys" out there who are on the knife-edge of faith. Perhaps you are one of them. We want you to know this: The Lord who has done great things for others wants to do the same for you.

He Gives Living Water

There is a place on the grounds of the Andersonville National Historic Site that is like an oasis in a desert. It is called "Providence Spring." During a heavy rainstorm on August 14, 1864, a spring suddenly gushed up from a hillside just inside the walls of the camp. Several men claimed to have seen lightning strikes at that spot just before the spring burst forth. This was an answer to thousands of prayers, for the water in the stream that ran through the camp was filthy and diseased.

Prisoners first reached the spring (which was on off-limits ground) by tying cups to tent poles, but the guards later allowed the men to trough the water into the camp. The day after the rainstorm, John L. Maile of the Eighth Michigan Infantry wrote in his journal, "A spring of purest crystal water shot up in the air in a column and, falling in a fanlike spray, went babbling down the grade into the noxious brook. Looking across the dead-line [the place near the wall beyond which prisoners who ventured would be shot], we beheld with wondering eyes and grateful hearts the fountain spring."

A pavilion was erected on the site in 1901. On it are engraved these words, "The prisoners' cry of thirst rang up to heaven. God heard, and with His thunder cleft the earth, and poured His sweetest waters gushing here."

That's exactly why we wrote this book. We want you to know there is a spring of purest water waiting to quench your spiritual thirst. It is the fountain of living waters Himself... instead of the broken cisterns of legalism that can hold no water (see Jeremiah 2:13).

We pray and hope you will turn the page and begin the journey home.

Part I
THE LIES THAT BIND

1

THE LAW KILLS

Paul's Story

It was a Sunday morning in April 1988. The sun was just peeking over the horizon in the small Tennessee town where my wife, Linda, and I (Paul) were staying. We were investigating the possibility of my pastoring a church there.

The previous day had been a busy one and a good one for me. Church members had gathered at an evening cookout, and we'd enjoyed meeting them. They were good people. I also had had the chance to travel around and see the local sights. I was excited about the area. Linda, unfortunately, had only seen the seedier side of town and called the place "crummy." I was looking forward to doing some sight-seeing with her after I had preached at church that morning. I was certain she'd warm up to the area and become as excited about it as I was.

Unfortunately, a cruel intruder was about to disrupt my neatly controlled world.

"Are you okay?" I asked her as she turned to me in bed. She had been restless, tossing and turning all night.

"I haven't slept very well," she replied.

"Well, we can rest a while longer. They're on Central time here. It's still early."

I felt confident my words would reassure her and that we could get some more rest. After all, I always knew just what to say. That was part of who I was.

Still unable to sleep, Linda got out of bed, went into the bathroom, and shut the door. As I dozed, I could hear the water running. I figured she was showering, so I cleared my head and focused on my message for the morning.

Then I heard a thump in the bathroom.

She must have bumped her elbow in the shower or something. No big deal.

Needing to finalize my thoughts for the sermon, I sat up in bed and shifted back into message-preparation mode. This was my main shot at showing this congregation what I could do from the pulpit. Preaching was my passion, and I was eager to perform well.

But something wasn't right. The water in the bathroom was running too long.

I'd better check and make sure everything's okay.

"Linda! Linda! Are you all right?"

There was no response, even though she couldn't have been more than three feet away from me. The headboard of the bed was right up against the wall that separated the bedroom and bath.

I cracked open the bathroom door and saw the water running in the sink, but there was no sign of Linda. I opened the door a little more and could see that she wasn't in the shower either.

Where in the world is she? What's going on?

I could tell something was wrong, but I wasn't sure what. The water was splashing into the sink, but other than that, the room was strangely quiet.

Panicking now, I shoved the door open and found myself pushing against Linda's prone body. She had fallen facedown on the floor.

Lord, what's happening?

I was struck by a feeling of helplessness—something I had never allowed myself to feel. I had always been the strong one, the one who knew just what to do. But this was something that would turn out to be way beyond me.

My mind forced away the dread that was already demanding entrance into my life. Refusing to cave into the fear, I swung into action.

I lifted my wife's head slightly off the floor. Her face was pressed in. Horrified, I noticed it would not go back to normal. It was awful seeing her that way. It was like someone had punched me in the gut, knocking all the wind out of me.

Linda was clutching a washcloth. A green one. She had apparently been holding it against her face, trying to relieve some pain or discomfort. Then she had fallen. And that was the thump I had heard.

I've got to act fast. What can I do to save her?

I forced myself to think this way, even though, through the shock of the moment, one thing was clear to me. Her body was lifeless. And I felt like death, too.

I can't cry. I've got to do something. But there's nothing I can do! This is it. But it can't be true. It's not happening.

Sadness. Shock. Confusion. Denial. The whole scene took on a surreal fuzziness. I just stood there like a stone while waves of guilt broke over me.

I brought this on her. She didn't want to move here. This was all my idea and I've done something terrible. I should have checked on her right away when I heard that noise. Me and my last-minute sermon preparations...

She hadn't been feeling well a few days ago. Why didn't I...?

My mind went back to some events of the past week. They had bothered me at the time, but not enough to do anything about them. We had been over at our friends' house and had our blood pressure checked. We had all done it...all of us except Linda.

Did she know then that her blood pressure was high?

A few days before that incident, I had come back from a conference on the church bus. I had asked Linda to pick me up at church, but she had said she was not up to it. *What in the world could keep her from being able to just drive the car to the church and pick me up?* She said she thought she had the flu, but by her description it sounded more like an ulcer. At the time I had urged her to get it checked out by a doctor. Later, I found out that stomach pains can be a sign of heart trouble.

Snapping out of my inner nightmare for a moment, I yelled for help from my close friend, in whose house we were staying. He immediately called 9-1-1, and within minutes Linda was at the hospital. DOA. A massive heart attack had taken her away from me. Apparently she had died instantly.

Out of Control

A confusing kaleidoscope of emotions enveloped me. This was all new territory to me. I had spent my entire life stuffing my feelings deep down where they couldn't do me or anyone else any harm.

A friend of mine had once said, "I've never seen Paul Travis out of control." Neither had I.

It was like I had a closet in my heart labeled "Painful Emotions" that I kept padlocked, with an armed guard protecting it. This unit was well trained to keep barred inside every feeling that could possibly cause me to lose control—anger, fear, confusion, sorrow, grief, helplessness, and hopelessness.

I was surprised to discover later that "the guards" had misinterpreted my orders. They had secretly kept *every* emotion locked inside. And so over time I had come to feel very little at all.

As I took in all that was going on, it was obvious that no locked door could contain my feelings any longer.

What will I do without her?

Fear, the emotion that I dreaded perhaps most of all, had burst out of its cage and was seeking to devour me. I tried as hard as I could to keep myself from feeling pain, but it wasn't working.

I've got to keep my feelings under control. That's the right thing to do. I've got to stay in control.

My eyes were tearing up, but I wouldn't let myself cry. I couldn't.

I stayed at my friends' house that morning during the worship service, saddened by Linda's death and my missing the chance to preach. The church, however, made other arrangements for the sermon that morning and assured me that everything had been taken care of.

Later on I held a Bible study with those who had dropped by to console me. As unbelievable as it may sound, I felt that I needed to preach the Word to those who came over. They listened intently as I performed well.

A Life of Performance

I had always performed well. Though I would likely have denied it vehemently, I was a legalist, a spiritual performer. Driven to work hard for God, I had already accomplished many things in my ministry. If there had been an Academy Award for "best performance by a leading actor in church," I would have been up there receiving that Oscar. In fact, I would have received the "Lifetime Performance Award" because from the womb to the tomb, I was bound and determined to do right, look right, and be right.

It was only then that I believed I would be all right. But I was wrong.

My wife Linda's death was just part of God's powerful and painful process of lovingly moving me from self-satisfied legalism into the joy of freedom in Christ. It served as the wake-up call, the two-by-four over the head to show me that I needed to allow God's truth to touch my heart and not just fill my mind. I needed to know that Paul Travis's neatly controlled world could fall to pieces in a moment's time. I needed to know that my efforts to keep my life in order were totally futile. Only then would I be set free from life as a performer and legalist.

Legalism—A Good Thing?

What exactly is a *legalist?* When we see the word "legal," we know that it refers to something that is lawful to do. Because we live in a fallen world and our culture is in moral decline, we realize that some things that are lawful are awful (for example, pornography, abortion, and so on). But generally speaking, we identify things that are legal as right, and things that are illegal as wrong.

So wouldn't a *legalist* (in a religious sense) simply be a person who tries to do right by keeping God's or man's law? And therefore, wouldn't *legalism* be a good thing?

At first glance, legalism sounds like a very good thing. A noble thing to be commended. But it is anything but commendable, as we shall see.

Webster's New World Dictionary offers two definitions of legalism:

1. strict, often too strict, and literal adherence to law

2. in theology, the doctrine of salvation by good works

The *World Book Dictionary* says, "Legalism is the strict adherence to law or prescription, especially to the letter of the law rather than the spirit." Following that same theme and building on it, in *The Dictionary of Religious Terms* Donald Kaufman writes,

Legalism is:

1. Emphasis on the letter rather than on the spirit of the law;

2. Belief in salvation by obedience to the law rather than by the grace of God or by faith;

3. Undue stress on legal details without balancing considerations of justice or mercy.

Legalism only demands that the law be satisfied.[1]

Though the law of God is "holy and righteous and good" (Romans 7:12), trying to keep it in order to be accepted by God is unholy, unrighteous, and not good at all. Man was never designed nor expected to keep God's commands on his own, nor was strict adherence to law ever God's way of making man righteous. It has always been *by faith*.

Seeking to achieve right standing with God by religious performance would be like expecting a mirror to wash the dirt off your face. The purpose of the mirror is not to clean you, but to reveal the dirt. In the same way, "through the Law comes the knowledge of sin" (Romans 3:20), not the power to remove it.

Bondage Versus Liberty

Unfortunately, as we saw earlier in the Barna research, God's people by and large have got things wrong, and the spiritual effects are deadly. Like a virus infecting a Bible software program, legalism can corrupt even the noblest of spiritual endeavors. It causes confusion and drivenness, a feeling like being trapped in a maze where every seeming exit ends up a dead end. The testimony of this woman is typical:

> I was plagued with condemnation for the first two years after I came to the Lord. It was preached at our church to pray and read the Word an hour a day, to share your faith each week, and so on. Not to mention being told to not listen to "worldly" music, not seeing "worldly" friends, and on and on the list goes. This was good advice but it was presented in such a way as to become a burden, and I felt like if I didn't keep up in these areas, I would

lose my salvation. My heart was to please the Lord, but feeling judged was really painful.

I tried to make everything look good on the outside, but I just couldn't do all the things I was supposed to do, and the pressure from others in the church was too much. I saw others trying in their own strength to conform to the image of Christ. I tried to do the same, though I knew I couldn't do it. Yet I questioned myself. Maybe I wasn't trying hard enough and that was why I was failing. Ultimately I realized that I just couldn't keep up with it all. The condemnation that I dealt with even after leaving that church was relentless. Finally I learned that all my efforts at changing myself are wood, hay, and stubble.

She's right. Jesus put it this way: "It is the Spirit who gives life; the flesh profits nothing" (John 6:63). What she needs (and what we all need!) is freedom in the Spirit. And Scripture promises that "where the Spirit of the Lord is, there is liberty" (2 Corinthians 3:17). But how to get there? It's easier said than done, and many have been desperately trying all their lives to find the trail that leads to spiritual liberty. But instead they find themselves stuck on a stony path that leads only to deeper frustration and bondage.

Adding to Grace

In his book *Grace Awakening*, Chuck Swindoll writes,

> Legalism is an attitude, a mentality based on pride. It is an obsessive conformity to an artificial standard for the purpose of exalting oneself... Legalism says, "I do this or I don't do that, and therefore I am pleasing God."[2]

Based on these definitions, it is clear both non-Christians and Christians can be legalists. Though Christian legalists are

in serious bondage and are missing out on the abundant life
Christ promised (John 10:10), non-Christian ones are in the
gravest danger, for they may very well be convinced they have
found the road to salvation. In reality they are on the path that
ultimately leads to eternal destruction.

According to another poll conducted by the Barna
Research Group in early 2002, 55 percent of Americans surveyed believe that our salvation can be earned. That means
that a majority of people in this nation are religious legalists!
And sadly enough, from a statistical standpoint this percentage has not changed over the past ten years.

The specific question posed by the Barna researchers was
"Can a good person, or one who does enough good for others,
earn eternal salvation?"[3]

Scripture clearly teaches that salvation is not by good
works of any kind, but by grace alone, through faith alone, in
Jesus Christ alone. Consider the apostle Paul's words to the
church at Ephesus:

> By grace you have been saved through faith;
> and that not of yourselves, it is the gift of God; not
> as a result of works, so that no one should boast
> (Ephesians 2:8-9).

Paul reiterates that crucial principle in his letter to the
Romans when he writes,

> There has also come to be at the present time
> a remnant according to God's gracious choice. But
> if it is by grace, it is no longer on the basis of
> works, otherwise grace is no longer grace (Romans
> 11:5-6).

The story of how the legalist rabbi Saul of Tarsus became
the gracious apostle Paul could be a book all on its own, but
for now it's enough to see that his inspired writings are clear:
Salvation is by grace, a free gift from God—and not as a result

of accumulating heavenly merits by good works. You simply can't earn "brownie points" with God by trying to be good.

According to the Bible, the "salvation equation" looks like this:

$$+ \frac{\begin{array}{l} \textit{God's grace} \\ \textit{Our faith in Jesus and His death and} \\ \quad \textit{resurrection alone to save us} \end{array}}{\textit{Salvation}}$$

Any time a person or church adds anything to that equation, they have crossed into legalism. In other words, faith in *Jesus* + *anything else* is no longer faith in *Jesus*, because any human standard of performance that we must attain or maintain in order to be saved negates the reality of faith. Any standard is a law, and adherence to any law in order to attain, gain, or maintain God's acceptance is in direct violation of grace. It is legalism.

God's grace is undeserved, unmerited, unearned. It is His free and abundant gift granted in spite of what we have done in sinning against Him. Grace is not the result of our good deeds, as Paul explains in Titus 3:4-7:

> When the kindness of God our Savior and His love for mankind appeared, He saved us, not on the basis of deeds which we have done in righteousness, but according to His mercy, by the washing of regeneration and renewing by the Holy Spirit, whom He poured out upon us richly through Jesus Christ our Savior, so that being justified by His grace we would be made heirs according to the hope of eternal life.

Earning Your Way to Heaven

Tragically, though nearly two-thirds of Americans attend church in any given year,[4] most have not heard or believed God's message of grace through the apostle Paul.

When it comes to the matter of salvation, a majority of Americans are indeed legalists. They believe that by accomplishing a certain measure (meeting a standard) of good works, they will be saved. In other words, if they jump through enough spiritual hoops, God will let them into heaven. Those hoops usually include a lot of good things like "attending church regularly, keeping the 'Ten Commandments,' donating money to church or charity, helping people, being baptized, confessing sins, praying, fasting, making religious pilgrimages," and so on. But how could you ever be sure you'd done enough?

What most people end up doing is justifying themselves in comparison to others: *Well, at least I don't do (name the bad action) like (name the person).* Or they try not to think too much about eternal issues at all. Doing their best to keep God happy, they hope and pray that at the end of their lives their good deeds will "outweigh" their bad (which is an essential belief of Islam). But one sin committed is enough to tip the scales against us so heavily that even the sum total of all our good deeds would not budge it one bit. James 2:10 warns, "Whoever keeps the whole law and yet stumbles in one point, he has become guilty of all." Even the moral "best of the best" is as bad off as the "worst of the worst," "for all have sinned and fall short of the glory of God" (Romans 3:23).

Again, the apostle Paul could not have made it clearer when he wrote,

> Knowing that a man is not justified by the works of the Law but through faith in Christ Jesus, even we have believed in Christ Jesus, so that we may be justified by faith in Christ and not by the works of the Law; since by the works of the Law no flesh will be justified (Galatians 2:16-17).

The majority of Americans are convinced that they can get salvation the old-fashioned way—they can *earn it.* It is human pride invading the spiritual. It is the independent American frontier spirit slapped onto the world of religion. No matter how noble, heroic, or logical the opinion might seem, and no matter how prevalent it might be, there is one big problem with it. It is absolutely wrong...and it is deadly.

Proverbs 14:12 and 16:25 repeat the same warning: "There is a way which seems right to a man, but its end is the way of death." You can try to climb your own ladder of "spiritual success," but eventually you will discover it is leaning against the wrong wall. Jesus Christ, on the other hand, proclaimed, "I am the way, and the truth, and the life; no one comes to the Father but through Me" (John 14:6).

Salvation from sin, then, does not come from trusting in the good works that we do, but in the Good Work that Jesus has already done by dying on the cross for our sin and rising from the dead! It is not by our effort but by His. That makes all the difference in the world. It is the difference between life and death.

George Barna concludes a chapter in his book *The State of the Church 2002* with this sobering statement:

> In the end these figures may be a wake-up call regarding the clarity and intensity of the teaching that people receive regarding salvation. While evangelicals, by definition, accept the notion of salvation by grace alone, and they are joined by millions of Americans, the undisputable fact is that most Americans consider themselves Christian, believe they will have eternal salvation, and base their view on the notion that salvation can either be a free gift of God or earned through good behavior. Somehow, despite the literally billions of dollars spent on evangelism and Christian education in the past quarter century, the true message of the gospel has failed to penetrate the minds and hearts of most Americans.[5]

That is a tragedy that should motivate us to preach God's Word in season and out of season (2 Timothy 4:2).

Earning Your Way to Acceptance

There is another tragedy, however. Millions of Americans who truly are Christian have failed to fully comprehend the gospel. It is as if they have one foot in the new covenant and another in the old.

When I (Paul) described myself as being a legalist, that is what I meant. I was a Christian legalist. I never believed that my *salvation* was dependent upon my good works, but I came to believe that my *sanctification* (growth in Christ) was. I trusted Christ for my salvation at an early age and was baptized when I turned 12. I didn't think that I had to perform in order to *enter into* God's grace. I just came to believe that I had to spiritually perform and do everything right in order to *grow in* grace. Can you see the difference?

I had adopted a form of the false teaching that the apostle Paul reacted to so strongly in the church at Galatia. He wrote, "Are you so foolish? After beginning with the Spirit, are you now trying to attain your goal [which for me was to be a good Christian] by human effort?" (Galatians 3:3 NIV). If the apostle had directed that question to me, if I were honest I would have had to answer, "Yes, that's exactly what I'm doing." And unfortunately, so are far too many Christians in our nation.

For the sake of simplicity, we offer this definition of Christian legalism, the malady we are focusing on in this book. *Christian legalism is seeking to attain, gain, or maintain acceptance with God, or achieve spiritual growth, through keeping a written or unwritten code or standard of performance.* It always results in life lived in the energy of the flesh rather than in the power of the Spirit, because the burden of responsibility is on our behavior rather than on God's enabling grace. It is the difference between "trying harder"...and trusting Him. It is also the difference between being *led* (by the Spirit) and being *driven* (by the flesh).

The Real Wages of Legalism

Christian legalism is a dead-end street that drains away spiritual vitality, steals our joy, dulls our passion for God, and drives many people into depression. Others it drives away from God Himself in bitter anger and defeat.

Many Christians are just tired out. Not necessarily sleepy… but *tired*. Worn out. Weary. To them, the words of Jesus in Matthew 11:28-30 seem almost a mockery. He said, "Come to me, all you who are weary and burdened, and I will give you rest. Take my yoke upon you and learn from me, for I am gentle and humble in heart, and you will find rest for your souls. For my yoke is easy and my burden is light" (NIV). To which so many of God's people say, "Yeah, right." Just when they think this oasis of spiritual life might actually be within reach, it fades away like a cruel mirage, obscured in a fog of more "do's" and "don'ts," "oughts" and "shoulds." All they're left with is a thirst that won't be quenched and a desert experience that won't quit.

The following woman's journey is tragic but not uncommon. Perhaps you can relate:

> As a young mother I became involved in a mainline church that I thought was Spirit-filled. Coming from a home where I was never good enough, I found that I was also not good enough for God. At least that's how I felt. My husband and I served in seven different ministries within the church, but were never accepted by those in leadership. Once I was reprimanded by a church member for not wearing a dress to church on Sunday nights. I felt there were many more rules than I could keep up with and wondered what we would need to do to be good enough.
>
> There were rules and regulations surrounding what was proper behavior for Christians. Unfortunately, those regulations were not from God's Word. Trying to be a good Christian, I did my best to comply and teach my children. Since the church

was hard on me, I felt I must be hard on my children so they would be pleasing to God.

Finally, I couldn't take it any longer. The kids were miserable and I was becoming angry. We changed churches but, it seems, the damage had already been done. Now, as teens, my children see Christians as hypocrites and hateful people. They do not want to be involved in church and only go because we require them to go.

I am involved in my new church and am learning that God loves imperfect people. But my heart aches to see what an outcome our involvement with a legalistic church has done to my children. Daily I see the results in their rebellion and walking away from God's will. As a parent, this is one of the hardest things to endure. I still struggle with resentment toward this church but I am trying to let the Lord heal the anger. And I pray for my children daily that He may be able to love them back into the Kingdom.

The Performance Trap

An article in *Discipleship Journal* from a number of years ago shows how easily the problem of legalism can creep into the lives of even the most committed Christian people. It was entitled "I Don't Feel Like a Very Good Christian." The subtitle was "Why does it seem that you can never quite measure up?" Here is an excerpt from that article:

I could tell something was bothering my wife one evening—she was quieter than usual and didn't look at me as much. Finally, after the kids were put to bed, she said, "I don't know what's wrong." "What do you mean?" I asked. "Well," she said, "I don't...I just don't feel like a very good Christian."

> I wasn't sure what to say. I wanted to tell her that of course she was a wonderful Christian, but she didn't look like she was quite ready to believe that. So instead I asked, "What do you think is making you feel like that?" "I haven't had a quiet time for a while," she confessed. "After chasing two small kids all day, I feel wiped out; I'm too tired to read the Bible and pray. Mornings are crazy, and the kids don't nap at the same time, so I haven't had devotions in weeks. I'm not even sure I have a relationship with God anymore."[6]

In this refreshingly transparent article, Kevin Miller confessed that his wife wasn't the only one in the family struggling in this way:

> That week I had written in my journal, "Lord, I want to live more simply, as Jesus did, but I love money as much as anyone. I should be out ministering in some way, maybe at the nursing home, but I haven't got going. I haven't been reading my Bible and praying like I should. And I want to lead family devotions on Sunday nights, but I've been so sporadic lately. I feel like I've failed you."[7]

We can really sympathize with this couple. They are sincere Christian people who truly want to live a life pleasing to God. But it is so easy to slip into this form of legalism—"performing for God" in order to grow spiritually. And it is not those who are half-hearted or spiritually lazy who struggle with Christian legalism. It is those who are highly motivated to serve who take the bait—the bait of gauging their spirituality based on the outward, exterior practices of the Christian faith.

Unfortunately, there is a hook hidden in the bait. And the hook is this lie: *My Christian growth is primarily dependent upon my efforts to maintain Christian disciplines or practices rather than upon God's grace.* And as long as a Christian believes this lie, he or she never truly enters into God's rest.

To a certain extent such believers are like the apostle Paul's countrymen, the Jews. In Romans 10:2 he described them in these terms:

> I testify about them that they have a zeal for God, but not in accordance with knowledge.

God through Hosea said, "My people are destroyed for lack of knowledge" (Hosea 4:6). In this case, the knowledge they are missing is the truth that will set them free (see John 8:31-36). And just as it is truth that sets us free, it is lies that keep us in bondage.

This "performance trap" is driven by a very subtle lie, because spiritual disciplines are an essential ingredient of spiritual vitality. Christian legalists, however, put the cart before the horse. Their belief system says, *If I perform spiritually, I will experience God's grace and blessing.* However, true Christianity says, *Because God is gracious and I am already accepted in Christ, God will bless me. I don't have to perform for Him, but I want to seek Him and serve Him because of His great love.*

In his book *The Myth of Certainty*, Daniel Taylor writes,

> Legalism clings to law at the expense of grace, to the letter in place of the Spirit. Legalism is one more expression of human compulsion for security. If we can vigorously enforce an exhaustive list of do's and don'ts (with an emphasis on external behavior), [we think that] we not only can control unpredictable human beings but have God's favor as well.[8]

But God's favor cannot be purchased by us or squeezed out of Him by means of a disciplined lifestyle. Though it cost Jesus everything, it costs us nothing. That is the nature of grace. And that is the message of the new covenant in Christ.

A Matter of the Heart

While defending his apostleship, Paul contrasted life under the law (which he called "the letter") and life in the Spirit:

> [This] confidence we have through Christ toward God. Not that we are adequate in ourselves to consider anything as coming from ourselves, but our adequacy is from God, who also made us adequate as servants of a new covenant, not of the letter but of the Spirit; for the letter kills, but the Spirit gives life.
>
> But if the ministry of death, in letters engraved on stones, came with glory, so that the sons of Israel could not look intently at the face of Moses because of the glory of his face, fading as it was, how will the ministry of the Spirit fail to be even more with glory? (2 Corinthians 3:4-8).

Under the old covenant, the Israelites sought to please God by keeping the commandments Moses wrote on stone tablets. Under the new covenant, God says, "I will put My laws upon their heart, and upon their mind I will write them" (Hebrews 10:16). It is no longer an external effort to achieve right standing with God, but an internal reality of righteousness. It is not by what we do, but by what He has already done in us as believers in Jesus.

Clearly, most believers in Christ are not trying to keep all the old covenant dietary (kosher) laws and ordinances in order to be "good Christians." But far too many of us have climbed up our own Mt. Sinai and have come down with a set of written (or unwritten) rules, laws, or codes that govern our spiritual life. Whether these rules come from your home, your church, a Christian organization, a book you've read, a seminar you've attended, or even your own interpretation of Scripture, all can easily become laws. And the law kills.

Many things we "do for God" are good things, like having a quiet time or memorizing Scripture or praying for others or evangelizing the lost. Nobody would ever deny that these are extremely valuable things that Christians who are growing in their faith often do. But when these things become rigid requirements to attain God's blessing or achieve spiritual growth, we have fallen from grace into legalism.

The curious thing about legalism is that you might look at a legalist and a person walking in grace and at times not be able to tell them apart. They could very well be doing the exact same things. The difference lies not on the outside but on the inside, in the realm of *motivation*. Why is he or she doing it? A person is a legalist therefore, not necessarily because of *what* they do or don't do, but because of *why* they do or don't do it.

How do you know if this is true of you? One way is to ask yourself this: How do you react if you *don't* do the things you feel you should do or need to be doing in order to be a "good Christian"? The law condemns. Do you feel condemned? Do you feel like a failure in God's eyes? Are you driven to redouble your efforts in order to do better "next time"? Do you tend to evaluate your spirituality by how regularly you are keeping up with or measuring up to certain standards? Do you feel like God loves you more when you perform certain Christian practices? Do you seem to feel a disheartening sense of disapproval from Him when you don't?

Freedom in Christ Is for *You*

The apostle Paul wrote, "It was for freedom that Christ set us free; therefore keep standing firm and do not be subject again to a yoke of slavery" (Galatians 5:1). God the Father delights in our presence and deeply enjoys having fellowship with us. We are His precious children—and He wants us to come to Him out of love and desire, not out of obligation or duty. True, there are times when we open our Bibles or go to church or begin praying simply because it is right and good. Our feelings may take time to warm up and catch up. But when our lives become predominantly an exercise in trying to do good works in the desperate hope of somehow pleasing God, something is very wrong.

When our "want to's" toward God fade and shift into "ought to's" or "supposed to's," the joy is drained away. We come to see the Father as more like a boss or a heavenly principal than as the God whose arms and heart are always wide open to us.

The law kills. It kills worship and joy. It kills spontaneity and creativity. It kills freedom. It kills relationships and families. It even kills churches.

But Jesus came that we might have life and might have it more abundantly (John 10:10). That is what He wants you to experience: not some kind of drudging, trudging religion, but a joy unspeakable—and freedom so real that "you will go forth and skip about like calves from the stall" (Malachi 4:2).

Perhaps you have felt like a spiritual failure, helpless to do better and hopeless to please God. Guilt and shame have hounded you on your spiritual journey to the point where you don't know whether to work harder or just quit. You've probably tried both. And neither has worked.

Maybe you've never made the connection between the nagging, gnawing guilt and shame you feel and a life lived under the law. Be encouraged. God wants you to be free. He sent His Son to purchase your freedom (Galatians 5:1).

This freedom *is* for you. We trust these next chapters will bring more liberating light to your life.

2

IN THE GRIP
OF GUILT

Rich's Story

It was my (Rich's) birthday. Late in my sophomore year at Penn State, I had just turned 20. I was determined to have a good time. And so were my partying buddies down the hall in our dorm. The beer was plentiful, the music was loud, and I didn't have a care in the world.

Though you would not have known it that night, I had given my heart to the Lord Jesus about 17 months previously. Knowing that I was a sinner in need of God's saving grace through Christ, I had had a definitive experience of salvation on Christmas Eve, 1972. But my early days in the faith were a rocky road.

Even though I tried hard at first, for some reason I didn't quite fit in with the Christian culture around me at the university. It seemed too cookie-cutter, with a huge emphasis on "doing things for God."

I'm sure some of the problem was with my pride and rebellious attitude, along with some misunderstanding, but I still felt like I didn't quite fit in or measure up. Everyone else seemed to be continuously giddy with joy while I was still wrestling with issues like "Can you really believe the whole Bible?" I had some deeply rooted insecurities, anger, and fears, and so I felt out of place in a culture of bubbly optimism. I also felt guilty for struggling and questioning. Increasingly I sensed an alienation from my brothers and sisters in Christ. I just wasn't able to play the part very well—and my guilt and anger increased to the point where I would take long walks late into the night, yelling at God for making my life miserable. I felt like a complete outcast. I was indeed living in the grip of guilt.

As time went on, I found it easier just to hang out with my non-Christian buddies. I knew they weren't perfect, and they knew I wasn't either. Neither they nor I tried to appear to be anything but what we were: friends who cared about each other and liked to party. In retrospect, it was pretty shallow, though it seemed to be emotionally safe.

My safety was shattered that birthday night as one of my buddies burst into the room, announcing that my older brother, Tom, was walking down the hall. It might as well have been the apostle Peter. Quickly hiding my beer bottle, I tried my best to look and act sober. I was feeling and acting guilty, and he hadn't even walked into the room!

I could tell that Tom felt uncomfortable. The feeling was mutual. He smiled kind of weakly, wished me a happy birthday, handed me a present, and waited for me to open it. It was obviously a book...which meant trouble.

My brother had come to Christ about nine months before I had, and he had been the first one to share the gospel with me. Unlike his prodigal younger brother, Tom had walked the Christian walk from the beginning.

I croaked a lame "thank you" as I gazed at the cover of *The Master Plan of Evangelism* by Robert Coleman. I saw a mixture of amusement and amazement in my friends' eyes. You see, I hadn't exactly made it my life's goal to convert my friends, though they knew I believed in Jesus. Mercifully, my brother left quickly after that. I could see the sadness in his eyes.

As the night wore on, I became increasingly drunk. Drinking was my way of escaping my haunting by guilt feelings. Sometime after midnight some of my buddies came up with the brilliant idea of wrapping me up in a bedsheet, putting me in the dorm elevator, and pushing all the buttons. I was so out of it that I couldn't get out of it (the sheet, that is). I felt increasingly rotten as I became the comedy floor show each time the elevator doors opened.

Somehow I managed to crawl out of the elevator into the lobby of our dorm floor. Extremely nauseated by now, I lay in a corner praying that I wouldn't throw up. I think I vowed to become a priest or something if God would keep me from vomiting all over the place. Guilt and shame were bad enough. Humiliation I couldn't handle.

After several more hours I started crawling down the hall toward my room, knocking on doors, hoping my friends would help me. No one did. Miraculously, I made it to my room, pushed open the door, and climbed into bed. My roommate, who was a strong believer in Christ, watched me come in but didn't say a word.

A few minutes later, my buddies came crashing into the room, excited to see the birthday boy. Noticing that my feet and lower legs were hanging over the foot of the bed, they decided to help get the rest of my body onto the mattress. Lifting me up by my ankles, they pushed me forward and drove my head into the wall. I should have been in agony, but I felt nothing.

Probably assuming I was dead and therefore no more fun, my friends left me alone with my roommate. I felt such incredible guilt and dread. I braced myself. *Here it comes. He's going to tell me what a rotten Christian I am. And he's right. But I don't care. I dare him to judge me and try to make me feel guilty!*

Expecting to be hit with a judgmental sledgehammer, I heard my roommate merely ask quietly, "Do you think this is glorifying God?"

That's it? That's all he's going to say? No lambasting, scolding, scalding, or rebuking?

In the light streaming in from the hallway I turned, anticipating a disgusted, frowning expression on my roommate's face. All I saw was that same sad look I had seen in my brother's eyes.

That was a turning point for me in my walk with Christ. I had suffered from guilt feelings that had driven me from God. But when I came face-to-face with grace—twice in one night—my defenses came down and my hard heart softened.

Believing in Grace, but Living by Guilt

Several years ago our ministry conducted an informal survey of college students at a Christian university in the Midwest. The survey asked a number of questions regarding the spiritual lives of the students, and more than half of the student body responded. It included the statement, *I still feel guilty for sins I have committed in the past.* Nearly 60 percent of those responding said they felt guilty "sometimes, often, or always." Only 10 percent experienced no such residual guilt at all.

Those of us who have observed the body of Christ over the years are not surprised at the results. While they are troubling, they are not unexpected. We would venture to say that what was taking place at that Christian educational institution is also happening in the typical American church. In general, we believers have done a far better job of pointing out people's failings and faults than we have of pointing them to the solution. Though we sing of God's "Amazing Grace," far too many of God's people have yet to truly experience it.

Brennan Manning, in his grace-book *The Ragamuffin Gospel,* writes,

> Put bluntly: the American Church today accepts grace in theory but denies it in practice. We say we believe that the fundamental structure of reality is grace, not works—but our lives refute our faith. By and large, the gospel of grace is neither proclaimed, understood, nor lived. Too many Christians are living in the house of fear and not in the house of love.[1]

In his book *The Vanishing Conscience,* teacher John Mac-Arthur explains that

> guilt feelings may not always be rational, but they are nearly always a reliable signal that something is wrong somewhere, and we had better come to grips with whatever it is, and make it right. Guilt functions in the spiritual realm like pain in the material realm. Pain tells us there is a physical problem that must be dealt with or the body will suffer harm. Guilt is a spiritual pain in the soul that tells us something is evil and needs to be confronted and cleansed.[2]

We agree with that statement, with one important qualifier. The spiritual pain of guilt feelings does not necessarily indicate that there is something evil in the person suffering from it! The evil that "needs to be confronted and cleansed" may be in the guilt-inducing legalistic system in which the sufferer finds him- or herself.

So what exactly is guilt? Does the Bible teach believers to feel guilty? Is there a difference between guilt and guilt feelings, and how does a legalistic system foster guilt feelings? These are some of the issues we will deal with in this chapter.

Guilt from Breaking the Laws of the Land

There are two main categories of real guilt that we deal with as individuals.[3] The first category is *legal guilt,* or *civil guilt.* If you run a red light or a stop sign, cheat on your taxes, steal things from the office, speed, and so on, you are guilty of breaking civil or criminal laws. You may not *feel* guilty for doing these things, but that doesn't matter. You are still guilty—and if caught and convicted, you'll pay a fine or do time in prison.

Many people, even believers in Christ, feel justified in taking advantage of the system if no authority figure is around, if they feel the system has gotten the better of them, or if keeping the law doesn't happen to be convenient. On the interstate highway, it is amusing to watch the scores of brake lights that suddenly flash on speeding cars when a police car is spotted up ahead. This is a reaction to a realization of civil guilt. Romans 13:5 admonishes us that "it is necessary to submit to the authorities, not only because of possible punishment but also because of conscience" (NIV).

The unfortunate thing is that too many people obey laws only because they fear being caught or punished, not because it is the right thing to do. Lawlessness is the bent of the natural, unsaved man, and societal laws are ordained by God to thwart cultural pressure toward sinful chaos. That seems to be the apostle Paul's point in the following phrases: "Realizing the fact that law is not made for a righteous person, but for those who are lawless and rebellious, for the ungodly and sinners..." (1 Timothy 1:9).

It is not legalism to keep the laws of the land, for it is God's will for "every person...to be in subjection to the governing authorities. For there is no authority except from God, and those which exist are established by God" (Romans 13:1). However, we must be careful not to think that our standing with God is measured by how law-abiding a citizen we are! That *would* be legalism. Nor should we violate the spirit of the law (its intended purpose) in order to rigidly keep the letter (exact wording) of it. Should we feel guilty over exceeding the speed limit when, for example, we are transporting a dangerously ill daughter to the hospital? The spirit of the law would say it is okay in this instance to go faster than the speed limit, just so long as the driver does not endanger other lives by doing so. Saving a human life is more important than rigidly obeying a traffic law.

Guilt from Breaking God's Law

The second type of guilt is *theological guilt*, a violation of God's law. This is a violation of God's character, for God's law is an expression of who God is. A harsh and harming word spoken in anger is sin because God is patient and kind. Sexual intercourse outside of marriage is sin, no matter how much love the couple might share, because God is holy and has forbidden such behavior. Ignoring a hurting person just because you are busy is sin (see the parable of the good Samaritan) because God is compassionate. When we sin, we are guilty of breaking God's law, regardless of whether or not we *feel* guilty. That is why we need the objective truth of God's Word to teach us right from wrong and to reveal His character, rather than simply relying on our emotions to dictate morality.

There are a variety of ways people try to deal with the reality of theological guilt. The first way we would call *justification by good works*. This was the mind-set of the Pharisee in the temple who puffed himself up and put the tax collector down. The Pharisee pulled out his spiritual résumé and started bragging about all his religious good works: "I fast twice a week, I pay tithes of all that I get" (Luke 18:12). He also engaged in *justification by comparison* by "praying," "God, I thank You that I am not like other people: swindlers, unjust, adulterers, or even like this tax collector" (verse 11).

Luke reports that Jesus "told this parable to some people who trusted in themselves that they were righteous, and viewed others with contempt" (verse 9). The Pharisee mistakenly thought that by doing certain things and by not doing other things, he had it made. He thought that because his behavior was more moral than the tax collector's, he was a shoo-in to heaven. But God looks at the heart, and it was the tax collector who cried out, "God, be merciful to me, the sinner!" who went home justified (verses 13-14).

Justification by religious pedigree also falls into the same category. This was the pre-converted Saul of Tarsus' method of achieving right standing with God—he was trying to pull himself up by his own religious bootstraps. Recalling his misguided efforts of self-righteousness, he testified of himself in Philippians 3:4-6,

> If anyone else has a mind to put confidence in the flesh, I far more; circumcised the eighth day, of the nation of Israel, of the tribe of Benjamin, a Hebrew of Hebrews; as to the Law, a Pharisee; as to zeal, a persecutor of the church; as to the righteousness which is in the Law, found blameless.

God's Prescription for Guilt

But God's way is *justification by faith in Christ.* We are absolved of all theological guilt through faith in the work of Jesus Christ on the cross. John put it this way:

> I write this, dear children, to guide you out of sin. But if anyone does sin, we have a Priest-Friend in the presence of the Father: Jesus Christ, righteous Jesus. When he served as a sacrifice for our sins, he solved the sin problem for good—not only ours, but the whole world's (1 John 2:1-2 THE MESSAGE).

Because of what Jesus did for us at Calvary and because of our receiving of that gospel (good news) message by faith, we can say with Paul, "Having been justified by faith, we have peace with God through our Lord Jesus Christ" (Romans 5:1).

When it comes to guilt—*theological* guilt before God—this is incredible news! This proclaims the end of all guilt before a holy God. We are truly declared innocent (justified) in Christ, and there is never again even the threat that we will be condemned for our sin! Read on in Romans:

> There is now no condemnation for those who are in Christ Jesus. For the law of the Spirit of life in Christ Jesus has set you free from the law of sin and of death. For what the Law could not do, weak

as it was through the flesh, God did: sending His own Son in the likeness of sinful flesh and as an offering for sin, He condemned sin in the flesh, so that the requirement of the Law might be fulfilled in us, who do not walk according to the flesh but according to the Spirit (8:1-4).

This is the Christian's Emancipation Proclamation. No more guilt! No more slavery to sin and death! No more fear that God will condemn! Notice that this Scripture passage teaches that God condemned *our sin—not us!*

We are truly free. We are truly forgiven.

Under a Greater Law

"Sin and death" is a spiritual law, just like gravity is a physical law. Gravity remains in effect upon a human body unless and until a stronger law or force takes over. The law of aerodynamics overcomes the law of gravity. When we are in an airplane that is flying, we overcome gravity.

What is "the law of sin and death" that Romans 8 talks about? The law of sin and death is simply this: "The person who sins will die" (Ezekiel 18:20). We overcome the law of sin and death by experiencing the greater law of the Spirit of life *in Christ Jesus.* In the flying plane, gravity is overcome. *In the risen Christ,* the law of sin and death is overcome! And every believer in Christ is *in Christ!*

Recently my son Brian and I went on a helicopter ride at a local fair. What a rush! For $20 we got the ride of our lives. Strapped safely into our seats, we took off like a rocket straight up in the air. There were no doors covering the side entrances to the chopper, and its walls were constructed of clear, hard Plexiglas, so I felt more "outside" than "inside." We swooped and soared over the interstate, a quarry, and the fairgrounds in a three-minute thrill. If my seat belt had not been securely fastened, that helicopter would have just dumped me out the side when we banked left!

Was I safe? Yes! Did I *feel* safe? Absolutely not! There are probably still fingernail prints on the handle inside that helicopter where I clung for dear life. I know now that I would have enjoyed the ride much more had I realized then how safe I really was!

The great news is that all believers in Christ, every one of them, have been 100 percent guilt-free (free from theological guilt before God) from the very moment they trusted Jesus to save them. The tragedy is that so few are experiencing the exhilaration of the joy ride of life in Him. They are not guilty, but they *feel* guilty.

Not *Guilty*—Rather, *Forgiven*

You might be surprised to know that the term *guilty* is almost never used in the New Testament in reference to a believer in Christ. Only one time is the Greek word *enochos* (meaning "liable to [a condition, penalty or imputation];—in danger of, guilty of, subject to")[4] used: in Paul's treatise on the Lord's supper in 1 Corinthians 11:27:

> Whoever eats the bread or drinks the cup of the Lord in an unworthy manner, shall be guilty of the body and blood of the Lord.

The context seems to indicate that some of the Corinthians were treating the elements of the Lord's supper just as though they were regular food. There was an atmosphere of selfishness, impatience, and gluttony at these love feasts, and the Lord was not pleased. In this case, the Lord Himself brought the judgment (in the form of physical discipline) upon those who had sinned in this way. Many of the church members were weak and sick, and some had even died, as a result of God's hand upon them.

Other than that single instance, the New Testament is silent about believers being guilty. But it says a lot about their being forgiven in Christ. Here is a sampling:

> In Him we have redemption through His blood, the forgiveness of our trespasses, according to the riches of His grace which He lavished on us (Ephesians 1:7-8).

> He rescued us from the domain of darkness, and transferred us to the kingdom of His beloved Son, in whom we have redemption, the forgiveness of sins (Colossians 1:13-14).

> When you were dead in your transgressions and the uncircumcision of your flesh, He made you alive together with Him, having forgiven us all our transgressions, having canceled out the certificate of debt consisting of decrees against us, which was hostile to us; and He has taken it out of the way, having nailed it to the cross (Colossians 2:13-14).

Do you realize that there is nowhere in the New Testament epistles where believers in Christ are commanded or compelled to *ask* God to forgive them? That might sound like downright heresy to you, but it is true!

What about 1 John 1:9, you say? In case you don't have it memorized, this verse says,

> If we confess our sins, He is faithful and righteous to forgive us our sins and to cleanse us from all unrighteousness.

Anything about *asking* God for forgiveness there? Nope. It just says that we are to confess or agree with God concerning our sin. In other words, we are to say the same thing about our sin that God says. First of all, we agree with God that it's wrong. Secondly, we agree with Him that it's already been paid for by Christ at the cross. And when we do this we experience to the fullest the forgiveness of our sin (its being taken away) and the cleansing from evil that we need in order to be restored to fellowship with the Holy One. We are forgiven because Christ died on the cross for our sins, not because we confess every sin.

Guilt That We *Feel*

You might be wondering, *Isn't there an emotional element involved when we sin? Shouldn't we feel guilty?* Those are great questions, and they bring us to one more aspect of guilt that we need to address. That is what has been termed *psychological guilt* or *guilt feelings*. This is our emotional response when we know that we have violated a divine or human standard of morality.

Godly Sorrow

The Bible, however, does not call this emotional response *guilt*—and so neither should we. Instead, the scriptural term used is *sorrow*. Notice the two very different forms of this sorrow discussed in 2 Corinthians 7:9-11:

> I now rejoice, not that you were made sorrowful, but that you were made sorrowful to the point of repentance; for you were made sorrowful according to the will of God, so that you might not suffer loss in anything through us. For the sorrow that is according to the will of God produces a repentance without regret, leading to salvation, but the sorrow of the world produces death. For behold what earnestness this very thing, this godly sorrow, has produced in you: what vindication of yourselves, what indignation, what fear, what longing, what zeal, what avenging of wrong! In everything you demonstrated yourselves to be innocent in the matter.

The apostle Paul, in his first letter to the church at Corinth, had reproved them for numerous failings, including tolerating in their fellowship a man who was having sex with his stepmother (1 Corinthians 5:1). The Corinthians responded with such a godly zeal to repent and make this matter right that Paul went to great lengths to commend them.

The realization of their sin was accompanied by *godly sorrow*. Godly sorrow is "according to the will of God" and is therefore a very good thing. It is good because it leads its sufferer to repentance, and it is good because it points to a heart that is truly broken over sin. God says He will never despise a broken and contrite heart (Psalm 51:17). It is knowing God's kind and forgiving nature that moves those who sin to repent (Romans 2:4). Godly sorrow comes through the Word of God which is "profitable for teaching, for reproof, for correction" (2 Timothy 3:16) and which is "able to judge the thoughts and intentions of the heart" (Hebrews 4:12). The Spirit of God uses the Word of God like a sword to reveal our sin and to urge us to repent.

Many Christians would call this the Holy Spirit's "conviction" of sin, but that is not really correct, because that ministry of the Spirit is to the world, not to the believer. In John 16:8-9 Jesus says of the Spirit, "He, when He comes, will convict the world concerning sin...concerning sin, because they do not believe in Me." However, the Holy Spirit does use the Word of God to produce in believers a godly sorrow that leads to repentance.

Worldly Sorrow

Worldly sorrow, on the other hand, does not come from God. It is a sense of remorse and regret for what we've done. But it does not lead to repentance and a sense of restoration before God. It leads to despair and death.

Worldly sorrow is the emotion that Judas felt when he realized he had betrayed innocent blood. It is a realization that one has sinned, and that is good. But it is also the failure to realize that Jesus has the solution to that sin—and that is not good. Failing to find the true and only solution to our sin is a deadly mistake.

Guilt That Is False

False guilt, however, is different. False guilt is the guilt feelings we experience when we think we have sinned, but actually haven't. Unfortunately, it is the emotion that countless people experience every day. Here's an example from one young woman's life:

I grew up in a church steeped in legalism, and its emphasis on rules deeply affected my life and my view of God. In our church, "going to heaven" was always about our performance. If we obeyed all the church rules, which of course were taught "from the Bible," then we could get to heaven. Some of those rules were, "Women may not cut their hair, though trimming the ends is permitted. Men must keep their hair short, off the collar. Men must shave their faces. Women must not wear jewelry, though watches and wedding bands are permitted. Women must not wear pants, for that would make them look like men. Women may not pluck their eyebrows. Shorts are never permitted." And so on. I can so clearly remember all the "thou shalt nots," but I don't remember any encouragement or ever being taught about a relationship with Jesus Christ and about God's wonderful grace and mercy.

What affected me most, though, is that I came to be best friends with the pastor's daughter. I usually spent Sunday afternoons with Judy in her home. The pastor (her dad) was just like the picture he painted of God. He had a lot of anger and was very strict with his children. I can still remember the fear on my girlfriend's face when her father, who was sitting downstairs in his easy chair, demanded that she get him another cup of coffee. No matter where we were in the house, she would hear his voice and drop whatever she was doing to run to serve him.

> This became my view of how God was. I was "externally" trying to live up to standards of being a Christian, but this effort left a gaping hole in my heart for love and acceptance. It is only in the last 5 years that 25 years of guilt and shame have come peeling away from my life.

Was this young woman's guilt legitimate? Should she have felt guilty when she did something the church said was wrong? We don't believe so.

Many churches will add to this woman's list the rule that their people (at least the truly committed ones!) will be there every time the church doors open. Even though it is a good and necessary thing to meet for fellowship with other believers (see Hebrews 10:24-25), does God want us to go to church for fear that He'll get mad if we don't? Clearly not. Is it wrong to question the value of attending services where people are merely "holding to a form of godliness, although they have denied its power" (2 Timothy 3:5)? No, we don't believe that is wrong either. Especially since the last part of 2 Timothy 3:5 tells us to "avoid such men as these"!

Here's another example of how churches can foster false guilt:

> I have been a Christian for 12 years, and I have always been careful to choose a church that is biblically based and stands strongly on Scripture. However, I have been challenged many times to be more submissive, more missions-hearted, more generous, more this, more that. My pastor is a very godly man and I know he teaches from the heart and the Word—but—after doing some reading I'm now wondering why I have never been told how loved and totally accepted I am in Christ. Today, now, just as I am. For years I have felt like

a struggling, failing, never-quite-good-enough Christian. Can it really be true that all God asks of me is to believe in the completed work of Jesus and trust Him to do the rest in my sanctification? What a breath of fresh air! My question is, how did the church get it all wrong? No wonder so many of us walk around under a cloud of guilt over how disappointing our efforts must be to our Holy God.

Heavy Burdens from Legalistic Systems

Not all churches have gotten it all wrong. Many are wonderful, vibrant, healthy safe havens of grace and truth. But some are not. Some have fallen into the same legalistic trap as the people whom Jesus encountered in the first century. The rules may differ, but the spirit is the same.

Jesus was crying out to those who were trapped under the legalistic system of the Pharisees when He said, "Come to Me, all who are weary and heavy-laden, and I will give you rest. Take My yoke upon you and learn from Me, for I am gentle and humble in heart, and you will find rest for your souls. For My yoke is easy and My burden is light" (Matthew 11:28-30).

But tragically, many of God's people all over the world are still under the pile—crushed by legalistic rules and regulations, wracked by false guilt. And there are at least four ways that legalistic families, churches, or other institutions can heap a heavy burden or put a yoke of slavery on believers.

The Bible—A Sledgehammer

First, frequently those under their teaching are not taught to come to Jesus—at least not to the real Jesus, the One full of grace and truth (John 1:14,17). They are taught to come to the Bible or to specific teachings of the Bible. Jesus Himself upbraided the Pharisees for loving the Scriptures but missing their point—to direct people to Him: "You search the Scriptures because you think that in them you have eternal life; it is these that testify about Me; and you are unwilling to come to Me so that you may have life" (John 5:39-40).

Often Old Testament passages of judgment and wrath are preached with great fervency. Even when New Testament commands are emphasized, if they are preached apart from the grace and forgiveness of God and the acceptance and new life we have in Christ, they can become spiritual sledgehammers—instruments of guilt and condemnation.

Even the *style* of preaching in some churches can contribute to God's people being unnecessarily crushed under a burden of guilt. Those who are already victims of a world system that has beaten them down Monday through Saturday need words of hope, not discouragement, on Sunday morning. Unfortunately, sometimes that does not happen. Dr. David Seamands, in his book *Redeeming the Past*, addresses this issue:

> All of these [problems of divorce, abuse, addictions, and so on] have helped make our society an assembly line for turning out disturbed people with damaged emotions. And many of these damaged emotions are deeply buried in layers of memory which will not respond to the kind of preaching we ordinarily hear. In fact, we can say some of our traditional preaching actually causes people greater fear and hardens their defenses so that those memories are driven still further underground. Even in sermons of comfort or encouragement, it is possible to present the Good News in such a way as to deepen people's despair.
>
> Many times when I asked people why they don't share their problems with their pastor they tell me it is because they already know what he will say. He will simply make them feel guiltier than they already do. When I pursue this further by

asking them how they know this, they usually reply, "I can tell by the way he preaches." It would be easy for evangelists and pastors to dismiss this judgment as unfair. The fact is that it hurts because it is so often true. *Too often our preaching discourages people even more and deters them from seeking the help and healing they so desperately need.*[5]

An Incomplete Understanding of Scripture

The second way in which legalism can produce unnecessary guilt is through preaching the Word of God without a proper understanding of the cultural context. An example of a teaching that can lead to that kind of situation is found in 1 Corinthians 11, where Paul urges women to wear head coverings while praying or prophesying (verses 5-6). Matthew Henry's comments on this are particularly noteworthy since he writes from a seventeenth-century British cultural context:

> The thing he [Paul] reprehends is the woman's praying or prophesying uncovered, or the man's doing either covered...To understand this, it must be observed that it was a signification either of shame or subjection for persons to be veiled, or covered, in the eastern countries, contrary to the custom of ours, where the being bare-headed betokens subjection, and being covered superiority and dominion. And this will help us the better to understand.[6]

Removing a biblical command from its cultural context is dangerous. You can easily end up keeping the *form* while missing its *function*. In this case, there is nothing inherently right or wrong about a woman's wearing a head covering in church. There is, however, something very wrong about a woman not being in submission to the proper authority, and that was Paul's point. In the first century that subjection was demonstrated by a head covering; in the seventeenth century it was just the opposite. In twenty-first-century America, head coverings have nothing to do with submission or shame, but are simply a factor of fashion and weather.

It is the responsibility of those who teach the Word of God and shepherd the flock of God to understand not just *what* Scripture says, but *why* it says it. A scholarly study of the history and cultural context in which the Bible was written can protect teachers from laying a legalistic burden on people today...a burden the Holy Spirit never intended.

Rules from Outside of the Bible

The third way in which legalistic systems can put a yoke of slavery on people is by encumbering them with a heavy load of additional things (not included in Scripture) to do or not do. These become requirements for acceptance by God, or acceptability to others.

Believers are made to feel guilty when they miss a church meeting, don't give sacrificially enough, don't witness enough, don't pray or read their Bibles enough. But who determines what is enough?

We say, "Enough is enough!" When men dictate to God's people (apart from the grace of God and the clear teaching of Scripture) how they should live life, this is spiritual control. When that control becomes damaging to sincere seekers of truth, that is spiritual abuse. Those spiritual abusers are the ones sinning, not those in their flock!

Here is just a small sampling of the rules and regulations from one Christian school in America. Unfortunately, the attempted micromanagement of lives that takes place here is replicated in numerous other institutions as well.

- "The following types of music are not permitted: a. Current popular music; b. Jazz, rock, rap, folk, 'Nashville' type, or new age music; c. Religious music performed in the folk, western rock, or gospel rock style."

- "Men and women students may be together at breakfast, but they must meet and part inside the facility lobby."

- "Computers may not be connected to Internet or e-mail services including wireless services."

- "Men's hair should be cut in such a way that it does not come over the ears, eyebrows, or collar...Men must be clean shaven—no beards or mustaches are permitted. Belts should be worn with pants which have belt loops. Socks should always be worn."

- As far as disciplinary measures are concerned, "Whenever students behave inappropriately with members of the opposite sex, they are 'socialed.' For two weeks they may not communicate with anyone of the opposite sex. The student signs a form stating he will abide by this regulation."

Is this final point giving a disciplinary measure for sexual immorality? Hardly. At this school, such a discipline could be meted out for an infraction as innocuous as a man being found in the women's parking area, or vice versa.

It is obvious that some of these rules and regulations are genuine efforts to try to protect the students' well-being. Some rules, unfortunately, are more likely designed to protect the school's image. The problem is, once you decide not to trust the Holy Spirit to guide someone in his or her life, where do you stop? You simply can't. You end up with a rule for every possible occasion—and in so doing you become ridiculously meticulous.

The original intention of these kinds of rules and regulations is to protect people from sinning. The system progresses as follows: We teach biblical principles that are designed to protect God's people from harm, but we fear that those we love "won't get it." So, to further keep them from sin, we build fences around those scriptural guidelines. And sometimes we build fences around the fences. Soon, the fences become the laws, and the original biblical guidelines are lost in the legalistic shuffle. For example, Scripture tells us that we should not be bound together with unbelievers (2 Corinthians 6:14). Clearly that verse prohibits a believer in Christ from knowingly marrying an unbeliever. So to keep that from happening, a fence is erected: *You cannot date unbelievers.* According to human wisdom, that makes all the sense in the world. In fact, it may be advisable in many cases. But then another fence is built to keep the first fence intact: *You should not have unbelieving friends* (lest you be somehow corrupted or tempted to date). The result is that eventually Christians are encouraged to "separate" from the world of unbelievers. But how can we be the salt and light of the world in isolation?

What happens is that we end up placing an insufferable load upon the shoulders of those who want to do what's right. Plus we provide major ammunition for those who are simply not going to go along with all the rules, in that we foster a rebellious spirit in them when they would otherwise not have had one.

Drivenness

A fourth way in which legalistic systems heap an unbearable burden on their victims is by robbing them of rest. Years back, Tim Hansel wrote the book *When I Relax, I Feel Guilty.* Too often that is the case. Driven to do more and more in order to be accepted or win some semblance of approval, many of God's people are restless, anxious, fearful, guilt-ridden slaves.

When a legalist fails to measure up to the standards set for him or set by himself, he experiences guilt. This can engulf him in a life of drivenness, keeping the pressure on to perform better and better. The lie that fuels this drivenness is the belief that "I am only valuable when I am working hard" or "God's love for me depends upon my performance."

Legalists feel guilty for what they have said and done, or what they have not said and done. But when all is said and done, they've still not done enough. So they often feel like worthless failures. Which leads to even more drivenness, and so on. Many driven performers find it nearly impossible to say "no." They are fearful that others will reject them if they refuse their requests...and rejection spells even more guilt and shame.

In his landmark book *Codependency*, Pat Springle expresses this clearly:

> Motivation by guilt is usually associated with the desire to avoid condemnation and the desire to perform, or measure up, to standards set by someone else or ourselves...Our motivation is characterized by "I have to" and "I can't" statements:
>
> I have to accomplish this or that task today.
>
> I have to go here.
>
> I have to help this person in this way at this time.
>
> I have to say yes.
>
> I have to control my anger and hurt.
>
> I can't fail in this assignment.
>
> I can't let her down.
>
> I can't let my anger get out of control.
>
> I can't say no.[7]

The Temptation to Manipulate by False Guilt

Those who are in ministry are not exempt from the temptations of trying to perform and avoid condemnation. In fact, they are supremely susceptible to taking matters into their own hands in order to try to advance the kingdom. Unfortunately, it is not always the kingdom of God that is at stake—sometimes it is the kingdom of the minister himself or herself.

It is very easy for anyone in Christian leadership (parents, preachers, teachers, and so on) to go beyond what the Scripture says regarding how we are to live. It is so easy to slip into guilt manipulation instead of grace motivation. Christian leaders are under tremendous pressure to perform, and most of them desire strongly to see their people walk with God. But sometimes they give in to the temptation to hurry up and try to change behavior without first seeking to change beliefs. And suddenly grace is replaced by guilt.

Don't misunderstand. God has placed pastors and teachers in His church to lead and instruct the people of God. And the Scriptures admonish us to obey our leaders and submit to them (Hebrews 13:17). We are to appreciate them and esteem them very highly in love for all that they do (1 Thessalonians 5:12-13). When they are operating under the empowering of the Holy Spirit and under the authority of the Bible, they are a precious gift, essential for spiritual health and growth. We are to pray continually for our spiritual leaders. They need it…and the godly ones would be the first to admit that!

The temptation to motivate by guilt, however, is a strong one because it can produce immediate results. The problem is that those results don't reflect real life-transformation. For example, people can be "guilted" into giving extra money for a special offering, bringing a guest in order to help the church break an attendance record, or signing up to volunteer for a needy ministry—all just by the sheer force of the pastor's personality. Often these people discover a growing sense of resentment in their hearts once they stand back and realize how they've been manipulated. Further, once the yoke of guilt is removed, their behavior generally reverts to its original state—that is, unless their resentment turns to rebellion.

Grace, on the other hand, is God's way of effecting change. The standard is internal, not external—transforming the heart, not just conforming the behavior. In general, it is a slower process because it gives people room to change under the patient transforming hand of God…and that simply takes time. Unfortunately, for some Christian leaders that poses a problem. They simply don't want to wait that long, so they engage in religious behavior modification, often using guilt as the driving force.

Discerning False Guilt and Finding Rest

If you have been trapped in a legalistic system of rigid rules, regulations, and standards, chances are you have grown to mistrust your own God-given discernment. You have relied on others to tell you what is right and wrong. *After all, they're the spiritual leaders.* You may have felt a "check in your spirit" (sensing something wasn't quite right), but you likely dismissed it as either rebellion or a critical spirit.

Don't be so quick to ignore that spiritual "intuition" in your heart. God has given His new-covenant people the precious Holy Spirit, who will guide us into all truth (John 16:13). He has written His laws on our hearts and minds (Hebrews 10:16). If we seek Him, the Holy Spirit will never fail to give us clear wisdom as to what is right and wrong, even when false guilt seeks to overwhelm our emotions. John gives us this assurance in his first letter:

> Little children, let us not love with word or with tongue, but in deed and truth. We will know by this that we are of the truth, and will assure our hearts before Him in whatever our heart condemns us; for God is greater than our heart and knows all things (1 John 3:18-20).

Through a Holy Spirit–directed and empowered study of God's Word, you can develop an inner witness of what is truth and what is error. This witness will expose deception and the false guilt caused by legalism. Then you will be able to walk in freedom, even when surrounded by a legalistic system. John again assures us,

> The anointing [presence of the Holy Spirit] which you received from Him abides in you, and you have no need for anyone to teach you; but as His anointing teaches you about all things, and is true and is not a lie, and just as it has taught you, you abide in Him (1 John 2:27).

As you abide in Christ, gaining confidence in your relationship with God and in your understanding of His Word, you will be able to stand firm against the false standards of legalism, just as our Lord Jesus and the apostle Paul did in their day. You will begin to see false guilt fade away. You will come to walk with Jesus, with His easy yoke and light load resting on your shoulders. And you will finally find rest for your soul.

3

IT'S A SHAME

Even when we look back at our lives from the vantage point of grace, there can still be pain. The following testimony is not written by an angry, bitter woman, but by a dear saint powerfully used by the Lord. As you will see, in her legalistic home she often felt guilty. But even more painful was her sense of shame.

> My dad was a very religious man who read the Bible for hours every day. He was an elder in our church and made sure our family was there every time the doors were open. But my dad's religion was often used as a rod of iron in our home.
>
> There were times when my dad would force me to pray and read the Bible aloud after disciplining me. I came to think of Bible-reading as a form of punishment, and the regimented, forced prayer times convinced me that God was angry with me. If my mom and I were enjoying ourselves while watching an interesting program, my dad would get a scowl on his face and turn off the TV. He would say, "Let's read the Bible." We were made to read Old Testament prophecy passages or

genealogies packed with long, almost unpronounceable names.

I felt pressured and fearful, like I wasn't able to do anything right and that fun was wrong. Worse yet, I came to feel that *I* was wrong...like there was just something wrong with *me*. Adding to my shame was the fact that my dad could never truly believe I was saved. Countless times he would ask me if I was ready for Jesus' return. He would say, "You better be praying that you are worthy when Jesus comes back!"

His six children seemed to thwart his ability to fulfill his purpose in life, which seemed to be about working hard to please God by obeying Scripture and using money wisely. It was the gravest of sins to waste money. He had very strict rules about everything that was done in our home. He wanted everything neat and orderly. He monitored the use of hot water and electricity. In the winter, we slept in bedrooms with no heat because he said we needed to save money, not because we lacked a heater or the money to use it. I remember seeing my breath on cold mornings in my bedroom while getting ready for school.

I lived with a terrible sense that I could never keep up with all the rules. There were too many, and my dad might change them at any moment. I lived in fear of doing something, anything, that would displease my dad. And more painfully, I lived with the realization that there was little I could do that *did* please him. One time my niece and I were reading Harlequin romance novels in my room, when my dad came in and grabbed them from us. With that awful scowl on his face he tore the books apart page by page. Though there wasn't anything sexual about them, he acted like we were complete sluts for reading them. We were both crying. It was horrible.

When I was young, the discipline we received was with a belt or switch. It was not really the method of discipline that was so painful. It was the trauma caused by his anger and the ferocity with which he struck my siblings and me. There was one time when the belt broke as he was whipping me. The buckle flew up and hit me in the face, and I got a black eye. I had to cover up what had happened. There were many times when I had cuts and welts on my legs that I had to cover up with heavy tights, even when the weather was warm. It was painful, embarrassing, and shaming.

His abuse was also verbal. When angry, my dad would say that I was lazy, that I was "a moron," and that I would never amount to anything. When I was a teenager, he would intently look at my face to examine my eye makeup. He would call me a "Jezebel" when he thought I was wearing too much. When he disapproved of my clothes, he would label me a "streetwalker."

The Torment of Shame

False guilt and false shame are fraternal twins, not identical ones, but they are often born from the same legalistic womb. They're illegitimate offspring of verbal, emotional, physical, sexual, and spiritual abuse. When they are in control of someone's life, they are cruel taskmasters.

Shame runs deep because it makes its home near the very core of our being. Nobody likes to feel guilt, but shame is worse. Guilt says that I did something wrong. Shame broadcasts the message that *I* am what's wrong. There is a huge difference, as Dr. Sandra Wilson points out in her book *Released from Shame:* "Shame is different than guilt. Guilt tells me I made a mistake. Shame shouts that I AM a mistake. If my behavior is wrong, I can correct it and change. If my very being is flawed, I am without hope for change."[1]

At least that is how we are made to feel, especially in a legalistic home or church situation. Fortunately, real change is not only possible but is part of your heritage as a child of God. You are truly "transformed by the renewing of your mind" (Romans 12:2). Not only that, but the torment and humiliation of years of living in shame can be healed by the Restorer, the Lord Jesus. He has come to "bring good news to the afflicted," to "bind up the brokenhearted, to proclaim liberty to captives and freedom to prisoners" (Isaiah 61:1). This is the year of the Lord's favor and grace, not of unflinching and cruel standards. And He has come to comfort those who mourn (61:2).

A Journey out of Shame

To be perfectly honest, I (Paul) didn't want to write this chapter. Not because it isn't important. It is vitally important because there are countless numbers of God's people who are still being crushed under a yoke of shame. But I also knew that it would mean facing some very painful memories in my own life, memories I would have much rather left alone. I knew it would mean facing my own shame, shame that piggybacked on the legalistic system in which I grew up.

But a remarkable thing happened as I allowed the Spirit of God to bring back to mind more and more things I had tried to forget. Facing the very thing I dreaded—the pain of my shame—became a doorway into a broader and brighter expanse of freedom. I pray your journey will be as fruitful, though I wish I could guarantee that it will be less painful. I can't. What I *can* guarantee is that the One who comforts the mourner will be with all those who are His in Christ. He wants to give you "the oil of gladness instead of mourning, the mantle of praise instead of a spirit of fainting, so [you] will be called oaks of righteousness, the planting of the LORD, that He may be glorified" (Isaiah 61:3).

I grew up on a small farm in the Finger Lakes region of western New York state. I don't remember a lot of joy as a child. What I do remember was performing hard to fit in and be accepted. I always tried to do my best, often going way beyond the norm. Pleasing people became my highway to happiness. I liked it when others saw how good I could be as I did things for people.

The problem with finding value through people-pleasing is that it is like an exercise wheel for a hamster. You expend a lot of energy, but you never get anywhere. The moment you stop performing, you find you are right back where you started. Only you are more tired this time. And yet you run some more and more and...It's called drivenness.

I tried to find my niche through athletics, tennis in particular. Right across the street from my home in Corning, New York, there was a building that became my tennis partner. I would spend endless hours hitting the ball against the front of the building. The hard work paid off. I always beat my teammates in singles, and so I became the number one seed at Northside High.

I remember my match against the top player at Bath High School. I was ready. Since I was considered one of the best players in the county, expectations were high for me to win. And I had a lot of confidence. I was looking forward to proving my value through performing well. (As you have probably gathered by now, that has been the theme of my life.)

The match started great. I won the first of three sets easily, 6-1. I played hard and aggressively, hitting some beautiful winners. But his strategy was to lob back everything I threw at him, waiting patiently for me to make the mistake. In my frustration, his strategy worked.

As the match wore on, my confidence wore away. After three sets, my opponent had become my conqueror: 6-1, 5-7, 6-8. I had lost the match I was expected to win. I felt like a whipped pup. Shamed, I realized that I had let my teammates, myself, and others down. The fact that people had expected me to win only made it worse. I was never the same on a tennis court again.

Shame-Based Identity

For me, shame became a crippler. I never seemed to be able to measure up to my own standards or the expectations of others. You see, the law doesn't have to come on tablets of stone to kill. It can come by way of one's own unrealistic expectations or the high hopes of others. The looks of disapproval or disappointment from other people can cruelly crush our sense of worth, and the mirror can become our mocker, reflecting back to us the face of a loser.

My mind became my worst enemy: *I failed. I'm useless. What do people really think of me? I'm not worth anything. There's something wrong with me. I should have done better.* I hated making mistakes, and I hated admitting them even more, because mistakes meant imperfection, and imperfection meant shame. I had been taught well that performance was the way to establish worth. If I didn't perform very well, then I wasn't very valuable. I had a shame-based identity and belief system.

I realized years later the dead-end street of such ill-logic. My own failings and growth helped me understand the devastation of a professional tennis player who came into my office for counseling. He told me of the time when he had just beaten the number-one tennis player in the United States. He had immediately called his mother on the phone to tell her the good news—and she had simply said, "You couldn't have." He had hung up the phone in disbelief and shame. His life of shame had affected his marriage, his job, and every aspect of his life.

What Is *Shame?*

In this chapter we want to examine the following issues: What is shame? Is there any place for shame in the life of a believer in Christ? How does legalism foster false shame, and what is the way out of a destructive, shame-based lifestyle?

The *Random House Dictionary* defines *shame* as "a painful feeling, a fact or circumstance that is a cause for regret; to cause to suffer disgrace; to undo." Similar are the terms *embarrassment, humiliation, injury to one's pride, disgrace, dishonor,* and *reproach.* J.I. Rodale's *Synonym Finder* lists *debasement, smear, tarnish, blemish, disrespect, depreciation, unworthiness, abasement,* and *disappointment.*[2]

Shame is a strong and disheartening sense of failure and worthlessness. It is clearly a deeply demoralizing emotion, which brings grief to the individual experiencing it. But it is more than a feeling. It is a feeling generated from a mind-set that says, *I don't measure up to what I should be, what others are, or what others expect of me.*

The Place of Shame in a Believer's Life

Living out of a shame-based identity is debilitating and defeating. But there is a legitimate place for shame, even in the life of a believer, and that's when there actually *is* something wrong with us or our behavior. God has placed a warning system for this in all of us. We call it our conscience. For instance, in 1 Samuel 24:5 we read, "It came about afterward that David's conscience bothered him because he had cut off the edge of Saul's robe." In other words, King David felt legitimate shame for touching the Lord's anointed king (verse 6). That warning bell within him was good and appropriate, motivating him to positive action—namely, he did not allow himself or his men to do further harm to King Saul (verses 7-22). Nor did he wallow in his shame, allowing it to plunge him into depression.

A conscience, however, is not an infallible guide to what is right and wrong. Apart from the presence of the Holy Spirit, it can become seared "as with a branding iron" (1 Timothy 4:2), no longer functioning as a moral alarm bell. On the other hand, many people have oversensitized consciences, especially those whose lives have been steeped in a shame-based, legalistic system.

Identity Comes First

The apostle Paul was very disturbed that the Corinthian believers were going to unbelievers to settle civil disputes. Not unlike in our society today, lawsuits were the rage in first-century Corinth. His words were quite scathing:

> I say this to your shame. Is it so, that there is not among you one wise man who will be able to decide between his brethren, but brother goes to law with brother, and that before unbelievers? (1 Corinthians 6:5-6).

If you have freely used shame as a means of seeking to motivate others, you might be quick to respond, "See? Even the apostle Paul shamed people into repentance! Therefore, shaming others is not an indicator of legalism." But let's look more closely at what Paul said.

True, Paul was saying in essence, "You ought to be ashamed of yourselves." But notice the context in which his case is presented. Paul was affirming the Corinthian believers in their identity in Christ and calling them to live life accordingly. In verse two he had asked the question, "Or do you not know that the saints will judge the world?" Already he had told them that they were saints by calling (1:2), not miserable, wretched sinners. Beyond that, Paul had informed them that the saints would also be judging angels (6:3)!

The apostle's point was that since the believers were saints who would one day judge unbelievers and even angels, why did they not settle matters by seeking out wise men in the church? Why were they allowing themselves to be judged by the very people they themselves would one day judge? It made no sense to Paul, and he saw it as bringing shame upon the body of Christ. They should have known better and done better.

However, it is important to immediately observe that Paul did not use shame as a club to browbeat the people of God. In 1 Corinthians 4:14 he says, "I do not write these things to shame you, but to admonish you as my beloved children." Paul had become their spiritual father through proclaiming the gospel to them and seeing them converted (verse 2). He called them his "beloved children"—and they were God's beloved children as well.

A Calling to a Higher Life

Clearly, Paul's use of "shame" was far different than the legalist's. The legalist relentlessly erodes away the dignity, value, and self-esteem of those in his path. The shame they feel is because they are convinced they are worthless. Paul's rare use of shame was based on the fact that believers are of immense value and worth, being saints and children of God. Therefore it is shameful for them to walk in a manner unworthy of such a high calling. He was calling the saints to a higher life, just as God was doing. He was not driving them deeper into a muck hole of failure and worthlessness.

The shaming legalist says, "See? You are nothing. You've always been nothing and always will be nothing! What you just did simply confirms what I've said."

The gracious servant of the gospel says, "You are holy, set apart from sin. You are a beloved child of God, with the high calling to walk in newness of life. Repent and do what is right, for sinning is not what you were made for in Christ."

In the former case, under legalism, all that results is worldly sorrow that leads to regret and death. In the latter, under grace, the result is godly sorrow that leads to repentance.

We expect sinful behavior from nonbelievers. But Christians have become new creations in Christ, and the higher way of righteous living is expected of them—not to gain God's acceptance, but because they already have it!

Real Shame, Real Change

Counselors today who negate the concept of real guilt and real shame do a disservice to people, like those "counselors" in Jeremiah's day who "healed the brokenness of My people superficially, saying, 'Peace, peace,' but there is no peace" (Jeremiah 6:14). The solution is not to throw out the real thing with the counterfeit, but to point people to the cross, where our real shame was placed on Jesus Christ. He "endured the cross, despising the shame, and has sat down at the right hand of the throne of God" (Hebrews 12:2).

Through Christ's death on the cross, our real acts of disobedience to God are forgiven, and the real corruption of our unsaved hearts is changed! You can rejoice that you have "been saved by the LORD with an everlasting salvation; you will not be put to shame or humiliated to all eternity" (Isaiah 45:17).

To be perfectly frank, we are disappointed when preachers quote Jeremiah 17:9 in reference to new-covenant believers in Christ: "The heart is more deceitful than all else and is desperately sick; who can understand it?" If that were the true condition of a believer in Christ, then we would all be wallowing in a shame-based identity system!

But Jeremiah was speaking of life under the old covenant. Look at what Ezekiel wrote concerning the condition of our heart and inner man under God's new covenant:

> I will sprinkle clean water on you, and you will be clean; I will cleanse you from all your filthiness and from all your idols. Moreover, I will give you a new heart and put a new spirit within you; and I will remove the heart of stone from your flesh and give you a heart of flesh [soft, tender, yielding]. I will put My Spirit within you and cause you to walk in My statutes, and you will be careful to observe My ordinances. You will live in the land that I gave to your forefathers; so you will be My people, and I will be your God (Ezekiel 36:25-28).

God has done away with the old system that shut us all up under sin and has brought us into a new, *grace-based* reality! In

Christ our hearts are new, not old. They are clean, not dirty. They are alive and healthy, not deceitful and desperately sick.

Our responsibility then as believers in Christ is as John exhorts us: "Now, little children, abide in Him, so that when He appears, we may have confidence and not shrink away from Him in shame at His coming" (1 John 2:28). We are to abide in Christ—to remain with Him, keeping our eyes focused on Him, listening to what He says, and doing what He commands, knowing that it is His strength that enables us to do so. Then there will be no shame, only joy, when Jesus comes to bring us home!

The Bondage of False Shame

Having examined the reality of legitimate shame, how do we know when shame is illegitimate? How does a legalistic system in the heart, home, or church contribute to false shame? The following testimony is tragic. It is the story of a sincere seeker who was ambushed by legalism on the road to liberty in Christ. But the grace of God proved stronger.

I see that legalism is usually preached by those that have never been in bondage (or so they say). They have no idea how heartbreaking it is for a child of God to finally get up the courage to seek help for his addiction and be met with an unrealistic church that is trapped in traditions. It plays right into the hands of the enemy. It leaves you confused and ashamed and distorts your idea of God and yourself. Legalism is a counterproductive lie that keeps people in bondage.

With tears for those children of God who are in bondage, this is my testimony. Legalism was one of the reasons I left the church in the first place, and it helped pave the way for the enemy to introduce me to a bunch of junk. A couple of years passed, then God, out of His grace, intervened in my life. I recommitted my life to Jesus, and the year that followed was one of the most wonderful years of my life. God laid the foundation to help me stand during the storm that was to come.

Satan remembered the seeds I had sown and he attacked. I was so confused, and I thought in a legalistic way. This was all the enemy needed to crush my mind. The more I found myself doing what is wrong, the harder I tried in my own strength to free myself. I was locked in a dark room, with the four walls of guilt, shame, fear, and hopelessness. (In reality, this room was already unlocked and open.) These four walls, along with tears, were what I experienced day after day.

I have heard of people who remain like this for years. But I could not take it any longer. I begged God for death rather than a life like this. But Jesus provided the way of escape. TRUTH. I have now found my freedom in Christ, and I am understanding who I am in Christ. God is showing me how to stand firm, how to put on the armor and use the sword, how to take every thought captive and allow my mind to be renewed. May my voice be another out of many that says, "JESUS IS THE BONDAGE BREAKER AND THE TRUTH SETS US FREE!"

Sources of False Shame

Illegitimate shame is born out of abuse, rejection, and the failure to keep legalistic standards. When we experience rejection from people who are supposed to accept us, it sends a message loud and clear to our hearts: *You are worthless. You are unlovable.*

When this rejection comes from within our own families, it is devastating. It will drive some people to try even harder to gain approval. It will rob others of the ability to receive true love and encouragement. It will drive some to the point of despair. Or it can push its victims toward deep rebellion.

When this rejection comes from the church, it can make us believe that God is impossible to please. Brennan Manning, in *The Ragamuffin Gospel,* bemoans this perception of God:

> The God of the legalistic Christian, on the other hand, is often unpredictable, erratic and capable of all manner of prejudices. When we view God this way, we feel compelled to engage in some sort of magic to appease Him. Sunday worship becomes a superstitious insurance policy against His whims. This God expects people to be perfect and to be in perpetual control of their feelings and thoughts. When broken people with this concept of God fail—as inevitably they must—they usually expect punishment. So, they persevere in religious practices as they struggle to maintain a hollow image of a perfect self. The struggle itself is exhausting. The legalists can never live up to the expectations they project on God.[3]

But God isn't that way at all. He is "compassionate and gracious, slow to anger and abounding in lovingkindness" (Psalm 103:8). Unfortunately, many people in bondage to legalism are trying desperately to connect with God on a level of performance-based acceptance. And that is one place where He cannot be found.

Shame Drives Us to Hide

Generally speaking, shame makes us feel naked and vulnerable and drives us to hide or cover up. After Adam and Eve sinned, they hurriedly sewed fig leaves together when they discovered they were naked but no longer unashamed (Genesis 3:7). And we have been doing the same thing ever since.

Not with fig leaves, but with our own twenty-first-century versions of them. Our more socially acceptable cover-ups include an obsession with dieting, physical fitness, or body sculpting; spending exorbitant amounts of money on purely cosmetic surgeries; keeping up with the latest fashions, or having the "perfect" house, car, children, and so on; working long hours to the detriment of our health and relationships; drivenness to obtain a never-ending stream of graduate degrees, athletic awards, promotions, titles; or trying with all our might to somehow please or appease the God we fear by adhering to a list of relentless religious rules and regulations.

As damaging as those things can be, unfortunately the world also offers a complete demonic menu of ways to "self-medicate" our shame. They include a whole array of drugs and alcoholic beverages, as well as pornography and other types of sexual immorality. This recent story in the aftermath of the scandal among Catholic priests is as tragic as it is true:

> Cardinal Bernard Law acknowledged…that some of his decisions regarding priests were wrong, and said he has a "far deeper awareness of this terrible evil" of clergy sexual abuse than he did ten months ago, when the scandal first broke. Victims of abuse, with whom Law recently met, urged him to speak out more publicly and frequently…"As I have listened personally to the stories of men and women who have endured such abuse, I have learned that some of these consequences include lifelong struggles with alcohol and drug abuse, depression, difficulty in maintaining relationships and, sadly, suicide," he said.[4]

Of course there is much more than Cardinal Law mentioned here. How many of these victims kept quiet because they were afraid of being rejected by the church? How many were trapped in their shame because they believed God wanted them to keep this dark secret and so "protect" the perpetrators (who were, after all, "men of the cloth"!)? How many turned away from God out of disgust for a religious system that would spawn such awful abuse? How many, as a result of being molested, were thrust headlong into a compulsion for pornography or sexual promiscuity, or were polarized the opposite direction into frigidity? How many young boys grew into young men who were tormented by homosexual thoughts, urges, and eventually relationships because of what was done to them? And how many still labor under the horrible burden of thinking they are evil and absolutely worthless because of what happened?

Sex and Shame

There is perhaps no greater area of shame for a person, even a child of God, than that which comes from the misuse or abuse of sex. This was, sadly, so true of my (Paul's) life.

I was always looked upon as different by other boys because I was brought up to live a clean life. I am grateful for the good, moral upbringing I had, but because of the strictness of my home I was forced to dress differently than the other kids. And of course it was considered a sin to fight, and so I was bullied around quite a bit. I thought I was being persecuted for the sake of Christ—but in retrospect, much of what I endured was because I came across as "odd for God."

When I was nine or ten years old some older boys grabbed me, picked me up, and took me to a small building out behind our school. Once we were in that building, they pulled down my pants and fondled me, laughing at me. I was humiliated.

What these boys did left a deep scar in my life. It caused me to totally change my thinking in regard to sexual things. I felt so dirty...but soon I found myself becoming very curious about sex. Unfortunately, it was a taboo subject in our legalistic home. It was understood that sex was bad and that you just didn't talk about it. I never felt the freedom to tell my parents what had happened to me, nor did I have an outlet to express my concern over my growing interest in sex. And so my curiosity grew in an unnatural way, for through the law comes the arousing of sinful passions (Romans 7:5).

The legalism of my youth was also producing a growing sense of isolation from other kids. And yet, like any normal boy, I wanted to fit in and feel a part of the gang. On one hand I felt dirty and shameful for my interest in sex and on the other hand I desperately wanted to please God. At times, my desire to be accepted overcame my need to do what was right.

The boys on the neighboring farm were willing to "let me in"—but only if I joined them in their sexual experimentations. And so I ended up playing naked with them in their barn.

I was so naïve that when a box of Kotex came in our mail, I asked my mom what it was. I was sternly reprimanded and never said another word. I also became curious about what a condom was, so I tried to get a boy to bring me one so I might see it.

Why am I telling you this? Well, the whole area of sex had been kept totally secret from me. And I understand now why counselors consider this kind of secrecy an actual sexual violation. They refer to it as *suppression*, which means that all normal sexual inquiry, expressions, and feelings are reprimanded. In my counseling training, I found out that preventing or discouraging our children from talking with us about sexual things is actually a form of sexual abuse.

But that is what shame does. Shame tells us to shut up and keep things hidden. In legalistic homes and churches there is an overemphasis on image and reputation. *Keep smiling and don't do anything to harm the family...or church...name.* Unwittingly, these institutions become, as Jesus dubbed them, "whitewashed tombs." Nice, bright, and shiny on the outside—but full of death underneath.

Renouncing the Hidden Things

If you are caught in a legalistic system that has pressured you to keep quiet about shameful things in order to preserve that system's image or reputation, you need to talk with someone you can trust. You need to "walk in the Light" (1 John 1:7) because, as we saw with the victims of molestations by Catholic priests, shame can kill. The apostle Paul put it this way:

> As we received mercy, we do not lose heart, but we have renounced the things hidden because of shame, not walking in craftiness or adulterating the word of God, but by the manifestation of truth commending ourselves to every man's conscience in the sight of God (2 Corinthians 4:1-2).

God's way of dealing with shame is to *renounce* things that we have hidden in shame—not *repress* them. According to *Webster's New World Dictionary*, the word *renounce* means

> to give up, usually by a formal public statement... to cast off; disown; deny all responsibility for or allegiance to.

This is a very strong word. It indicates the most radical, urgent jettisoning of something deemed wrong or destructive. Once a belief or behavior has been renounced, it can no longer have a detrimental effect on the person.

Webster's definition of *repress* is also enlightening:

> In psychiatry, to force (ideas, impulses, etc. painful to the conscious mind) into the unconscious, where they still modify behavior or remain dynamic; to prevent (unconscious ideas, impulses, etc.) from reaching the level of consciousness.

You can sweep things under the rug, but eventually you'll stumble and fall over them. Or you can be rid of them forever. The *Steps to Freedom in Christ* (available through your local Christian bookstore) can provide a very helpful framework through which you can find release from the shame of your past. And chapter 11 of this book will provide some very important help as well.

Manipulating God's People Through Shame

It is challenging enough to deal with the real issues of sin in our lives in a thorough manner. Legalism, however, generates shame where there should be none. The Pharisees were constantly trying to make Jesus and His disciples feel ashamed for things that they did which were not in the least bit wrong. This shame-manipulation was a feeble effort at trying to control a Man and His new system that deeply threatened their power.

They objected when Jesus' disciples picked heads of grain and ate them on the Sabbath. This, in their narrow thinking, was "work" and was therefore unlawful. Jesus rebuked them: "If you had known what this means, 'I desire compassion, and not a sacrifice,' you would not have condemned the innocent" (Matthew 12:7). The legalist almost always demonstrates a far greater concern for *laws* than for *lives*.

"Sunday Religion"

Elsewhere Jesus corrected the Pharisees' tunnel vision by proclaiming that the Sabbath was made for man, not man for the Sabbath (Mark 2:27). The day of rest was intended to be a servant to mankind, providing restoring rest for spirit, soul, and body. It was never intended to be a cruel master, forbidding us from going about our normal daily lives and helping others (see Matthew 12:9-13).

How ridiculous that some people today forbid doing anything but "religious" activities on Sunday! Strictly speaking, Sunday isn't even the Sabbath anyway—it is Friday sundown to Saturday sundown. Missing a worship service on Sunday for a legitimate reason is not a sin. However, making people feel ashamed if they miss a Sunday service *is* a sin! Obviously, we are not to forsake the assembling of ourselves together (Hebrews 10:25)—and a habit pattern of neglecting fellowship may indicate a serious spiritual problem—but we dare not turn this into a law to bully people into coming out every time the church doors are open!

I (Rich) can recall one woman in a church where I was a member who was the self-appointed watchdog of the congregation. She had an uncanny knack of knowing who was there and who wasn't every Sunday. (Perhaps she kept a ledger!) At any rate, she would always sidle up to her victims on the first Sunday of their return and announce, "We missed you last week." It was the glint in her eye, I think, that tipped me off that this was simply her way of saying, "Gotcha!" To be perfectly honest, I often muttered under my breath as she walked away with her smoking gun, "Well, I certainly didn't miss YOU!"

Divorce

Another example of an area in which many people have suffered great shame at the hands of fellow Christians is the matter of divorce. Often those who are, or have been, involved in a divorce are not accepted equally at church. Perhaps they are expected to go to a special class during Bible or Sunday school classes. Most of the time they are silently labeled as second-class believers, and they suffer from rejection and shame.

Our desire, though, should be to reach out to them in love and acceptance because God does. He doesn't accept any of us on the basis of our behavior, but on the basis of who we are.

> Accept one another, just as Christ also accepted us to the glory of God (Romans 15:7).

> ...to the praise of the glory of His grace, by which He made us accepted in the Beloved [Christ] (Ephesians 1:6 NKJV).

Understanding this concept will greatly help. When we accept other believers based on *who they are,* not *what they do,* we accept them as people—whether or not we accept their behavior. And it is all by God's grace—His undeserved favor:

not because of what they have done but because of what Christ has done on the cross.

When John Kennedy was president of the United States, during the Cuban missile incident many dignitaries assembled in the Oval Office of the White House to discuss the crisis. A photo of this meeting reveals that, while these leaders were in serious discussion over the events, trying to decide what to do, little John Kennedy was playing under the president's desk, and one of his shoes was lying on the floor at the president's feet. Now, all the VIPs had had to show credentials to enter the office; but the president's son hadn't. If you were to ask how this could be, the answer would be this: It was because of who he was—family.

I now realize that when I (Paul) was a pastor, I subtly avoided people who were divorced. I didn't look forward to their joining my church. Shame on me! That was legalism—and it was wrong. Certainly, there are qualifications for certain offices in the church, but we are to accept every believer as a brother or sister in Christ—a member of our spiritual family.

Shame from Disagreement

Legalists often try to bring shame to other Christians because they do not interpret Scripture the same way or have the same convictions they do. *But in the Scripture, there are important principles given that should govern our behavior in matters not specifically mentioned in the Bible.* For instance, 1 Corinthians 6:12 gives us the principle that "all things are lawful for me, but not all things are profitable...I will not be mastered by anything."

It is certainly not right to exercise freedom when it would cause a brother to be damaged (which would clearly be unprofitable). Paul told us, "It is good not to eat meat or to drink wine, or to do anything by which your brother stumbles" (Romans 14:21).

What each of us is to do is to allow the Holy Spirit to form our convictions. The following verses give the Lord's counsel:

> Put on the Lord Jesus Christ, and make no provision for the flesh in regard to its lusts (Romans 13:14).

> Whatever is not from faith is sin (Romans 14:23).

> Do you not know that your body is a temple of the Holy Spirit who is in you...? Therefore glorify God in your body (1 Corinthians 6:19,20).

The point we are making is this: We have no right to criticize or shame people just because they differ from us in their convictions. "Who are you to judge the servant of another? To his own master he stands or falls; and he will stand, for the Lord is able to make him stand" (Romans 14:4). The key is living to the glory of God. "Whether, then, you eat or drink or whatever you do, do all to the glory of God" (1 Corinthians 10:31).

It is amazing but sadly true that just about anything can become a source of false shame for God's people: having a TV set or pool table, connecting to a cable provider, keeping your kids in public schools, speaking in tongues, not speaking in tongues, having a Christmas tree in your home, enjoying country music, going to the theater to see a movie, not using the King James or some other certain version of Scripture, wearing certain styles or colors of clothes and not wearing others, keeping your hair at a certain length (for both men and women), and so on.

No matter where you draw or don't draw the line, you can almost always count on somebody pointing a gnarly finger at you in disapproval. For many people, such attempts at legalistic control are merely a passing annoyance. But for others who are spring-loaded toward a shame-based identity, such criticism can be devastating.

As we have seen, shame is just one of the terrible consequences of an overwhelming trauma. How unspeakable that

Christians often feel compelled to compound that trauma with yet another blow of rejection and shame! May God bring us sorrow over this and lead us to accept His forgiveness and His power to change.

Living Out God's Amazing Grace

If you are one of God's people who are haunted by a constant low-grade fever of shame, this is a fight for your life. We encourage you to pray and ask the Lord for grace-filled relationships that can help you heal. We urge you to persist in seeking them out. As much as we love and value the local church, the reality is that some fellowships are deeply dysfunctional, operating out of a guilt- or shame-based value system. If you are sincerely seeking to walk with God, and week after week you find yourself damaged and wounded by the preaching or the people in your church, you need to leave. Find a fellowship where God's Word is preached and His amazing grace is lived out, not just sung about!

It is a tragedy that some people find more grace and acceptance in a local bar or local AA meeting than they do in the local church. We conclude with a story about an AA meeting that ought to be a model for every home and church seeking to walk in love, truth, and grace:

> On a sweltering summer night in New Orleans, sixteen recovering alcoholics and drug addicts gather for their weekly AA meeting. Although several members attend other meetings during the week, this is their home group. They have been meeting on Tuesday nights for several years and know each other well. Some talk to each other daily on the telephone, others socialize outside the meetings. The personal investment in one another's sobriety is sizable. Nobody fools anybody else. Everyone is there because he or she made a slobbering mess of his or her life and is trying to put the pieces back together. Each meeting is

marked by levity and seriousness. Some members are wealthy, others middle class or poor. Some smoke, others don't. Most drink coffee. Some have graduate degrees, others have not finished high school. For one small hour the high and the mighty descend and the lowly rise. The result is fellowship.

The meeting opened with the Serenity Prayer followed by a moment of silence...That night, Jack was the appointed leader. "The theme I would like to talk about tonight is gratitude," he began, "but if anyone wants to talk about something else, let's hear it."

Immediately Phil's hand shot up.

"As you all know, last week I went up to Pennsylvania to visit family and missed the meeting. You also know I have been sober for seven years. Last Monday I got drunk and stayed drunk for five days."

The only sound in the room was the drip of Mr. Coffee in the corner.

"You all know the buzz word, H.A.L.T., in this program," he continued. "Don't let yourself get hungry, angry, lonely, or tired or you will be very vulnerable for the first drink. The last three got to me. I unplugged the jug and..."

Phil's voice choked and he lowered his head. I glanced around the table—moist eyes, tears of compassion, soft sobbing the only sound in the room.

"The same thing happened to me, Phil, but I stayed drunk for a year."

"Thank God you're back."

"Boy, that took a lot of guts."

"Relapse spells relief, Phil," said a substance abuse counselor. "Let's get together tomorrow and figure out what you needed relief from and why."

"I'm so proud of you."

"...I never made even close to seven years."

As the meeting ended, Phil stood up. He felt a hand on his shoulder, another on his face. Then kisses on his eyes, forehead, neck and cheek. "You old ragamuffin," said Denise. "Let's go. I'm treating you to a banana split at Tastee-Freeze."[5]

So many of us are filled with shame, desperately *saving face* when what we need is *saving grace.*

May our hearts, homes, and churches become such safe havens of grace and truth. Until that happens, the gospel will have little or no impact on our lives, our families, or our culture. And that truly would be a shame.

4

FUELING FEAR

So far we've hit some heavy issues head-on, and there's more to come. But for a moment we want you to take a deep breath, relax, and enjoy the following short essay. It is titled "Why God Called You."

There are many reasons why God shouldn't have called you. But don't worry. You're in good company. Moses stuttered. John Mark was rejected by Paul. Timothy had ulcers. Hosea's wife was a prostitute. Amos' only training was in the school of sheepherding and fig tree pruning. Jacob was a liar. David had an affair. Solomon was too rich. Jesus was too poor. Abraham was too old. David was too young. Peter was afraid of death. Lazarus *was* dead. John was self-righteous. Naomi was a widow. Paul was a murderer. So was Moses. Jonah ran from God. Miriam was a gossip. Gideon and Thomas both doubted. Jeremiah was a bullfrog (just kidding!)—he was depressed and suicidal. Elijah was burned out. John the Baptist was a loudmouth. Martha was a worrywart. Mary wouldn't help serve. Samson had long hair. Noah got drunk. Did I mention that Moses had a short fuse? So did Peter, Paul—well, lots of folks did.

But God doesn't require a job interview. He doesn't hire and fire like most bosses, because He's more our Dad than our Boss. He doesn't look at financial gain or loss. He's not prejudiced or partial, not judging, grudging, sassy or brassy, not deaf to our cry or blind to our need.

As much as we try, God's gifts are free. Satan says, "You're not worthy." Jesus replies, "Says who? *I* am worthy—and in Me, you are too!" Satan looks back and sees our mistakes. God looks back and sees the cross. He doesn't calculate what you did back in '98. It's not even on the record.

Sure, there are lots of reasons why God shouldn't have called us. But if we truly love Him and hunger for Him, He'll use us in spite of who we were, where we've been, or what we've done.[1]

Trapped in the Snare of Fear

We all need such words of grace. So many of God's people are bound up in a legalistic system, afraid they just don't or won't measure up. A denominational leader once told me (Neil), "As I travel and talk to our pastors I have come to the conclusion that their number-one motivation in ministry is the fear of failure."[2] I thought that was a little exaggerated until I asked the students in a Doctor of Ministry class what they feared the most. All of them said in one way or another that they feared failure.

One survey examining the personal and professional lives of ministers revealed that 50 percent of them feel unable to do all their job requires. And 70 percent said their self-esteem was lower now than when they first entered the ministry!

A pastor came to me (Paul) and declared, "I'm quitting! I'm resigning my church!"

"Why?" I asked him, curious about his reasons for throwing in the towel.

"I haven't had one person join our church this past year."

It was clear the man meant what he said. His face mirrored the deep sadness and fear inside his heart. He saw himself as a complete failure and was taking all the blame and responsibility for the lack of growth in his congregation. My heart really went out to him, having been a pastor many years myself.

After spending some time counseling him, he wondered if there might be something in his past that was blocking his progress in life and ministry. He had no idea what it might be, but he was willing to pray with me for the Lord to reveal it.

As we prayed together, the Lord brought back to his memory a time when a loved one had sexually abused him. Since he had totally forgotten the incident, he wondered whether the memory might be false.

I assured him, "You prayed and asked the Lord to show you the root of any blockage in your life. If the Lord indeed has brought back this very significant event to your mind, then He can confirm it. What He has begun, He is able to complete. You can be sure that He loves you and wants you to be free. Let's pray for the Lord to confirm this to your satisfaction."

A few weeks later a death in his family brought some relatives together at the funeral. At the cemetery, a conversation with a close relative confirmed to this man what God had revealed to him in prayer.

After completely facing his pain and making the choice to forgive, he experienced peace and freedom. His whole countenance changed. You could see the joy in his face. The fear of failure was gone—and with it the sense of condemnation. He was free to be loved, and to love in return. The apostle John informed us that this will happen when we truly connect with God's love:

> We have come to know and have believed the love which God has for us. God is love, and the one who abides in love abides in God, and God abides in him. By this, love is perfected with us, so that we may have confidence in the day of judgment;

> because as He is, so also are we in this world.
> There is no fear in love; but perfect love casts out
> fear, because fear involves punishment, and the
> one who fears is not perfected in love. We love,
> because He first loved us (1 John 4:16-19).

Unconsciously, this pastor had been driven to perform in order to compensate for the damage done to his sense of worth through the abuse. He had believed the lie that his performance determined his value, and so he had come under a self-imposed law system that judged him as a failure. Since by his definition he had not performed well, he had then come to believe that his value in life was gone. He had become trapped in a snare of his own making, and he had found that his version of the law had become his prosecutor, judge, jury, and executioner. That is how our self-made laws operate.

But legalism resulting in fear is not limited to the pastorate. We wonder how many top executives, athletes, politicians, and performers are privately tormented and driven by a whip on their back: the fear of failure—and with it, the fear of rejection. There are also many sincere believers in churches all over the world who are in the same spiritual boat.

Legalism Fuels Fear

In this chapter we want to examine the role that fear plays in the lives of those involved in a legalistic system—both the entrapped and the entrappers. We will also specifically examine how legalism fuels the fear that leads to perfectionism. Finally, we will share some thoughts about "control," though we will tackle that issue even harder in chapters 5 and 6.

The following testimony illustrates how legalism can easily generate a life of fear:

> After I received Christ as my Savior, I was
> encouraged to be baptized and to join a good
> church. The church where I was saved seemed as

good as any, so my husband and I became official members. The other Christians there were so eager to help me grow. And as a young mother, I was grateful for all the help I could get.

As time went by, however, it seemed that the preaching and teaching in my church always revolved around "do's and don'ts." I was told that I must be at church every time the doors opened— Sunday morning and evening services, Wednesday evening prayer meetings, Thursday night visita tions, and so on. It all seemed like "the right thing" to do. But no matter how much I did it wasn't enough. If I didn't meet all these obligations I was made to feel like a failure as a Christian woman. The more involved I became, the more rules were mandated by the church leaders. "Don't go to the movie theater. No dancing. No 'mixed' swimming. Ladies are not allowed to wear pants!" They always managed to pull out a Scripture to justify each new rule.

For years I tried desperately to keep their rules and tried my best to live right and fit in. In spite of all my efforts, my life was only getting harder and harder. I found myself agonizing over the most mundane things, like getting dressed in the morning. I would experience anxiety and stress, fearing that perhaps my skirt was not quite long enough. I found myself more and more fearful of not doing everything just right. Eventually my life began to fall apart. My marriage subsequently ended in divorce, and it became painfully clear that I could never measure up.

A tremendous amount of healing has taken place in the life of this dear saint. She has come to understand her identity in Christ and has learned to place her trust in the Word of God rather than the word of men. But she is still a bit gun-shy, wary of how easy it is to get sucked into the system and lose her life—not for Christ and His kingdom...but for the needs, demands, and opportunities of church and ministry.

Conforming and Performing

Many believers are like this woman, desiring to fit in with the church culture. But in striving to do so, they have succumbed to the pressure to conform and perform. This pressure usually comes by way of feelings or fears of disapproval, embarrassment, or a lack of love from those people important to us. Sometimes it can come by way of overt rejection.

Even the strong and bold apostle Peter feared rejection by his Jewish friends, and so he catered to the legalistic racism of his past. Paul described his confrontation of Peter's hypocrisy in Galatians 2:11-12:

> When Cephas [Peter] came to Antioch, I opposed him to his face, because he stood condemned. For prior to the coming of certain men from James, he used to eat with the Gentiles; but when they came, he began to withdraw and hold himself aloof, fearing the party of the circumcision.

Legalism uses peer pressure to force conformity, because a rule-based system requires rigid adherence to regulations. The focus is on an exterior *conforming of behavior* rather than an interior *transforming of character*. A dim view is taken of any quest for individuality, which is labeled as rebellion or insubordination. Often harsh reprimands or even rejection are the painful paybacks for questioning or even *thinking*. For a new Christian or for a family whose friendships center around the church, the prospect of such shunning is devastating.

Nobody likes to be rejected. Rejection is one of the most painful experiences that humanity suffers. Unconditional love and acceptance are some of the deepest and basic needs we all have, but by definition we cannot do anything to qualify for unconditional and voluntary love. It is simply a gift of God's grace. Too many of God's people, however, labor under the false assumption that if they live perfectly everyone will accept them. So they are squeezed into a life of perfectionism in the vain hope of attaining acceptance. But there was only One who ever lived life perfectly...and they crucified Him.

Perfectionists: Tyrannized by the Law

Jesus was perfect, but He wasn't a perfectionist. He was "full of grace and truth." The law system of the Pharisees placed a heavy yoke of slavery on people, but Jesus' yoke was and is easy, and His load, light. Jesus sets captives free, but legalism puts people in bondage, fueling the fire of fear that produces a perfectionist lifestyle.

In his book *Escape the Trap*, Richard Walters defines perfectionists as

> people who believe they must think and act without flaw, often scolding and punishing themselves when they don't meet this unattainable goal. This approach to life leaves a trail of frustration and only breeds more problems. Perfectionists remember the past with regret, don't enjoy the present as much as they might, and usually dread the future.[3]

Perfectionists live under the cruel tyranny of the law. Whether the standards are imposed from the outside or from within the victims' minds, the demand for perfection is relentless and insufferably unfulfilled. Nothing is ever good enough.

As unbearable as life can be for the perfectionist, his or her tendencies inevitably spill over into the lives of others. In a home this can lead to an almost intolerable burden. Perfectionists will likely make the people around them miserable with their perfectionism. The pillows need to be fluffed a certain way. The bed must be made with no creases. The house has to be spotless. The car can have no dirt on it or in it. The stamps must be straight on the envelopes. Report cards must have straight A's. Athletic performance *will* be stellar. Disapproval is meted out swiftly, as the following testimony illustrates:

I have been married to a legalist husband for 21 years. Neither I nor my children feel like we can ever measure up to his expectations of us. His key verse in life is, "Be perfect as your heavenly Father is perfect." He feels like it is his God-given duty to hold up the standard of perfection to us. If we fail to measure up, he visibly disapproves and gives us the silent treatment.

In his own life, outwardly he strives for perfection. His church attendance has been impeccable. His tithing is more than 10 percent of his gross income. He works hard, does not lie, does not allow PG-13 movies into the home, and lives a "righteous" life. We sacrificially served as missionaries for more than half of our married life, several of those years in Africa.

Despite his holy exterior, he has a great void in love. All of our children are gifted and well-behaved, but they avoid their father and are angry that they cannot be good enough for him. They are angry because they can't earn his love. More and more, they associate our church with their father's legalism and resist going. They want nothing to do with his form of religion. Our home is a battlefield. By God's grace both my children and I are beginning to experience a new side of God's love and grace. But the kids are suffering. They crave his love and acceptance and can't seem to get it.

Legalists feel incapable of truly resting in the gracious, accepting arms of God. Many fear that they're just not worthy of being loved. Although that love is what they desperately need, the lies they have believed refuse to let them relax. Consequently, those around them are not relaxing either, but are living life walking on eggshells.

Things...Not People

Legalistic perfectionists major on law instead of love, on rules instead of relationships, because *things* are more quantifiable than *people*—they can be measured or controlled. *At least*, so the perfectionist thinks, *I can make sure something in my life is acceptable.*

There is a measure of pleasure gained in controlling and maintaining order, but it never serves to alleviate the deep fear and insecurity inside the perfectionist's heart. Ironically, perfectionists actually believe that they are helping others to "do better" by their constant reminders, criticisms, and naggings. But recipients of such "helpful" advice are far more likely to get bitter than get better.

My (Rich's) insensitive perfectionist standards drove my wife, Shirley, to tears one day. Neglecting the fact that she was already at the end of her rope with two small children, I produced "the law" for our home. I am embarrassed to share with you my not-so-inspired "10 Helpful Hints for a Happy Home":

1. If you are done with it...*put it away.*

2. If you leave the room...*turn it off.*

3. If you drop it...*pick it up.*

4. If you get it dirty...*clean it up.*

5. If you open it...*close it.*

6. If you spill it...*wipe it up.*

7. If you take it off...*hang it up or put it in the hamper.*

8. If you use it all up...*throw it away.*

9. If you mess it up...*straighten it up.*

10. If you do it now...*you won't forget about it.*

Shirley didn't even get to my *really* helpful hints at the bottom of the page (which I will spare you from having to read) before she started crying. Once I realized what a mess I'd made, I sheepishly asked forgiveness...and placed my "law" into a file that should be entitled "What Not to Do in a Marriage."

Perfect, Not Perfectionist

The sad thing is that a great number of people, like the father in the previous testimony, truly believe that God expects perfection in our behavior. Like that man, they solemnly quote Matthew 5:48: "Therefore you are to be perfect, as your heavenly Father is perfect." And away they go to try harder and do better.

When Jesus made that statement in the sermon on the mount, it was for the purpose of exposing the futility of self-made righteousness. He was not dangling a religious carrot of God's-approval-based-on-flawless-performance in front of His listeners. In actuality, He was raising the bar so high that all who had any vestige of hope of attaining right standing with God by self-effort would fall to the ground in utter exhaustion and despair. Jesus was not trying to prod us to "just try a little harder" or "do a little more" for God so we could earn His smile. He was bringing us to the point of desperation where we would stop trying altogether...and start trusting Him as our righteousness.

Once we give up, Jesus moves in. A lifeguard will wait for the swimmer in distress to expend all his energy at saving himself before moving in for the rescue. So will Jesus.

To the perfectionist, Jesus whispers, "You don't have to try and be perfect anymore, because I was perfect *for* you—and in Me, you *are* perfect."

In *The Message,* Eugene Peterson paraphrases Hebrews 10:11-14 this way:

> Every priest goes to work at the altar each day, offers the same old sacrifices year in, year out, and never makes a dent in the sin problem. As a priest, Christ made a single sacrifice for sins, and that was it! Then he sat down right beside God and waited for his enemies to cave in. It was a perfect sacrifice by a perfect person to perfect some very imperfect people. By that single offering, he did everything that needed to be done for everyone who takes part in the purifying process.

Through Christ and in Christ we have been made perfect and holy, acceptable and accepted. There is absolutely nothing that we can do to improve upon that which Christ has already done. Is our Christly perfection of spirit always mirrored in perfect behavior? Of course not, and it never will be this side of heaven. But our *acceptance* in Christ is perfect—no matter how far we fall short of the glory of God.

That reality should result in resting, not rushing. Trusting, not trying. Working, not worrying. Serving, not slaving.

The irony is, the harder you fight against sin and the harder you try to be perfect, the stronger sin's pull will be on you, and the more you will fail in your performance. But when you are caught up in the grace of God, exulting in the acceptance that is already yours in Christ, you are able to live the righteous life you've always desired.

Insecurity and Dishonesty

There is nothing wrong with striving for excellence by the power of the Holy Spirit. But if we gauge our acceptability by God or acceptance of ourselves by our performance, we will suffer. For instance, there is a lot of pressure in the workplace to be a perfectionist. You want to please your boss with your good works because it may affect your salary or promotion. The perfectionist may be more efficient and get the job done right, but at what price to co-workers, family, and personal health? Stress-related illnesses are the management dilemma of the twenty-first century.

Perfectionists live on the ragged edge of anxiety and fear all their lives. For how can they ever be sure they are doing enough to measure up? They simply can't. That is why legalistic perfectionists tend to be very insecure people. According to the *Gale Encyclopedia of Psychology,*

> Perfectionist anxiety can cause headaches, digestive problems, muscle tension, and heart and vascular problems. Anxiety can cause "blanking" or temporary memory losses before events such as musical performances or academic exams. Perfectionists also hesitate to try new activities for fear of being a beginner at an activity, even for a short period of time. Negative effects of perfectionism are felt especially when an individual is a perfectionist in all areas of life, rather than in one realm, such as an artistic or scientific pursuit, which might allow room for mistakes in other areas of life.[4]

In addition to the more overt compulsions of legalistic perfectionism, there is a covert issue as well—the inability to be emotionally honest. This phenomenon manifests itself every Sunday morning in churches around the country. Consider the following "normal" conversation:

"Hey, Joe! How're you doing? Great to see you, brother!"

"Praise the Lord! Great to see you, too. Things are great. How 'bout with you?"

"Couldn't be better. God is good."

"Amen. Well, see ya later!"

And off go Joe and his friend, having done nothing but rub their coatings of spiritual veneer against each other. No matter that Joe just had a knock-down drag-out fight with his family on the way to church and feels totally unworthy to worship

God. No matter that his friend can't stand his job and feels angry and trapped. True fellowship never happened. Why? In an environment of legalism, you are not allowed to be real. To be real means to admit imperfection—which leaves you vulnerable to reproof, rebuke, or even rejection by sanctimonious saints.

And so we become masters at masking our emotions in order to survive what can be the scariest hour of the week, the Sunday morning worship service. In some cases, we become so good at hiding what we feel that we deny our feelings altogether.

Right after my wife's death, the Lord impressed upon me (Paul) the need for counseling. I wanted to help others, but I had come to realize I was the greatest one in need. The first part of my counseling involved a personal inventory—making my life completely transparent to the counselor. That wasn't easy for me. Here's an excerpt from that conversation:

Counselor: Did you have any anger when Linda died?

Paul: No!

Counselor: Then how did you feel?

Paul: I felt hurt.

Counselor: You said that you felt hurt, but you also said you had no anger. Is that right?

Paul: That's right.

Counselor: How do you feel when people lose their temper?

Paul: I don't like it and I don't appreciate it.

Counselor: Do you often lose your temper?

Paul: No, I don't!

Counselor: Do you believe Christians should get angry?

Paul:	No, I don't believe they should.
Counselor:	Paul, you don't think you have any anger because you don't believe that a Christian should have anger. So you just bury it and deny it. You don't believe that you have any anger because you can't feel it. You probably have been stuffing your feelings all along.
Paul:	Do you really think so?
Counselor:	You have not only stuffed your feelings, but you have probably concreted over them. If you really felt hurt, then you had anger!
Paul:	No, I didn't have any anger; I just felt hurt.
Counselor:	Feeling hurt produces anger. Paul, you need to allow yourself to feel the hurt and anger. Ephesians 4:26 says, "Be angry, and yet do not sin." You need to face reality and accept the truth. Jesus said in John 8:32 that the truth shall make you free.

No Performance Needed

As I came to understand my identity in Christ, I was freed up so I no longer needed to be an emotional perfectionist. I realized that I don't have to keep a tight lid on emotions that might make me look weak or even (God forbid!) *human.* Jesus was angry and yet never sinned. He cleansed the temple and drove out the moneychangers. He turned over the tables, not the people. His anger was under the control of the Holy Spirit, and it produced righteous action.

When I heard this, I knew that God was speaking to me. It was so freeing to think that I didn't have to fear the truth, even the truth of how I really felt. The crisis of losing my wife and the subsequent counseling opened up my heart and life to the Lord like never before. I learned that I was free to accept myself, just the way I was, because God did. All this was in spite of my not doing everything right or performing perfectly.

If you struggle with the fear of measuring up or with perfectionist tendencies or with both, we cannot give you a better word than this: Your journey for love and acceptability ended at the cross. Jesus died to make you acceptable to God just as you are in Christ. No strings attached. No performance needed, either perfect or imperfect. Isn't it time you stopped striving and struggling for what you already have? Isn't it time to enter into the rest that God provides? But in order for this good word to make a difference in your life, you must *believe it*, as the author of Hebrews wrote:

> Let us fear if, while a promise remains of entering His rest, any one of you may seem to have come short of it. For indeed we have had good news preached to us, just as they also; but the word they heard did not profit them, because it was not united by faith in those who heard. For we who have believed enter that rest (Hebrews 4:1-3).

Controllers: Tyrannizing Others with the Law

Closely akin to fear and perfectionism is "control." Perfectionism is trying to manipulate your world or your own life in order to gain a sense of acceptance, approval, or well-being. Control is trying, in the energy of the flesh, to manipulate other people in order to feel safe and secure, get your own way, advance your career, or make yourself look good or feel happy.

We try to exercise control for one or more of the following reasons:

- *Pride:* we sincerely think we know what is best

- *"Success":* things seem to go better when we are in charge

- *Pain:* having been hurt in the past, we try to shield ourselves now from further hurt

- *Greed:* we want what we want when we want it

- *Insecurity:* we dread rejection, failure, the future, and so on

- *Unbelief:* we don't really think God will come through for us

But do you realize that even God does not control people? Though He whispers to us and woos us with His love, He does not control. He has given the human race tremendous dignity by giving people a will, with which they can choose right or wrong, love or hate. It has involved a huge risk—and mankind by and large has devastated the world by abusing this freedom, but God has so ordered His universe.

Therefore, no person has the right to control another. The devil tries to control through temptation, accusation, deception, and intimidation, but that is not God's way. As God's people, we are to be like Him. So we can love, even discipline in love, but we dare not try in our strength to force another person to do our bidding. We may end up gaining a measure of outward conformity, but inwardly we will have only succeeded in fostering rebellion or breaking another person's spirit. Both are terrible sins, and they result in terrible tragedies.

Unfortunately controllers are spawned out of legalistic systems—in the home, the church, the school, and so on. Fathers, for example, are given the moral responsibility to raise their children in the discipline and instruction of the Lord, and Paul warns them not to be too heavy-handed, crushing a child's spirit and provoking that child to anger

(Ephesians 6:4). But one woman confided in me that when she was a child her dad had been so controlling that he would stand behind her when she peeled potatoes and make sure she did not remove too much potato. He would listen outside the bathroom door to make sure those who were showering were not using too much hot water. He would inspect the lawn when he came home from work to make sure there were no weeds. Everyone in the house made sure ahead of time he would find none.

Not surprisingly, this woman, her siblings, and her mother would celebrate when they received a call that Dad was coming home late that night from work. I wonder if he ever knew that…and if he did, if he would have cared.

Fear of Losing

Though you might not expect that a controller is often a fear-driven person, Dr. Les Parrott III brings out this hidden reality in his book *The Control Freak:*

> If you are a self-confessed Control Freak, you know just what I mean. Though few people around you suspect it, you're well aware of the worry and distress that too often plague your days. On the one hand, you must live up to the impossible self-image you have created for yourself (strong, competent, etc.) but on the other hand, you deeply doubt your ability to do it. Anxiety is the result. And you know how anxiety fuels your desire to create a world that runs just the way you want it to. You know how it causes you to compulsively control not only your environment but also the people in it. You count on their compliance. You get frustrated when their needs and feelings interfere with your own. The result is more anxiety, and that fuels more unhealthy attempts to control it.[5]

The ways that controllers control are exhaustive and exhausting. They include manipulation (deceit, self-pity, guilt, shame); criticism; cold, silent treatment; passivity (making others take responsibility); ignoring or forgetting on purpose (especially in response to authority figures); angry hostility and intimidation (abuse, threats, ridiculing); physical punishment; sexual abuse or sexual neglect (with a spouse); overprotection (smothering); negative body language; use of strong personality (to try to persuade or railroad); pulling rank; yelling, screaming, or crying; people-pleasing; arguing; excessive planning and organizing; rejection and shunning.

To the controller, to lose control means to *lose*. Life for the controller is about winning—being on top and being in charge. It is a power game played by those who are terrified to admit that someone else might be right or better or smarter or more blessed by God. So they hold on for dear life, but it isn't life that they're holding on to. Eventually everyone comes to realize how pathetic controllers really are...usually everyone except the controllers themselves.

The controller becomes like Samson who "awoke from his sleep and said, 'I will go out as at other times and shake myself free.' But he did not know that the LORD had departed from him" (Judges 16:20).

A Controller in Action

Early in my experience of fatherhood, I (Rich) shifted from comforting dad to controlling dictator in my home. I'm not sure how it happened, but I know that some of it was the result of fearing that my children would not turn out exactly the way I envisioned for them. Consequently, our home became a place where I constantly delivered orders, and responded to noncompliance or imperfect performance with disapproval and harsh words.

I was saying "no" way too much. My older daughter, Michelle, was feeling the sting of my strictness. Even her cousin, who did not see me very often, could tell something was not quite right.

One day, in tears, Michelle confessed that she didn't feel like she could talk to me about anything that was really on her heart, because I had become so hard. This broke my heart—but my heart needed to be broken.

The key issue at the time was Michelle's desire to have her ears pierced and to get earrings. Somehow I had embraced "the law" that she couldn't (because I thought girls in general shouldn't) get her ears pierced until she was 13 years old. She was 10 at the time. It took the Lord's inquiring, "Where did you get that rule?" for me to realize it wasn't in the Bible. It's not even in the Apocrypha!

Secretly I went to a local jewelry shop and set up an appointment for Michelle to get her ears pierced on the day after Christmas. On Christmas I gave her a card with the appointment on it, as well as two beautiful sets of earrings.

Suddenly I became Daddy again…and that was a breakthrough moment in our relationship of love and trust. As puberty bears down on this precious girl, she is going to need to know that Daddy is on her team. So I told her so—and because I quit trying to control, she believes me. Dads, the hugs are worth it!

The epilogue to this story came one day while I was driving three of our children to school, including Michelle. She mentioned that the day before in class they had had to write about their hero. Racking my brain to figure out who she would have chosen, I said laughing, "And you picked me, right?"

To my amazement and joy she replied, "That's right, Daddy."

"Why am *I* your hero?" I asked, stunned.

She answered, "Because you're funny, you cheer me up when I'm sad, and you're always there for me."

Grace had made all the difference in the world.

Growing Out of Control

As I continue to grow out of the life of a controller, my advice to others on the same journey is simple: Try to say "yes" whenever it is possible (and safe and wise) to do so. There are a lot more times when "yes" is okay than you may have thought. Catch your children doing something right and reinforce that with praise. Too often our children only hear from us when they do something wrong. How right to conclude with this piece of wisdom from Diane Loomans:

> *If I had my child to raise all over again,*
> *I'd build self-esteem first and the house later.*
> *I'd finger-paint more and point the finger less.*
> *I would do less correcting and more connecting.*
> *I'd take my eyes off my watch and watch with my*
> *   eyes.*
> *I would care to know less and know to care more.*
> *I'd take more hikes and fly more kites.*
> *I'd stop playing serious and seriously play.*
> *I would run through more fields and gaze at more*
> *   stars.*
> *I'd do more hugging and less tugging.*
> *I'd see the oak tree in the acorn more often.*
> *I would be firm less often and affirm much more.*
> *I'd model less about the lover of power and*
> *More about the power of love.*[6]

5

THE POWER OF PRIDE

Sinner. Prostitute. Whore. She wore her label like a scarlet letter. Everybody knew her, and everybody knew what kind of life she led. Some snickered when she passed by, others whispered behind her back, others pulled out their wallets. But they all despised her.

She was handy to have around whenever people started feeling a bit guilty for their own sins. "Well, at least I'm not as bad as that *prostitute*," they would say, spitting out the word. For a moment, they'd feel better about themselves.

The orthodox religious leaders of the day, the Pharisees, would not be caught dead near her—at least not in broad daylight, and certainly not during a meal. That was simply not kosher.

It must have been a shock to see her walk in on a private meal at Simon the Pharisee's house. Here's a retelling of that story from Luke 7:36-50:

> One of the religious elite, a Pharisee named Simon, invited Jesus over to his house for dinner, and Jesus accepted the invitation.
>
> Things were going along pretty much as expected—Simon checking out Jesus and Jesus reading Simon like a book. Then a Pharisee's worst nightmare occurred.

115

There happened to be a particular streetwalker, a lady of the evening, who heard on the street that Jesus was eating over at Simon's place. So she grabbed a bottle of very expensive perfume that she had purchased with her...uh...salary, and which she normally wore when she was...er...working, and took off for Simon's house.

Simon nearly choked on his lox and bagels when she slinked in.

Her being there was bad enough, but then things really turned ugly. At least in Simon's way of thinking. She didn't just say "Hi" to Jesus and then "Hasta luego." Oh no, she hung around behind Jesus. Then she started to cry, dripping her disgusting tears all over Jesus' feet.

At that point Simon simply had to turn away. It was too much for any good Jew to take. She dried the tears that had fallen on Jesus' feet with her hair! Then she started kissing his feet, and she just kept on and on and on...

The party was already ruined when out came the perfume. She poured that pricey fragrance all over Jesus' feet! What a waste. The whole stinking house was filled with the smell of it.

Simon couldn't believe his eyes.

But there was one silver lining to the cloud that had descended on his house. The whole scene only served to confirm to Simon what he had already suspected and hoped were true. This guy Jesus was a fraud.

He muttered under his breath, "If Jesus were anything special, he'd know what sort of human sewage this woman is. It's obvious he's not a prophet. I knew it all along."

Jesus answered Simon as if the Pharisee had been talking out loud rather than to himself.

"Simon, I'd like to have a word with you."

"Go ahead, Teacher. Shoot."

So Jesus shot. "Have you heard the story about the two men who went into a bank to take out loans? One borrowed $50,000 and the other borrowed $5000. But neither of them could pay off the loan.

"Remarkably, the bank manager just decided to forget about the whole thing and he canceled both debts. Which of the two guys who owed the bank money will love the bank manager more? Take a wild guess."

Rolling his eyes and letting out a big yawn, Simon replied, "I suppose it would have to be the one who was forgiven the $50,000 debt."

"Simon says correctly," Jesus responded.

Jesus then turned his attention back to the woman who was still behind him. He smiled at her and said, "Simon, do you see this woman? I know you do, even though you are trying hard to ignore her. When I came here for this meal, my feet were dusty, and it is customary to have your guest's feet washed. You didn't lift a finger to do that, but this woman has washed my feet with her tears and dried them with her hair.

"Furthermore, when I entered your house, you did not give me the polite greeting of a kiss on the cheek. But ever since I set foot in this place, this woman has been kissing my feet.

"Nor did you pour oil on my head as a greeting, but she has anointed my feet with this perfume."

By this time the woman's eyes were as big as saucers. Jesus had accepted her love! It was the first time a man had ever loved her for anything except...Her heart was about to burst with joy.

On the other hand, Simon's eyes grew narrower and narrower with rage. He felt like ending the meal and shooing both this man and woman out of his house like pesky flies. But common courtesy would not permit that, and neither somehow would Jesus.

"Simon, here's the point: This woman, who we all agree has sinned terribly in her life, has been forgiven of all those sins, because she loved greatly. But the one who has been forgiven little, loves little."

Turning again to the woman, he said, "Your sins have all been forgiven."

Shocked, Simon and the others at the table whispered to each other, "Who does he think he is, forgiving people's sins! Why, the nerve of the man!"

Ignoring them, Jesus smiled again at the woman and said gently, "Your faith has saved you. Now go in peace."[1]

The legalism of Jesus' host manifested itself as prideful self-righteousness. Simon, like all Pharisees, did not believe himself in need of much (if any) forgiveness. He loved the law a lot because he saw it as his ticket to finding favor with God and exerting power over people. But he loved Jesus little, for he had stuck his thumb in the religious pie, pulled out a plum, and said, "What a good boy am I!" After all, who needs God when you're already doing so well on your own?

The Evil Power Behind Legalism

Pride empowers legalism. Pride says, "I don't need anyone else's help. I can make it on my own." Pride says, "We are better than others because of who we are or what we do or don't do." Pride says, "I'm too important to bother with you." Finally pride says, "We have the right to tell you how to live because *we are right.*"

But God says in His word that He opposes the proud (James 4:6). There is perhaps no quality of man more anti-Christ than pride. Jesus, by His own testimony, lived in complete and continual humility in dependence upon the Father. He said, "Truly, truly, I say to you, the Son can do nothing of Himself, unless it is something He sees the Father doing; for whatever the Father does, these things the Son also does in like manner" (John 5:19).

Neither was Jesus' life a self-promoting exercise in ambition. Numerous times He would warn people not to broadcast His identity or accomplishments (for example, Matthew 16:20; 17:9; Mark 7:36).

Nor did Jesus live in smug separation from the riffraff of society. He was mockingly labeled a "friend of tax collectors and sinners" (Matthew 11:19), a title we believe He enjoyed immensely. (You simply don't gain such a reputation by being squeamish around earthy people.)

Jesus frequently used metaphors to describe Himself ("I am the vine," "I am the bread of life," and so on). But when He got down to the bottom line of His character, Jesus chose two words, saying, "I am *gentle* and *humble* in heart" (Matthew 11:29).

Pride and Christlikeness simply cannot coexist. That is why legalistic systems are so abhorrent to God, because legalism and pride are joined at the hip.

In this chapter, we will examine three aspects of legalistic pride: traditionalism, self-righteousness, and judgmentalism. They constitute the unholy trinity of prideful legalism, and they represent different facets of the kind of control that legalists try to exercise over the people around them.

Legalistic Pride Gives Birth to Traditionalism

The first thing that comes to mind when we think of *traditionalism* is resistance to change. Many people—and Christians are no exception—are afraid of change. Change is threatening because it by nature disturbs and disrupts the status quo. If the status quo changes, those who hold the reins of power fear losing control. Those who are happy with things "as is" will seek to preserve traditions in order to preserve comfort. As Mark Twain observed, "The only thing that likes change is a wet baby."

The problem with traditionalism, however, is that in addition to the element of fear, there is also the element of pride. Traditionalism says, "Not only do we not want to change because we don't like change, but we *do not need to change*—and in fact, we *should not change*, because the way we are doing things is the right way!"

Traditionalism Versus Traditions

A clear distinction needs to be made, of course, between *traditionalism* and *traditions*. In the book *Real Worship*, Warren Wiersbe explains,

> Our English word, tradition, comes from two Latin words that together mean "to give over, to pass on." It works like this: the older generation identifies the things they think are important and passes them along to the next generation for safe-keeping and for their enjoyment and use. Each new generation evaluates this heritage, rejects what it considers no longer useful, and passes along to their children and grandchildren what-ever is left...The problem really isn't tradition, because tradition is simply the content of what one generation hands to another. The problem is tra-ditionalism, which is the worship of traditions to such an extent that few people dare to examine them or try to change them.[2]

Traditions can be good or bad. In some cases the Scriptures speak of them in a very positive light. Paul wrote in 2 Thes-salonians 2:15, "Brethren, stand firm and hold to the traditions which you were taught, whether by word of mouth or by letter from us." In that case he was clearly referring to the apostolic teachings that we now know as Scripture. So strong was the need to hold on to these truths that Paul warned, "We command you, brethren, in the name of our Lord Jesus Christ, that you keep away from every brother who leads an unruly life and not according to the tradition which you received from us" (2 Thessalonians 3:6).

It is imperative that churches and families pass on the timeless truths of Scripture. In Judges 2:10-15 we are told of a time when a generation did not pass on the things of the Lord: "All that generation also were gathered to their fathers; and there arose another generation after them who did not know the LORD, nor yet the work which He had done for Israel" (verse 10). Verses 11 and 12 then describe how the new generation did evil and "forsook the LORD, the God of their fathers, who had brought them out of the land of Egypt."

On the other hand, not all traditions are valid or worthy of being passed down. In Colossians 2:8 the same apostle Paul sternly admonished the believers to "see to it that no one takes you captive through philosophy and empty deception, according to the tradition of men, according to the elementary principles of the world, rather than according to Christ."

Traditionalism Leads to Neglect of the Truth

When the traditions of men are elevated to a scriptural or near-scriptural level of authority, then you have *traditionalism*, one of the common manifestations of legalism. Jesus blistered the ears of the Pharisees because they couldn't understand why His disciples ignored the elder's traditions. His words recorded in Mark 7:6-8 ought to still ring in the ears of every legalistic traditionalist today:

> Rightly did Isaiah prophesy of you hypocrites, as it is written: "This people honors Me with their lips, but their heart is far away from Me. But in vain do they worship Me, teaching as doctrines the precepts of men." Neglecting the commandment of God, you hold to the tradition of men.

The legalist finds security in doing things the same old way. As others have wryly suggested, the seven last words of a church are, "We never did it that way before." Traditionalism is taking tradition to the extreme—not simply appreciating it, but viewing any change as contrary to the will of God.

For instance, nowhere does the Bible support believers in the traditions of having to meet together at eleven o'clock Sunday morning, having Sunday school before the worship service, being 12 years old before being qualified for baptism, singing only hymns on Sunday mornings, using collection plates, sitting on pews, having a steeple on the roof of the church building, and so on. God expects us to seek Him for wisdom and expects us to be open to putting the new wine of the new covenant into the new wineskins of new approaches and strategies (Matthew 9:17).

Greg Morris, in an insightful newsletter called *Leadership Dynamics,* offers four warning signs of church traditionalism, which he describes as "speaking a language a lost world does not understand":

1. "We begin to worship our history...We lose our effectiveness when our memories are greater than our dreams."

2. "We are more concerned with forms than with function."

3. "We are more concerned with management than with ministry...We become 'gatekeepers' rather than 'trailblazers,' adopting a defensive posture and therefore failing to impact the lives of those around us."

4. "We substitute motion for direction...As Eddy Ketchursid wisely stated, 'If your horse is dead, for goodness' sake dismount.' "[3]

The nineteenth-century philosopher Soren Kierkegaard once told a story about a village inhabited by ducks. On

Sundays the ducks would waddle out their doors to the church down the street. They waddled into the sanctuary and squatted in their favorite pews. The duck choir would waddle in, and the duck pastor would waddle up to the pulpit and open the Bible. And he would read, "Ducks! God has given you wings! With wings you can fly! With wings you can mount up and soar like eagles. No walls can confine you! No fence can hold you! You have wings. God has given you wings, and you can fly like birds." Excitedly, all the ducks shouted "AMEN!"—and then they all waddled home.¹

Traditionalism is a stronghold that has a *strong hold* over many churches, and it is very difficult to uproot.

Legalistic Pride Gives Birth to Self-Righteousness

The second facet of legalistic pride is *self-righteousness*. Jesus saw this manifested in the Pharisees of His day and often spoke against it, as in Luke 18:9-14:

> He...told this parable to some people who trusted in themselves that they were righteous, and viewed others with contempt: "Two men went up into the temple to pray, one a Pharisee and the other a tax collector. The Pharisee stood and was praying this to himself: 'God, I thank You that I am not like other people: swindlers, unjust, adulterers, or even like this tax collector. I fast twice a week; I pay tithes of all that I get.' But the tax collector, standing some distance away, was even unwilling to lift up his eyes to heaven, but was beating his breast, saying, 'God, be merciful to me, the sinner!' I tell you, this man went to his house justified rather than the other; for everyone who exalts himself will be humbled, but he who humbles himself will be exalted."

The self-righteous have the tendency to believe they are better than other people and their church is superior to other

churches. It can be as overt as viewing one's own denomination as "the best" and thinking that another legitimately
Christian denomination is "of the devil." Or it can be as covert
as secretly smiling when word comes that another congregation is struggling or going through a split. In fact, all of us have
been guilty at times of turning a prayer meeting (or allowing
it to be turned) into a gossip session. We "share prayer
requests" about other brothers and sisters in Christ who are
hurting, while in our hearts the feeling of spiritual superiority
swells up.

Usually what it takes is a healthy dose of God's loving (yet
painful) discipline in our own lives to wake us up to the reality
that just because things are going smoothly in life doesn't
mean we are better than others.

In this regard, A.W. Tozer talks about "fallow ground" in
his book *Paths to Power*. What he writes is a clinical diagnosis
of the self-righteous person:

> The fallow field is smug, contented, protected
> from the shock of the plow and the agitation of the
> harrow. Such a field, as it lies year after year,
> becomes a familiar landmark to the crow and the
> blue jay. Had it intelligence, it might take a lot of
> satisfaction in its reputation: it has stability; nature
> has adopted it; it can be counted upon to remain
> always the same while the fields around it change
> from brown to green and back to brown again.
> Safe and undisturbed, it sprawls lazily in the sun-
> shine, a picture of sleepy contentment.
>
> But it is paying a terrible price for its tran-
> quility. Never does it see the miracle of growth;
> never does it feel the motions of mounting life nor
> see the wonders of bursting seed nor the beauty of
> ripening grain. Fruit it can never know because it
> is afraid of the plow and the harrow.
>
> ...The man of fallow life is contented with
> himself and the fruit he once bore. He does not

want to be disturbed. He smiles in tolerant superiority at revivals, fastings, self-searchings, and all the travail of fruit bearing and the anguish of advance. The spirit of adventure is dead within him. He is steady, "faithful," always in his accustomed place (like the old field), conservative, and something of a landmark in the little church. But he is fruitless. The curse of such a life is that it is fixed, both in size and in content. *To be* has taken the place of *to become*. The worst that can be said of such a man is that he is what he will be. He has fenced himself in, and by the same act he has fenced out God and the miracle.[5]

Measuring Godliness

Self-righteous legalism is fed by the flesh, which always seeks to quantify spirituality. The flesh is always trying to come up with ways to measure godliness. But true spirituality cannot be gauged by a checklist or analyzed by an accountant. Jesus said that "the wind blows where it wishes and you hear the sound of it, but do not know where it comes from and where it is going; so is everyone who is born of the Spirit" (John 3:8). To Nicodemus, a Pharisee, these words did not compute, and so it is with every legalist.

When I (Paul) was a boy, much of my life centered around the church. I earned many of the awards and prizes that were offered, for I was very deliberate in my performance. In order to go to vacation Bible school at our church, I rode my bicycle 12 miles one way. Many of the people in our area couldn't understand why we didn't attend the local church but went so far away.

We children were never allowed to go to the movies, play cards, or go to dances. Dad never allowed Mother to cut her hair. We never purchased anything on Sunday and were not allowed to throw a ball or swim on "the Lord's day." Secular music was never allowed in our house. The elementary teacher used to tell my parents, "Paul will never grow up to know life if you don't allow him to go to the movies." This developed some religious pride; we were supposed to be better than others. I remember getting into an argument at school because I said that I had never used a swear word in my life. One of the boys made fun of me and laughed at me, and he told the teacher. They just could not believe that I had never sworn. I felt I was paying a price because of my stand for Christ. At that time, standing up for Christ meant keeping all these self-righteous standards, thus proving in our legalistic minds that we were better than others.

One of the ways to recognize the creeping crud of self-righteousness in our own lives is to take a hard look at how we react when questioned or criticized. Do we tend to get defensive? Are we startled or even shocked when a brother or sister in Christ confronts sin in our lives? (If that is the case, you have probably surrounded yourself with too many "yes-men" or "yes-women" who have put you up on a teetering spiritual pedestal.) Are we tortured by the thought that others may not see us as perfect or at least as "really spiritual"? Do we shun close accountability relationships because we want to keep up the aura (delusion) of elitism? Do we manage to maneuver ourselves into positions of serving others while sending out the message loud and clear that we don't need anyone serving us? Even worse, do we *actually believe* that others really need us to serve them, but we don't really need them?

These are searching questions for all of us, and we are not excluding ourselves from the list either. We believe there is a very real danger that lurks in the shadows of the flesh, much closer to our hearts than any of us like to think. And that danger is the thought—at first merely a temptation—that we are (or our church is, or our organization is) just a little bit more spiritually on the ball than others. Be very careful when others start calling you "anointed," "dynamic," "cutting-edge," "very gifted," "prophetic," or "apostolic." You might actually start believing it.

Legalistic Pride Gives Birth to Judgmentalism

The final area of legalistic pride and control we want to examine is *judgmentalism*. A biopsy on this "growth" always turns up cancer.

Judgmentalism always involves one person (or church) putting down another person (or church) based on a legalistic standard of performance. Quite often the judgmental person is trying to take the place of God in the other's life. In Matthew 7:1-5, Jesus sternly warned,

> Do not judge so that you will not be judged. For in the way you judge, you will be judged; and by your standard of measure, it will be measured to you. Why do you look at the speck that is in your brother's eye, but do not notice the log that is in your own eye? Or how can you say to your brother, "Let me take the speck out of your eye," and behold, the log is in your eye? You hypocrite, first take the log out of your own eye, and then you will see clearly to take the speck out of your brother's eye.

There are several very important principles to be gleaned from this passage. First of all, judging other people is wrong. First Corinthians 4:5 says, "Do not go on passing judgment before the time, but wait until the Lord comes who will both bring to light the things hidden in darkness and disclose the motives of men's hearts; and then each man's praise will come to him from God." Judgment is attacking another person's character or motives—and it is characterized by a lack of love.

Second, because of the sin in their own lives, those who judge others are disqualified from seeking to "straighten somebody out." Pride and lack of love prevent many Christians from being able to see another person and their needs clearly. What they end up doing is whacking people in the head with the two-by-four protruding out of their own eye. (A plank is not a very effective tool in removing a speck of dust from someone's eye.)

Third, we *are* called upon to help others, once our own issues of judgmental pride and lack of love are dealt with. In fact, part of God's breaking process is accepting the reality that our own coldness and harshness are far bigger issues than the issues that are afflicting our brother. Once we are humbled, then we can gently and kindly "take the speck out" of another's eye with the tissue of tenderness rather than with the log of legalism.

In fact, love is the primary prerequisite for being able to see clearly and serve others effectively, as Paul showed in Philippians 1:9-11:

> This I pray, that your love may abound still more and more in real knowledge and all discernment, so that you may approve the things that are excellent, in order to be sincere and blameless until the day of Christ; having been filled with the fruit of righteousness which comes through Jesus Christ, to the glory and praise of God.

No Love...Just an Idol

The prerequisite of love is missing in judgmental people, who can be very mean-spirited and cruel at times, as the following testimony underscores:

> Adherents of legalism spend a great deal of time focusing on other people's sin. They often place themselves on a pedestal while denigrating others. I was a young teenager when I first accepted Jesus Christ as my Savior. I met Jesus in a Pentecostal church and the experience was very exhilarating. I had grown up in a very conservative, traditional church, and the Pentecostal fire was

very engaging. The passion with which the preachers spoke was altogether different than the quiet, soft-spoken conservative approach.

However, many of these preachers seemed to be attacking people all the time. They blasted sinners of every variety imaginable and even spoke openly against other Christian leaders. These attacks began to leave me disillusioned because Jesus was very merciful in dealing with most sinners. As a result, I left the church and even worse, I turned my back on Jesus.

Fortunately, over time I came back to the Lord. My relationship with Jesus has been renewed and reinvigorated. Nevertheless, my testimony illustrates how too much focus on God's law can have a negative impact in the lives of believers. And while it is important to use discernment in evaluating our relationships, it is more important to deal with our own sins and walk with Jesus.

Psalm 115:4-8 gives us insight into why legalists can become so mean-spirited:

> Their idols are silver and gold, the work of man's hands. They have mouths, but they cannot speak; they have eyes, but they cannot see; they have ears, but they cannot hear; they have noses, but they cannot smell; they have hands, but they cannot feel; they have feet, but they cannot walk; they cannot make a sound with their throat. Those who make them will become like them, everyone who trusts in them.

An inviolable biblical principle is that *we become like the god or God we worship*. Although judgmental legalists believe they worship the God of the Bible, in reality they don't. Legalism creates its very own god—a harsh, strict, law-keeping, law-enforcing god—then becomes like the god it worships.

No wonder judgmentalism drives people away from the church, for who would want to serve such a god? The tragedy is that in causing people to flee from its false god, legalism can also drive them away from the True God as well.

In testimony after testimony, we have heard the sad histories of those who have run for their lives from judgmental, legalistic churches, only to leave Jesus behind as well. But the grace of God can penetrate where legalism has barred the doors, and many people have come back. Here's another such story:

> When I was 24 years old I began attending an Independent Baptist church. I had been drinking and using drugs, then I had a baby out of wedlock. After all that I was drawn back to the church as I was looking for a spiritual home for my four-year-old son. Plus I was looking for love and acceptance.
>
> At first it seemed like a loving and joyful church, very outspoken and evangelistic. I enjoyed being a guest and attended services and many activities. The problems began when I chose to become a member. I went through the membership classes and was told the following: 1) As a church member I MUST wear a dress to church on Sundays. Pantsuits were not acceptable. 2) My son's hair needed to be cut short. 3) I was to call all the men in the church "Brother So-and-so" (I asked to please be called "Sister _____" then…and was looked at as if I were being contrary and unreasonable). The list went on and on.
>
> I began to question these rules right away. I was told that God loves obedience and that if I refused to do these things, I could not become a member. I chose not to become a member and left. It was

another seven years—more drinking, drugs, and promiscuity—before I was willing to try the "church" again. These people and their lack of love and tolerance chased me FAR away from the possibility of a desire to come back to Jesus. If He were that judgmental, I wanted nothing to do with God.

Fortunately a church eventually reached out to me in love and showed me just how much God desires me—just as I am. I now have 13 years of sobriety, and I witness to God's love and acceptance to everyone I can. Thank goodness there are still people who present God as He is. Is sin terrible? Yes, it is. Does the Holy Spirit begin a transformation after a person is saved and growing? Yes, He does! Do pastors trust God to do this? Many do not.

Expressing Grace

As we have said before, we believe that those who seek to control others through strict standards and rigid rules genuinely believe they are helping people stay away from sin. But as we will see more fully in a later chapter, it is grace that motivates us to righteousness, not a heavy-handed fixation on sin. In fact, a critical, judgmental spirit that browbeats people with the law will drive them to commit the very sin you preach against. As Paul reveals in Romans 7:8, "Sin, taking opportunity through the commandment, produced in me coveting of every kind; for apart from the Law sin is dead." But Titus 2:11-12 tells us,

> The grace of God that brings salvation has appeared to all men. It teaches us to say "No" to ungodliness and worldly passions, and to live self-controlled, upright and godly lives in this present age (NIV).

To express grace toward others we need to differentiate between *principles, preferences,* and *prejudices.* The Bible is filled with principles that give us wisdom in living life. An example of a principle of church life is, "Worshiping God together in song is good and healthy and right." A preference, on the other hand, would be, "I like contemporary choruses more than hymns" (or vice versa). A prejudice would be, "I will not attend a church service with hymns (or choruses or musical instruments or...)."

There is nothing wrong with having preferences, just so long as they operate under the umbrella of biblical principles. We all have preferences. That is part of our uniqueness as individuals. But when our lives cease to be governed by principles, our preferences become our god—and they inevitably turn hard and inflexible. Eventually we end up hunkering down in our bunkers of prejudice. We cease to operate in grace and become judgmental.

A Critical Spirit Judges and Isolates

Biblical principles are unchanging and should never be compromised. And in the arena of preferences, we need to exercise much grace and godly tolerance toward those who differ from us. But when it comes to prejudices, only the most radical surgery is appropriate. We must recognize them as the stubborn sin they are and repent. Otherwise we are doomed to judge others wrongly, as happened in one of the most famous stories Jesus ever told.

This story, which we have come to call "the parable of the prodigal son," is really about *two* lost sons. Maybe you have never seen it that way before, but the fact is, one was lost out in the world, and the other was lost at home. Henri Nouwen, in his book *The Return of the Prodigal Son*, describes the lost condition of the older one.

> The lostness of the elder son, however, is much harder to identify. After all, he did all the right things. He was obedient, dutiful, law-abiding, and hardworking. People respected him, admired him,

praised him, and likely considered him a model son. Outwardly, the elder son was faultless. But when confronted by his father's joy at the return of his younger brother, a dark power erupts in him and boils to the surface. Suddenly, there becomes glaringly visible a resentful, proud, unkind, selfish person, one that had remained deeply hidden, even though it had been growing stronger and more powerful over the years.[6]

Let's tune in on Jesus' story starting in verse 28 of Luke 15. As you recall, once the younger, partying son came home, his older brother angrily refused to join the celebration of his brother's return.

> His father came out and began pleading with him. But he answered and said to his father, "Look! For so many years I have been serving you and I have never neglected a command of yours; and yet you have never given me a young goat, so that I might celebrate with my friends; but when this son of yours came, who has devoured your wealth with prostitutes, you killed the fattened calf for him." And he said to him, "Son, you have always been with me, and all that is mine is yours. But we had to celebrate and rejoice, for this brother of yours was dead and has begun to live, and was lost and has been found."

Notice the critical spirit of the elder brother! Had he talked with his younger brother and asked him what he had actually done with all the inheritance? No! He could've gambled it away or drunk it all away or spent it on luxurious accommodations and frivolous purchases. But the elder brother had already judged him in his heart as having blown all the money on prostitutes.

It seems that those trapped in legalism enjoy pointing out the defeats and mistakes of others, whether real or imagined. They are professional critics. When going home from church, they give a critique of the service. They don't allow the Word of God to pierce their hearts, they dissect the sermon. They don't enter into worship of God in spirit and truth, they criticize the style or skill of the worship leaders.

Legalists, like this elder brother, do not understand relating to God as a child to his Father. Instead they are more like employees, faithfully serving while being unable to connect with all the glorious riches that are theirs through Jesus. And so they are robbed of the joy of their salvation, unable to enter into the true celebration of freedom in Christ.

As with the elder brother, who refused to call his sibling "my brother" and would not join in the celebration, there is a haughty separatist attitude in the heart of those trapped in legalism. Though the licentious stance of "If you can't beat 'em, join 'em!" is wrong, so is the legalist stance of "If you can't beat 'em, separate from 'em!" Jesus entered the world of the sinner (though never the world of sin); He wasn't standoffish, and He never displayed a "holier than thou" attitude. Rather, this one thing is powerfully clear from the Gospels: *Jesus loved people, and He wanted those around Him to know that the Father loves people, too.*

Love: God's Bottom Line

Because of the trauma that hurting, wounded, and even just plain sinful people have already experienced, it is imperative that they be surrounded by loving, grace-oriented people if they are going to have any hope of recovery. In light of the parable of the prodigal son, our philosophy of ministry is, *Make sure you get the prodigal to the Father before the elder brother gets to him!*

Jesus said, " 'You shall love the Lord your God with all your heart, and with all your soul, and with all your mind.' This is the great and foremost commandment. The second is like it, 'You shall love your neighbor as yourself.' On these two commandments depend the whole Law and the Prophets" (Matthew 22:37-40).

The bottom line for God is *love*. Jesus puts such a high premium on it that He once warned a hard-working, never-quitting, doctrinally sound church that they were in danger of having the plug pulled on their whole operation. John recorded Jesus' important letter in Revelation 2:1-7:

> The One who holds the seven stars in His right hand, the One who walks among the seven golden lampstands, says this: "I know your deeds and your toil and perseverance, and that you cannot tolerate evil men, and you put to the test those who call themselves apostles, and they are not, and you found them to be false; and you have perseverance and have endured for My name's sake, and have not grown weary. But I have this against you, that you have left your first love. Therefore remember from where you have fallen, and repent and do the deeds you did at first; or else I am coming to you and will remove your lamp-stand out of its place—unless you repent...He who has an ear, let him hear what the Spirit says to the churches. To him who overcomes, I will grant to eat of the tree of life which is in the Paradise of God."

Without love, we are nothing (1 Corinthians 13:2). Without love, all our good deeds profit us nothing (verse 3). Without love, we are without God (1 John 4:7-8). Isn't it time to return to love, or maybe discover it for the first time? Either way, the Father is watching and waiting...with love.

6

ENEMIES OF FREEDOM

When I (Rich) joined the staff of Campus Crusade for Christ fresh out of college, I was well-prepared for raising my financial support. But I was not prepared for what I would find in the body of Christ. When I was a student involved with Crusade at Penn State, my buddies and I had been too busy trying to see our campus reached for Christ to concern ourselves with doctrinal details and denominational preferences. I was zealous, but naïve. I'll admit that much.

As I started visiting the homes and churches of people of a variety of denominational persuasions, I got an education real fast. I had foolishly thought that every Christian I met would be as excited about reaching high school students for Christ as I was. Unfortunately, that was not the case. The mere fact that I was on the staff of Campus Crusade for Christ raised the eyebrows of some.

Ambushed

I remember walking into the office of the pastor of an independent fundamental church. The handshake I received was firm but not warm. Though I was always a little uneasy when I first met a pastor, usually they put me at ease, eager to hear my testimony and calling. Not this time.

Maybe it was the black suit and dark tie. More likely it was the feeling that I had just been called in to the principal's office and was the naughty student, that gave me a sense this was not going to be pleasant.

I watched the pastor's eyes as he glanced inquisitively at the Bible I was carrying with me. "What version of the Scriptures is that?" he asked.

"It's a New American Standard," I replied.

Shaking his head with disapproval, the pastor firmly corrected me. "God has been blessing the King James version of the Bible for hundreds of years. He cannot bless another version." (I wonder if that pastor would have been so adamant about the KJV if he had known that its original, 1611 edition also contained the Apocrypha!)

Almost immediately, the assistant pastor came in and ushered me into another room, where we sat on hard, wooden chairs across a table. *Ah, the interrogation room,* I thought. And that's what it became. For about 20 minutes I was lectured on why my Bible was wrong, my doctrine was wrong, Campus Crusade was wrong, our presentation of the gospel was wrong, and on and on. I was too stunned to know what hit me or even to make a decent rebuttal.

Once it became quite clear this church was not going to be one of my prime supporting churches, I hastily said goodbye and let myself out. I'm sure the pastor and his assistant felt they had given me the truth and perhaps helped me to get back on "the straight and narrow," but I left that office shaken, discouraged, and confused. Though those men were likely born-again believers, they were used by the enemy to steal joy, kill vision, and destroy hope. They attacked my freedom in Christ and wounded me in the process.

Oppressed

But enemies of freedom do not come only in the independent fundamental variety. They can also wear the tag "orthodox," or "evangelical," or "reformed," or even "charismatic."

Early in my ministry with Freedom in Christ, I was conducting a youth retreat outside of Atlanta, Georgia. I had just finished speaking on our need to forgive others from the heart. I was giving the students and leaders an opportunity to seek the Lord regarding those they needed to forgive, when the retreat director had to step out for a while. I should have known we were in for trouble.

The director was one of the godliest, most well balanced Christian men I have ever met, and I respected him highly. Unfortunately, most of his volunteers or student leaders were not nearly so mature.

Almost immediately upon his departure, some of the youth group's loose cannons started firing. They jumped up front and told everyone that it was time to receive the baptism of the Holy Spirit. Quickly, small groups of eight or ten students and leaders surrounded their prey—those who had not yet spoken in tongues.

With harsh, persistent badgering, those who "had the gift" besieged those who did not. It was out of control and out of order. I felt a tremendous oppression descend on the place, and so I grabbed a prayer partner and we just began praying. It was grievous to watch the tortured expressions of those who just couldn't "get it" (the gift).

If the scene had not been so sad, it would have been amusing when the director walked back in and surveyed the scene. Shaking his head, he apologized to me, saying, "I can't leave these people alone for ten minutes!"

It is a wonderful picture of God's glorious grace that the next night a genuine, Spirit-led (not human-orchestrated) revival broke out!

Stealing Freedom, Hurting Christians

Though coming from opposite ends of the Christian doctrinal spectrum, both of these stories illustrate the same truth.

When even sincere followers of Christ seek to force-feed others with their particular brand of legalism or elitism, they act as enemies of freedom—and people are hurt, sometimes even traumatized.

It should not surprise us when we see freedom opposed. In the Bible, every time we see someone express spontaneous freedom or live a life of liberty, they become a lightning rod for controversy and opposition.

On one such occasion, King David was exuberantly worshiping God, dancing with joy through the streets of Jerusalem as the ark returned to that city. Part of David's unfettered joy was no doubt because this time the ark was being brought to town with God's blessing (2 Samuel 6:12-15). Three months earlier the ark had been improperly carried on an oxcart. At one point, when the oxen nearly dumped the ark on the ground, a man named Uzzah had irreverently reached out to steady the ark and was struck dead by the Lord for doing so (6:1-7). King David, filled with anger and fear, dropped the ark like a hot potato at the home of Obed-edom and went home a defeated man (verses 8-11).

But this time, the ark's homecoming was without incident, and David was filled with delight, to the point that he stripped off his outer robe as he danced before the Lord (verse 14). Unfortunately the local wet blanket, David's wife Michal, was watching the procession from the palace window. She despised David in her heart (verse 16).

After David had presented offerings to the Lord and distributed gifts to all the people, he burst into his house, ready to bless those waiting for his return. But Michal rebuked him venomously: "How the king of Israel distinguished himself today! He uncovered himself today in the eyes of his servants' maids as one of the foolish ones shamelessly uncovers himself!" (verse 20).

The party was over. Michal had stolen the joy right away from David. Angrily, the king declared that he had danced before the Lord with Him as his audience, not her, and that

God would bring honor to the king for his humility (verses 21–22).

God's judgment then came upon Michal, not David. For the rest of her life her womb was as barren as her heart (verse 23).

David is not alone in being persecuted for exercising freedom. As we noted in chapter 5, the elder brother angrily protested the party thrown in his prodigal younger brother's honor, despite the father's pleas for understanding (see Luke 15:11-32).

Mary, the sister of Martha and Lazarus, was bitterly scolded by Judas Iscariot for anointing the feet of Jesus with a pound of very costly perfume—perfume of pure nard. Judas sanctimoniously declared that the perfume should have been sold and the money given to the poor. But Jesus came to her defense and proclaimed His approval of her extravagant worship (see John 12:1-7).

When Jesus was entering into Jerusalem on "Palm Sunday" (see Luke 19:37-40), the Pharisees couldn't stand the explosion of joyful praise from His disciples' lips. When they implored Jesus to quiet the crowd, He would have none of it. Jesus told them that if the crowd became quiet, the stones would cry out.

RECOGNIZING THE ENEMIES OF FREEDOM

Jesus' ongoing confrontations with the religious leaders demonstrate the battle between law and grace, bondage and freedom—a battle that would never end during His time on earth.

Although He never missed a chance to expose the error of the scribes and Pharisees, there is one section of Scripture in which He lets them have it with both barrels. That passage is found in Matthew 23, in which Jesus holds nothing back in confronting the enemies of freedom in His day. Though these words were spoken by our Lord nearly 2000 years ago, the sins of hypocrisy and legalism have not changed much since the first century. By studying Jesus' words, we can pick up important clues as to how to recognize religious oppression today.

Ungodly Power and Influence

Jesus' first criticism was that "the scribes and the Pharisees have seated themselves in the chair of Moses" (Matthew 23:2). Moses, of course, was the giver and enforcer of the law. He was one of the religious leaders' heroes. Jesus, however, had warned them previously, "Do not think that I will accuse you before the Father; the one who accuses you is Moses, in whom you have set your hope" (John 5:45).

The scribes and Pharisees had "seated themselves" in Moses' chair as the religious heads of the people. God hadn't put them in that position; they had done it themselves. Therefore, the first danger sign of hypocrisy and spiritual abuse is when *leaders maneuver themselves into positions of power by their own personality, persuasiveness, or ingenuity.*

Once they arrive in positions of power and influence, they are difficult to dislodge. They will fight for their lives to stay there. Ted Engstrom, former director of World Vision and a man acquainted with spiritual authority and leadership, has said, "Power is the most serious problem in Christianity today."[1] And in her insightful work *The Religion of Power,* Cheryl Forbes writes,

> Although the religion of power is the antithesis of Christianity, Christians participate in it. Some people practice power consciously and willingly, quite often because they believe that power is necessary to promote Christianity throughout the world. Others may practice the rituals of power without consciously admitting that they do. They don't need to; their instincts for the rituals are unerring, like knowing how to breathe.

Whether it is conscious act or unconscious instinct, the reason given is to do God's will or to fulfill a God-given task. At some point the reason may change to something more self-centered, probably will change as power grows, but a Christian who moves into power usually believes that he is justified in doing so. He may believe that he needs power to protect the faith, influence government and political leaders, create an organization or movement to benefit mankind and glorify God. He overlooks, however, the inescapable truth that whoever attempts to wield power will find out that power wields him.[2]

Today's religious power brokers crave the large congregations (and with them, the large salaries), the biggest ads in the papers, the prominent names on the church marquees. They make sure that people "toe the line" and obey the leadership, no matter what. If criticized, they are quick to rebuke others for "touching the Lord's anointed" (which, by the way, referred in the Old Testament to a government leader—a king—not a religious leader!). One local pastor was so irate over this that he broadcast his anger to the entire community on the sign outside their church: "The minister cannot lead if the flock does not follow."

The following testimony is one of many we received that describe many a church under the control of a power broker:

> We are in the process of breaking away from a very legalistic church. It's been very painful. Our main concern is our children finding "freedom" in Christ. We have been under the instruction of a preacher who is against women in pants, women with slits in their skirts or dresses, shorts on men; he has a Sunday school class for "Preacher Boys"

> to train them up early. Isn't this the parents'
> responsibility? What if this isn't their gift?
>
> There is to be no talking among friends and
> members of the church about concerns with the
> pastor, who has ALL authority...almost more
> than God in this church! If we discuss a sermon
> negatively it's considered gossip, and we are pub-
> licly rebuked if found out. Just about any discussion
> other than the weather is gossip! It's been a heavy
> load, but God is keeping our eyes open, and we are
> praying for His direction as we are breaking away
> from an almost "cultlike" atmosphere.

It's All on the Outside

Secondly, Jesus criticized the scribes and Pharisees for being glory-grabbers, limelighters who made sure people noticed how "spiritual" they were. His words are pointed (Matthew 23:5-7):

> They do all their deeds to be noticed by men;
> for they broaden their phylacteries and lengthen
> the tassels of their garments. They love the place
> of honor at banquets and the chief seats in the
> synagogues, and respectful greetings in the market
> places, and being called Rabbi by men.

In the law, Moses had instructed the people to "bind [the commandments] as a sign on your hand and they shall be as frontals on your forehead" (Deuteronomy 6:8). A phylactery was a small piece of parchment-type material on which were written certain portions of the law and which was then tied to the head or arm. The tassels Jesus referred to were also spoken of in the law (Numbers 15:38-39). They were sewn on the ends of garments as reminders of the commandments.

Notice Jesus did not upbraid the Pharisees for wearing phylacteries or tassels, but for making them more prominent than normal, ostentatiously forcing people to notice how "spiritual" they were. Adam Clarke comments,

> Even the phylactery became an important appendage to a Pharisee's character, insomuch that some of them wore them very broad, either that they might have the more written on them, or that, the characters being *larger,* they might be the more *visible,* and that they might hereby acquire greater esteem among the common people, as being more than ordinarily religious. For the same reason, they wore the *fringes* of their garments of an unusual length...As these hypocrites were destitute of all the life and power of religion *within,* they endeavoured to supply its place by *phylacteries* and *fringes without.*[3]

Image-Creation

To the Pharisees of yesterday and today, image is everything. That is the second warning regarding legalism. *Pharisees do everything to create and maintain a strong religious image, but inwardly they are spiritually anemic.* That's why Jesus so often referred to them as "hypocrites"—play-actors pretending to be something they were not.

In the movie *The Wizard of Oz,* Dorothy wants to get home, the lion needs courage, the tin man needs a heart, and the scarecrow needs a brain. So they all go off to see the wizard, the wonderful wizard of Oz. When they finally meet the wiz, they find him to be a huge head with a loud, intimidating voice and hostile demeanor. All the fire and smoke surrounding him help to create the exact image he wants.

In order to gain his blessing, the four must perform a service for him (a typical religious transaction when dealing with a Pharisee). They actually succeed in accomplishing his almost suicidal requirement of killing the Wicked Witch of the West and bringing back her broom. Then the four adventurers actually have the audacity to hold the wizard accountable and ask him to do what he said he'd do! In their book *The Subtle Power of Spiritual Abuse,* David Johnson and Jeff VanVonderen pick up the story here and make an important point:

> With a thunderous roar, the Wizard demands to know how these four dare to challenge him ...It's at this moment that Dorothy's dog runs over to a small room and pulls back a curtain, and what is revealed to us is a simple, flesh-and-blood man who has long been hiding behind a mask of power. He operates behind a curtain pulling levers, making smoke, fire, and noise. The result *looks* impressive but is only a façade. Even when exposed he roars, "Pay no attention to the man behind the curtain!" The "Wizard" is in fact a power abuser. He controls a whole city with a façade that postures power and punishes people for noticing.
>
> ...It is sad to think how often religious power brokers control their spiritual kingdoms with power façades. They rain Bible verses on people about authority, submission, judgment, prosperity, or the end times. They penalize people for noticing that "the man behind the curtain" is just human, with no authenticity and no authority at all.[4]

The legalistic religious leaders of Jesus' day had become professionals at amassing symbols of power. The right seats, the right greetings, the right places at the right times, the right clothes, the long public prayers, the ostentatious giving of money, the not-so-subtle evidences of fasting, and so on. Jesus exposed them because every one of their power trips was contrary to the kingdom of God, in which "the Son of Man did not come to be served, but to serve, and to give His life a ransom for many" (Matthew 20:28).

Mystique, Not Reality

To borrow from another well-known tale, Jesus was something like the little boy in the story "The Emperor's New Clothes." Frustrated with everyone's "oohs" and "ahhs" over their leader's nonexistent beautiful garments, he declared of the emperor, "But he hasn't any clothes on!" Most of the Pharisees failed to realize that they, like the church in Laodicea, were wretched and miserable and poor and blind and naked (Revelation 3:17).

Cheryl Forbes's comments are again right on target:

> The issue here is symbol—small and great. No symbol is unimportant. Each one marks us, names us, or defines us. The longing to be known and named and understood is one of the deepest human instincts. But that desire may work against us and for the god [power]. Power promises, "I will name you. I will define you. I will tell others who you are. And I will start today." So we begin amassing symbols, clothes, furniture, space, and finally, people, who are the ultimate symbol. By the time we begin seeing other human beings as symbols, or even as tools who can be useful to us..., the god has won.[5]

That is why Jesus warned His followers not to accept the titles "Rabbi," "Father," or "leader." There is only one supreme rabbi (teacher) and that is the Lord Jesus Himself. There is only one Father, who is the very source of life and love: God the Father. And there is only one Leader, Christ (Matthew 23:8-10). Jesus wanted to level the playing field and take away the "clergy mystique" that the Pharisees had built up. "You are all brothers," Jesus said, and He reminded them again that "the greatest among you shall be your servant" (Matthew

23:11). Unfortunately, that message of servant leadership was lost on the religious leaders of Jesus' day...and it is still lost to twenty-first-century Pharisees.

Blocking the Way of Freedom

A third characteristic of enemies of freedom is that *by their lives and teachings they actually turn people away from grace and the joyful freedom that is ours in Christ.* Jesus rebuked the scribes and Pharisees for shutting off the kingdom of heaven from people and not allowing them to go in (Matthew 23:13). The Pharisees in Jesus' day were actually blocking people from the way of salvation by their rejection of Jesus. Christian Pharisees block God's people from the way of freedom by making the Christian life a cumbersome journey of religious performance. They are like the scribes and Pharisees in Matthew 23:4 who "tie up heavy burdens and lay them on men's shoulders, but they themselves are unwilling to move them with so much as a finger."

The following testimony is almost unbelievable in regard to how viciously people can oppose the message of freedom. It is the story of a seminary graduate who found freedom in Christ, but then had the "audacity" to teach it at a Christian school:

> It was like a light bulb had gone on. I finally understood the truth of freedom! I began studying God's Word on freedom in Christ. I was amazed that no one had told me about this. When the summer was over I was so excited to be able to come back and tell my students the truths I had learned...I wanted my students to learn freedom early.
>
> [After I had gained permission to teach the material], we hadn't been studying freedom for more than two weeks when I started to get calls from parents about the teaching. They wanted to

meet with me about it. My principal set up the meeting, and I met with them. These parents proceeded to tell me in the meeting that I was "evil," "New Age," and "demonized" because I was discussing freedom in Christ in my class. I had some students get very upset with me and tell me that they did not want their thinking to change.

This became a very big deal in our school and our area. Some of the administration, parents, and board members did not like the idea of being free. These parents began campaigning for me to stop the teaching and to get me removed from the school. There was a group called "The Fundamental Bible Study Group" that got together once a week. During their study they were also praying that I would get fired or removed from the school.

The battle is not over for this weary warrior, but he has been granted some freedom to teach on our liberty in Christ. Lest you think this man is a troublemaker or rabble-rouser, we'd like you to hear his heart:

I want my students to quit playing the religious church game and start living a life that is full of joy and excitement in Christ, free to be themselves and not conform to some religious system and church tradition—rather, free to be transformed by the blood of Christ. This has been a difficult road and I am continuing to fight the battle... Legalism can try to steal your joy, as Paul says in Galatians, but I am not letting it. If I lose my job, then I'll lose it on the basis of God's Word and teachings.

Somehow we believe that in that great cloud of witnesses surrounding this brave teacher, there is one in heaven by the name of the apostle Paul who is watching…and cheering!

Obsession with the Trivial

A fourth characteristic of freedom's enemies is that *they obsess over the minutiae of life while missing the boat on what really matters to God.* In other words, they sweat the small stuff. Jesus reprimanded the Pharisees for such practices when He declared,

> Woe to you, scribes and Pharisees, hypocrites! For you tithe mint and dill and cummin, and have neglected the weightier provisions of the law: justice and mercy and faithfulness; but these are the things you should have done without neglecting the others. You blind guides, who strain out a gnat and swallow a camel! (Matthew 23:23-24).

Under the Jewish kosher dietary laws, the eating of both camels (Leviticus 11:4) and gnats (11:20) was forbidden. The Pharisees, not wanting anything unclean to enter their mouths, would literally try to strain out the small insects that would get into the wine while it was being made. While drinking wine, they would strain it through their teeth and then pick out the bugs.[6]

Jesus' point was that the Pharisees worked very hard to keep from making the tiniest blunder in breaking the Mosaic law—as if that were the most important thing. But when it came to matters of the heart, they were in essence chowing down on a camel, filling their lives with the uncleanness of pride, cruelty, and lovelessness—a spiritual filth they could not or would not see.

David Johnson's remarks in *The Subtle Power of Spiritual Abuse* are again to the point:

What is the meaning in this for us today? Again and again we see that the issue of inverted spiritual values is alive and well in the church. Many have grown up in churches that teach: Never let wine touch your lips, never play cards,... never dance, never go to movies, and never smoke. To avoid some behaviors may in fact be a very good thing to do. But what if those same externally "clean" people are full of bitterness, anger and malice? In the church where I grew up, we very carefully monitored external behaviors, carefully sifting out even such "evils" as bowling. I used to wonder why bowling was so evil, while being a dried-up old sourpuss was okay.[7]

A former pastor of mine (Rich's), was brought before his denominational leadership because he stood for the truth that Christians are identified as saints in the Bible and not sinners (though we still sin). He taught that believers can come under demonic control, but in Christ they can walk in freedom. Teaching such "heresy" eventually brought about his being stripped of his ordination to serve within that body.

While he was still pastoring his small congregation, he asked an elderly lady (who held most of the church's purse strings) what the gravest of sins was.

Pointing a finger at him, she replied, "Sabbath desecration!"

I told him later he should have responded calmly, "No, actually the worst sin is judging someone else as evil because of 'Sabbath desecration'!"

The woman who writes about her experience below was seeking love but only got law. Her testimony bares the heart of the legalistic system, which is fixated on the trivial—and it also shows the life-changing power of grace:

> I grew up in a legalistic church that acted like a stumbling block, preventing me from

understanding what a relationship with Christ meant. Though I was heavily involved as a child, by the time I got my driver's license I "drove away" from the church. That is exactly how it felt. I did not feel like I was leaving God, but I was leaving the church.

I started to drift when I became best friends with the pastor's daughter. I was in his home regularly, typically on Sunday after church. When I saw the pastor with his anger and abuse toward his children, I started to lose my desire to be a Christian. I was already a teenager with a poor self-image (due to my own dad's anger). I was then told that I could not wear makeup, pluck my eyebrows, and so on. Why didn't I ask what all that had to do with a relationship with Christ? This pushed me out of the church. What I desperately needed was to hear that God loved me unconditionally. Instead I was reminded every time I went to church that if I did any of these things, I was bound for hell.

Twenty years later, after three divorces and a multitude of failed relationships, I heard of a grace-filled church that would accept you as you are. I "tiptoed" into the back of the church for several months until I was able to trust them.

I will never forget that first day. People were dressed casually...women wore slacks and makeup! Free coffee and doughnuts were served every Sunday, and you were encouraged to bring them into the auditorium! I loved the church and am still attending to this day.

I have since developed an unquenchable thirst for Christ. It has been a training process from God to learn that He loves me, He really loves me!...even when I mess up. Every time I think of that, it brings tears to my eyes (like now). What freedom to know that my salvation is not dependent on my following rules, but on what Jesus Christ did for me on the cross! And that freedom creates in my heart a desire to do His will.

Blindness to the Work of God

Jesus once chose to use a real-life example to expose the spiritual blindness of the Pharisees. Jesus had healed blind people before, but this time He decided to kill three birds with one mud ball. First, He corrected the cultural belief of that time that all illness or infirmity was a result of a person's sin or the sin of their parents. In reference to a man born blind, He said,

> It was neither that this man sinned, nor his parents; but it was so that the works of God might be displayed in him (John 9:3).

Second, Jesus spat on the ground and made clay out of the spit, applied it to the blind man's eyes, and healed him. A little gross to our way of thinking maybe—but to the Pharisees, absolutely infuriating. It was the Sabbath when Jesus did this (John 9:14), and according to the religious leaders, a person simply must not work on that day. To the Pharisees in their human traditions, it was okay to spit on a rock on the Sabbath...but woe to the man who would spit on the dust. To spit on the dust would create mud—which was *work!*

Seeing the bondage of such laws, Jesus cut right through the Pharisees' man-made traditions. They responded by badgering the healed man and his parents...and finally throwing him out of the synagogue. This gave Jesus the opportunity to confront the third issue: the blind man's sin problem (which had not caused his blindness, but rather his spiritual death).

Notice how Jesus spoke to the healed man versus how He spoke to the Pharisees. The difference is like day and night:

Jesus heard that they had put him out, and finding him, He said, "Do you believe in the Son of Man?" He answered, "Who is He, Lord, that I may believe in Him?" Jesus said to him, "You have both seen Him, and He is the one who is talking with you." And he said, "Lord, I believe." And he worshiped Him. And Jesus said, "For judgment I came into this world, so that those who do not see may see, and that those who see may become blind." Those of the Pharisees who were with Him heard these things and said to Him, "We are not blind too, are we?" Jesus said to them, "If you were blind, you would have no sin; but since you say, 'We see,' your sin remains" (John 9:35-41).

And that is why the Lord Jesus so severely criticized them, saying,

Woe to you, scribes and Pharisees, hypocrites! For you clean the outside of the cup and of the dish, but inside they are full of robbery and self-indulgence. You blind Pharisee, first clean the inside of the cup and of the dish, so that the outside of it may become clean also (Matthew 23:25-26).

Wanting to drive home His point with great power, Jesus then compared the scribes and Pharisees to whitewashed tombs, full of dead men's bones. On the outside they appeared beautiful and righteous, but inside they were "full of hypocrisy and lawlessness" (Matthew 23:27-28). They trivialized what a relationship with God was all about, reducing it to meticulous adherence to a rigid regimen of rules and regulations while blatantly ignoring the condition of their own hearts.

Envy and Lovelessness

After years of persecuting Jesus and seeking (unsuccessfully) to trap Him with some moral riddle or technicality of law, the religious leaders finally gave up on debating Him. Instead they came together to devise a plan to eliminate Him. In the dark, hidden, smoke-filled office of the high priest they plotted.

Beware! That kind of backroom politicking is still going on today.

What was it about Jesus that infuriated the scribes and Pharisees so much? Why did they come to the point of conspiring to do away with Him?

According to Matthew 27:18 and Mark 15:10, it was envy. The scribes and Pharisees hated Jesus because He was popular. He was a threat to the power they held over the people. Their fear of losing that power is captured in John 11:48 when they confess, "If we let Him go on like this, all men will believe in Him, and the Romans will come and take away both our place and our nation." Their frustration turned to blaming each other when they saw the multitudes adoring Him. "The Pharisees said to one another, 'You see that you are not doing any good; look, the world has gone after Him'" (John 12:19).

Little did they know how right they were when they said they were "not doing any good." For legalism never does anyone any good!

"Instead of truly knowing God as our divine parent and serving him by taking responsibility for each other as brothers and sisters, we *use* God and others for our own purposes,"[8] writes Richard Quebedeaux in *By What Authority?*

These legalistic religious leaders were Jesus' worst enemies, and it was they who spearheaded the movement to have Him crucified. This is strange—because of all the people of the day, they were the most learned in the Scriptures and were the most loyally devoted to their religious beliefs. But it is possible to be so rabidly loyal to laws that love is left out. In his book *Be Loyal,* Warren Wiersbe comments, "God wants mercy, not religious sacrifice. He wants love, not legalism."[9] He's exactly right. Jesus Himself said so in Matthew 9:10-13:

> As Jesus was reclining at the table in the house, behold, many tax collectors and sinners came and were dining with Jesus and His disciples. When the Pharisees saw this, they said to His disciples, "Why is your Teacher eating with the tax collectors and sinners?" But when Jesus heard this, He said, "It is not those who are healthy who need a physician, but those who are sick. But go and learn what this means: 'I desire compassion, and not sacrifice,' for I did not come to call the righteous, but sinners."

The God of This World Is the Enemy of Freedom

So far we have taken a look at the human enemies of freedom. There is, however, an even greater enemy of Jesus and of all believers, one who is bent on robbing God's people of joy and freedom. That is the devil himself. Although the religious leaders were the point men orchestrating the betrayal, arrest, mock trials, scourging, and eventual crucifixion of Jesus, Satan was the mastermind behind the strategy.

How do we know that Satan was actively working behind the scenes to orchestrate the persecution and crucifixion of Jesus? Consider the following Scriptures:

> You are seeking to kill Me, a man who has told you the truth, which I heard from God; this Abraham did not do. You are doing the deeds of your father...If God were your Father, you would love Me...You are of your father the devil, and you want to do the desires of your father. He was a murderer from the beginning, and does not stand in the truth because there is no truth in him (Jesus speaking to the Jewish leaders, John 8:40,42,44).

> I will not speak much more with you, for the ruler of the world is coming, and he has nothing in Me (John 14:30).

He, Jesus said to the chief priests and officers
of the temple and elders who had come against
Him [to arrest Him], "Have you come out with
swords and clubs as you would against a robber?
While I was with you daily in the temple, you did
not lay hands on Me; but this hour and the power
of darkness are yours" (Luke 22:52-53).

It is clear from the Word of God that Jesus' human enemies were actually puppets and that Satan (the ruler of this
world) was pulling their strings, manipulating their thoughts,
and corrupting their hearts to accomplish his foul will.

Satan's "Elementary Principles"

What about the system of legalism itself? Is there any evidence from Scripture that Satan has his claws in that mix?
Absolutely. Remember how Jesus referred to Satan as the
"ruler of the world"? In 2 Corinthians 4:4, the apostle Paul calls
him the "god of this world," who actively blinds unbelievers'
minds to the truth of the gospel.

This reference to "god of this world" can be a bit confusing, especially in light of other Scriptures that declare, for
instance, "the earth is the LORD's, and all it contains, the
world, and those who dwell in it" (Psalm 24:1). Maybe we can
clarify.

The triune Creator God birthed the world through Jesus
Christ and sustains it through the word of His Son (Hebrews
1:1-3). It is our Lord God who is on the throne overseeing the
heavens and the earth, not the devil.

But Satan is the god, or ruler, of the world system that
operates through the lust of the flesh, the lust of the eyes, and
the boastful pride of life (1 John 2:15-17). Though God loves
the world of people (John 3:16), we believers are not to love
this world system of anti-God philosophies and practices
(1 John 2:15).

Though human beings can be the devil's puppets, the vessels he works through on earth, ultimately "our struggle is not against flesh and blood [people], but against the rulers, against the powers, against the world forces of this darkness, against the spiritual forces of wickedness in the heavenly places" (Ephesians 6:12).

So what are these spiritual rulers (demonic powers) up to? Do they have a direct hand in designing, developing, and defending legalistic systems? In Colossians 2:15-22, the apostle Paul makes it abundantly clear that they do:

> When He had disarmed the [demonic] rulers and authorities, He made a public display of them, having triumphed over them through Him.
>
> Therefore no one is to act as your judge in regard to food or drink or in respect to a festival or a new moon or a Sabbath day—things which are a mere shadow of what is to come; but the substance belongs to Christ. Let no one keep defrauding you of your prize by delighting in self-abasement and the worship of the angels, taking his stand on visions he has seen, inflated without cause by his own fleshly mind, and not holding fast to the head, from whom the entire body, being supplied and held together by the joints and ligaments, grows with a growth which is from God.
>
> If you have died with Christ to the elementary principles of the world, why, as if you were living in the world, do you submit yourself to decrees, such as, "Do not handle, do not taste, do not touch!" (which all refer to things destined to perish with use)—in accordance with the commandments and teachings of men?

We must be on guard. Our adversary, the devil, prowls around like a roaring lion, seeking to devour his prey (1 Peter 5:8). He speaks through men, exploiting their weaknesses to create religious–legalistic systems that kill—and he speaks directly to men, implanting lies into their minds. The following testimony provides a strong warning against listening to the enemy's whisperings:

When I repented and received Jesus I was on fire, and I wanted to know everything all at once. I read a lot of books and Scripture and searched out what was true. So many wonderful truths popped out to me that made me feel so good. But then I stumbled on things that were legalistic...After a while, God seemed so distant and I wondered, "Where is God in all of this?"

I realized why He felt so far away. I understood why I wasn't experiencing the Spirit of power, love, and a sound mind. I was confused and full of doubt. It was because God has nothing to do with legalism. I prayed a lot about being free, but it never changed until I acknowledged the pattern— the guilt, confusion, doubt, divisions in the Church. My own mind was the problem, but how could I be thinking this way if Jesus really lived inside me? It was because the deceiver was whispering in my ear. The father of lies was trying to murder me spiritually.

I got up one morning and read the Gospel of John out loud, word for word and declared that this was the truth that my life was to be lived by. Through reading the Gospel I noticed certain things about Jesus. There are no specifics about His dress, no records of His being a slave to laws. All we have is a humble King who couldn't be recognized or accepted by religious leaders.

I now realize that if I am religious and legalistic I can't possibly recognize my Savior any better than the Pharisees. Jesus will deliver us from lies if we ask Him to and trust Him to. It has been a process for me, and each day is part of the journey of living and learning. However, legalism can happen in one's own consciousness without any traditional upbringings or church history. Satan tries to make us feel like we have to work to please God, even though we know we can't! Each day I learn a little more and am thankful that I have a relationship with God based on faith, grace, and love. I'm thankful that the I AM loves me just as I am.

Get Reacquainted with the One Who Sets Captives Free

Today, maybe you find yourself trapped in a legalistic religious system. You want out but don't know how to get out. You see in Scripture that God's commandments are not burdensome (1 John 5:3), but you feel weary and heavy-laden (Matthew 11:28)—you feel distressed and downcast like a sheep without a shepherd (Matthew 9:36). You feel like you are being eaten alive by leaders who are much stronger and more powerful than you are.

The prophet Ezekiel spoke a strong word to such oppressors and enemies of freedom:

> Woe, shepherds of Israel who have been feeding themselves! Should not the shepherds feed the flock? You eat the fat and clothe yourselves with the wool, you slaughter the fat sheep without feeding the flock. Those who are sickly you have not strengthened, the diseased you have not healed, the broken you have not bound up, the scattered you have not brought back, nor have you sought for the lost; but with force and with severity you have dominated them...Behold, I am against the shepherds, and I will demand My

sheep from them and make them cease from feeding sheep. So the shepherds will not feed themselves anymore, but I will deliver My flock from their mouth, so that they will not be food for them (Ezekiel 34:3-4,10).

Knowing also that sheep can be cruel to one another as well, Ezekiel spoke this word to sheep (people) who were oppressing others:

> As for you, My flock, thus says the Lord GOD, "Behold, I will judge between one sheep and another, between the rams and the male goats. Is it too slight a thing for you that you should feed in the good pasture, that you must tread down with your feet the rest of your pastures? Or that you should drink of the clear waters, that you must foul the rest with your feet?...Behold, I, even I, will judge between the fat sheep and the lean sheep. Because you push with side and with shoulder, and thrust at all the weak with your horns until you have scattered them abroad, therefore I will deliver My flock, and they will no longer be a prey; and I will judge between one sheep and another" (Ezekiel 34:17-18,20-22).

Perhaps you have been a victim of or know someone who has been a victim of a legalistic religious system—either in a home, church, school, or workplace. Feeling weak and downtrodden spiritually, emotionally crushed, and relationally alone, maybe you are wondering whether there really is a God...or if He *is* around, whether He can be found in a church. To you and for you there is also a word from Ezekiel. A different word. A word of hope.

> Thus says the Lord GOD, "Behold, I Myself will search for My sheep and seek them out. As a

shepherd cares for his herd in the day when he is among his scattered sheep, so I will care for My sheep and will deliver them from all the places to which they were scattered on a cloudy and gloomy day...I will feed them in a good pasture, and their grazing ground will be on the mountain heights of Israel. There they will lie down on good grazing ground and feed in rich pasture on the mountains of Israel. I will feed my flock and I will lead them to rest," declares the Lord GOD. "I will seek the lost, bring back the scattered, bind up the broken and strengthen the sick; but the fat and the strong I will destroy. I will feed them with judgment" (Ezekiel 34:11-12,14-16).

In the pages ahead, we want to reintroduce you to the Good Shepherd, who laid down His life for the sheep (you and me)—the Good Shepherd, who calls all His sheep by name and whose voice they hear. His voice is not rigid, harsh, and controlling. Rather, His voice is gentle, kind, and calming.

Right where you are...that's where He wants to meet with you. Maybe you're in your home, or in a crowded place all alone. Maybe you are sitting in a coffee shop wondering what went wrong between you and Jesus. Maybe you are questioning whether He gives a rip about you anymore. So you sit, bruised and wounded, almost out of hope and nearly out of time.

You have experienced what the enemies of freedom can do. Now isn't it time to get reacquainted with the One who came to set captives free?

For you, Isaiah penned these words:

> Like a shepherd He will tend His flock, in His arm He will gather the lambs and carry them in His bosom; He will gently lead the nursing ewes (Isaiah 40:11).

We pray that you'll read on. Good news is on the way. Good news for *you!*

Part II

THE YOKE
THAT FREES

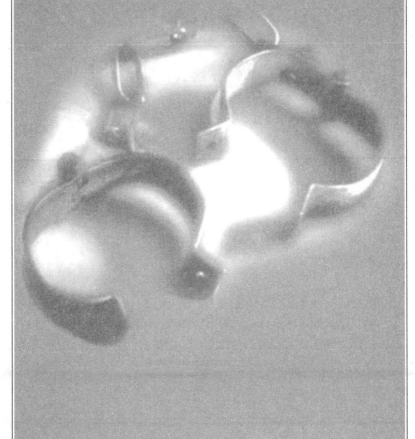

7

GRACE TO YOU!

I t is the God-given heritage of every child of God to walk in the freedom of grace—to be eager and able to know, love, and worship Jesus without the chains of a legalistic system dragging them down. That is the purpose of our writing: by God's grace to point the way toward breaking the bondage of legalism in your life, so that you can be ushered into a deeper reality of Christ. The Christian life is not rules but relationship,

> for you have not received a spirit of slavery leading to fear again, but you have received a spirit of adoption as sons by which we cry out, "Abba! Father!" (Romans 8:15).

Grace Is a Family Matter

I (Rich) can remember the time when our oldest son, Brian, was still in diapers. If I would go away on a trip, or even if I had only been gone a few hours, he would be the first to greet me, running toward me and yelling, "Daddy! Daddy!" Of course my heart would melt, and my arms would open wide and I'd pick him up.

Sometimes my nose would catch the drift before my arms would catch his body. Then I would notice the "ten-pound payload" bumping along behind him as he ran...if you catch *my* drift!

When this occurred, did I command him to stop his advance immediately? Did I run the other way? Did I demand that he "clean up his act" (he couldn't have even if I had wanted him to!) before I would accept him? Did I roll out the list of rules and regulations he had to measure up to before I would welcome him?

Of course not! I received him as he was. Was he perfect? Far from it. But I accepted him because he was my *son*, and because my love for him was not based on his potty perform-ance.

So it is with God and us. He is our Father, our Daddy. Now that we have become believers in Christ, we have not entered into a new form of slavery (based on law) that makes us afraid to fail or afraid of being punished. Instead, we are now *family*. Loved and accepted—just as we are. We are totally unable to clean up our act apart from Him—and that makes us cry out for Him and reach out for Him to hold us.

That's the power of grace...to you, to me, to all of God's children.

Receive His Love, Believe His Word

In the first half of this book we have attempted to diagnose the root problems and symptoms of legalistic lives and legal-istic systems. We did that because a problem well-defined is a problem half-solved. We hope that along the way we also gave you enough encouragement to keep reading.

In this second half, we want to provide the antidote to legalism. Not just a treatment of the symptoms, but a cure for the disease itself. We want you to hear God's voice speaking to you and saying, "Grace to you..." We want you to receive His love and believe His Word.

We begin with a testimony that we trust will bring you hope...hope that grace may become more to you than a theological concept or the theme of a hymn—a living reality in your life.

I grew up in a legalistic church and got married at age 26. My husband and I should have known we were in trouble that first Sunday, as we had to decide where to attend church. I had been taught that all other churches were going to hell, and I just assumed my husband would go with me. He wouldn't, so I went with him.

This caused me to study the Word of God and wrestle with the issues we disagreed on. God began a work in my heart, but I had the hardest time believing God sent Jesus to die for me and that there was nothing I needed to do to add to what He had done. I could not imagine it was a free gift! One day I accepted the Lord Jesus into my life. He has been so REAL in my life, answering many prayers, bringing me through hard times, and letting me experience God's tremendous PEACE and STRENGTH during those difficult times. Looking back, it was so hard to see that what Jesus was after was a personal relationship with me, and that He comes to live in us.

I praise the Lord that my mom, who belonged to that legalistic church, years ago told me that she saw Jesus in my life. I also praise God for the time I spent with her the days before she died. On August 31, while feeding her breakfast, I responded to her comment, "I'm so tired" (she had fought breast cancer and lung cancer for five years). I said, "I know you must be tired—it's been a long, hard fight, but you won't have to fight much longer." I made affirming statements about what Jesus did for us on the cross—that it was not our work but His, that saved us. Mom agreed with each statement. I had tried to witness to her for many years, but she had resented grace theology. For the first time I had true peace about where Mom would spend eternity.

She died the next morning at 2:50 A.M. I cannot tell you what power God gave me to make it through that night with my legalist sister, who always takes control...and did that night. I had such peace. I did not retaliate for any of my sister's condemning comments.

God is so good and real. A mighty fortress and refuge. This girl (me) who was stuck in legalism found God to be real and demonstrated to her family how a person finds grace and comfort in her Father...even as her mother is dying.

In this chapter, we want to deal a death blow to the guilt fostered by legalistic systems. In order to do so, we first want to look at an aspect of Christ's death on the cross that perhaps you had not thought about before: how you have been set free both from slavery to sin and slavery to the law by His death. Secondly, we want to face head-on the lies that you may be believing about our heavenly Father: that He is a cosmic killjoy, bound and determined to crush the fun out of life. Finally, we want to expose the activity of the "accuser of the brethren," who has made it his goal to keep believers under a yoke of slavery and guilt.

Freedom Through Death

The greatest battle of all time was fought and won by Jesus Christ on the cross. The battle still rages because the enemy of our souls is cruelly committed to keeping obscured the full revelation of the truth of what happened on that day.

In regard to the unsaved, Satan, the god of this world, has "blinded the minds of the unbelieving so that they might not see the light of the gospel of the glory of Christ, who is the image of God" (2 Corinthians 4:4). But by the grace of God,

His Holy Spirit opens the eyes of those who have been blinded, and they come to see that "God demonstrates His own love toward us, in that while we were yet sinners, Christ died for us" (Romans 5:8). Suddenly, the gospel moves from history to *His* story to *my* story, and we are saved from the penalty of sin—eternal death—by trusting in Christ's finished work on the cross as the full payment for *our* sins.

But as remarkable as that revelation is, that is not all that was accomplished by Christ on the cross. In order to be fully freed from the bondage of legalism, we must go beyond knowing that our sins were placed on the cross. We must see that *we* died with Christ as well. In Christ we received a new lease on life, but before we could enter into that life, the old you and me had to die.

If God Says It's True...

Perhaps you have read the following Scriptures and scratched your head, wondering what they could possibly mean. Deciding that such truths were too complicated for the average Christian, you decided that such "heavy" doctrines were better left to theologians. Maybe you just chalked them up to "positional truth" and moved on, unaware that they have power to transform *today*. We run into many Christians who will say of these verses something like, "Well, that's just the way God *sees* us," as if God were simply unable to look below the surface of things. They act as though the Lord were suffering from a serious bout with denial—refusing to face reality, as if He were looking at us through rose-colored glasses.

Think of it this way. If *God* sees us a certain way, is that not the way it is? Is that not the way *we are*? Are not God's knowledge and wisdom perfect? Can we not, therefore, trust that what God says about us in His Word is truly the truth? It may sound too good to be true—but if God says it is true, it *is* true. Our experience may say, "This could never be true!" Our feelings may shout, "There's no way that's the truth!" But is the reality of what is true or untrue based on our limited experience or on our constantly changing emotions—or on God's perfect, unchanging Word?

So take a look at these Scriptures with an open mind, as if you had never seen them before. Ask the Lord to bring *revelation* to your heart, that *"the eyes of your heart may be enlightened"* (Ephesians 1:17). God does not want to merely *inform* you—He desires to *transform* you.

> I have been crucified with Christ and I no longer live, but Christ lives in me. The life I live in the body, I live by faith in the Son of God, who loved me and gave himself for me (Galatians 2:20 NIV).

> Are we to continue in sin so that grace may increase? May it never be! How shall we who died to sin still live in it? Or do you not know that all of us who have been baptized into Christ Jesus have been baptized into His death? Therefore we have been buried with Him through baptism into death, so that as Christ was raised from the dead through the glory of the Father, so we too might walk in newness of life. For if we have become united with Him in the likeness of His death, certainly we shall be also in the likeness of His resurrection, knowing this, that our old self was crucified with Him, in order that our body of sin might be done away with, so that we would no longer be slaves to sin; for he who has died is freed from sin (Romans 6:1-7).

Dead to Sin, Alive to God

Something has radically changed in you and me because of Christ. We are not simply the same people we always were... with eternal life slapped on for good measure. We are radically (at the core) different. Changed. Metamorphosized. We are a new race (1 Peter 2:9), a new form of creation (2 Corinthians

5:17) that was not in existence 2000 years ago. We are dead to sin. We have been freed from sin's control! We are no longer its slaves!

I know we tend to think of only our sins being placed on Christ, but that's not the complete picture. It wasn't as if our sins were vacuumed out of our bodies and somehow spiritually injected into our Lord. We ourselves (the old you and me apart from Christ) were placed on the cross with Him along with all our sins. When Jesus died, we died with Him. When Jesus was buried, we were buried with Him. When He rose from the dead, we rose, too—as new, spiritually alive, set-free-from-sin's-control people!

You might be saying, "Dead to sin? Me? You gotta be kidding! I sin every day, all day, and I spend a lot of my non-sinning time trying to *keep* from sinning. You might as well tell me I'm dead to breathing!"

For starters, you need to understand what "dead to sin" does mean and doesn't mean. First of all, it does not mean you no longer sin. As believers in Christ we all still sin—and if you have any question about that personally, we suggest you talk to your spouse, children, or close friends!

Secondly, being "dead to sin" does not mean that temptation no longer happens. Temptation can still be very strong for even the saintliest saint. It's like the case of the 80-year-old Christian man who was asked by a group of teenage boys when sexual temptation goes away. His answer was, "Sometime after age 80, I suppose!" From now until we physically die, we are subject to temptation. But to be *tempted* is not to sin; to be tempted is to be human. Jesus Himself was tempted in all the ways we are, yet He never sinned (Hebrews 4:15).

Being dead to sin means that you are actually, really, genuinely no longer its slave, and that sin is no longer your master. That controlling relationship has been severed through Christ, and we are now "alive to God"—joined to Him instead.

How Dead People Deal with Sin

When temptation attacks, we are no longer helpless slaves who have no recourse but to obey their master. Having received Christ as our Savior, we can *now* choose by God's grace to say "No!" to sin and "Yes!" to God. Titus 2:11-14 spells it out:

> The grace of God that brings salvation has appeared to all men. It teaches us to say "No" to ungodliness and worldly passions, and to live self-controlled, upright and godly lives in this present age, while we wait for the blessed hope—the glorious appearing of our great God and Savior, Jesus Christ, who gave himself for us to redeem us from all wickedness and to purify for himself a people that are his very own, eager to do what is good (NIV).

Is there anything in those verses about following a list of rules and regulations to stop sin arrows in mid-air? Not in my Bible. That's because the Christian life is a relationship of grace, not of scrupulous adherence to laws.

Maybe you are thinking, *If only this could be true! If only I could have some kind of spiritual experience that would make this true for me.* The truth is that the only experience you require already occurred 2000 years ago (when Jesus died on the cross and we died with Him)—and the only way we can enter into that experience is *by faith.* Faith is saying our "Amen!" to what God says is true. It is our step of trust to agree that God *is* telling the truth, regardless of what we might think or how we might feel. It is the choice of our will that, in time, results in our thoughts and feelings lining up with that choice.

Romans 6:11 says, "Consider yourselves to be dead to sin, but alive to God in Christ Jesus." Counting ourselves dead to sin does not make it true. It *is* true (because God said so), therefore we count it to be so.

If I receive my savings-account statement from the bank and it says I have $5000 in the account, I count that to be true. My considering it to be true doesn't make it true, however. It already is true! That money is sitting there earning interest whether I choose to believe that bank statement or not!

So it is with you. If you are in Christ, sin *has* lost its power to control you—whether you believe it or not. If you choose to believe and continue to believe this truth, it will become progressively more evident in your experience, but it will never be truer of you than it is right now!

As you grow in Christ, you will learn, when temptation comes, to choose to believe the truth and say, "I am alive in Christ, and sin is no longer my master."[1] Then looking to Jesus for grace to help, you will then stand back in amazement and watch as sin is shown to be the defeated foe it is.

An Example from Marriage

When I (Rich) said "I do" (and fortunately Shirley did, too), she and I were legally married. At that moment when we were pronounced husband and wife, we both died to singleness—35 years of it for me, 34 for her. There was a combined 69 years of living as singles being poured into that marriage! We *had been* lifelong singles, but at that moment we *truly became* newlyweds. The Bible says that we, two individuals, became one!

During the wedding ceremony we felt excited, but I wouldn't say we "felt married" (13 years later I'm still not sure what that *feels* like). Neither did we do a particularly great job of acting married when we got to our hotel that night. We were both nervous and embarrassed. There was nothing wrong with being naked in each other's presence—in fact, there was everything right about it—but it sure *felt* weird. Fortunately we got the hang of that, but marriage (and its consequent "deadness" to singleness) hasn't come easily.

There were many "single" habits that we carried over into our married life. Shirley certainly had hers, but in the name of self-interest (my continued good health!) I'll just mention some of my own. I was used to coming and going as I pleased—I had to learn to inform Shirley of my whereabouts so she wouldn't worry. I was used to being in control of my schedule—I had to learn to include Shirley in my plans. And when it came to money, I really fought being married...but that's too painful a story!

Now I wouldn't dream of being single (especially with four kids!). I know I'm married and dead to singleness. I see myself as married and no longer single. Nobody has to convince me that I'm a husband. I *know*. It affects the choices I make in life. I consult Shirley when we have decisions to make or major expenditures coming up. We pray together for our home, our relationship, our family, and other things.

Am I still tempted to act like I'm single? Of course. I said I was dead to *being* single, not dead to *acting* single. The deadness to singleness occurred in a moment. The living out of that reality takes a lifetime of growth, but it is all still based on the validity of that wedding ceremony. By the way, if the Lord has called you (either temporarily or for a lifetime) to singleness, that is a good thing. To experience the fullness of your calling, however, you must die to *independence* and come alive to *interdependence* (in the body of Christ), as must every believer.

A Practical, Everyday Truth

Though I (Paul) knew the Scriptures that spoke of my death and resurrection with Christ, I wasn't really applying these truths to my everyday life. I didn't realize that I was deeply steeped in legalism and performance. My experience with Christ only served to thrust me into hyperperformance and crippling drivenness. I could not seem to do enough for God.

While I was in Bible college, a man named Rudy Peterson came to speak at a chapel service on campus. As he spoke of our union with Christ, what he said caught the ears and hearts of many students. Rudy was on fire for Jesus, and many students caught the flame. I was one of them.

Rudy remained on campus for several days, much to the chagrin of the administration, which was more concerned about academics. Many of the students were being revived by God, however, and they could not focus on their classes.

Almost everyone seemed affected, but it was just a small group of us that met with Rudy in the upper room of a nearby church. We spent hours in worship and prayer, with the liberating truths of our dying and rising with Christ deeply penetrating our minds and hearts. We wept with our faces to the floor, repenting before God and embracing by faith this new (to us!) truth.

God used that meeting with Rudy and the other students to sow the seeds of freedom in my life, seeds that have grown into a full-time ministry of seeing captives set free by Christ.

The problem with most Christians is that they do not see themselves as being "dead to sin and alive to God in Christ Jesus." So they work hard to protect themselves from sin by building walls of laws around themselves. And since they are convinced that the Christian life is well-summed up as "trying hard to obey God's commands," they keep trying harder.

Children of God, that is exactly how the devil wants you to fight sin—trying hard to beat this evil enemy by gritting your teeth and keeping the commandments. By doing so you have fallen right into the trap of legalism. And you *will* fall...and fail. Count on it. "It is the Spirit who gives life; the flesh profits nothing" (John 6:63). Sin cannot be defeated by mere human energy, ingenuity, or determination.

Once you understand that you are truly dead to sin and that it is no longer your master, the tables are turned. Suddenly victory over sin's enticement becomes attainable. You come to realize sin is deceitful (Hebrews 3:13) and it never delivers on its promises. In fact, sin is actually your deadliest enemy, waging war against your soul (1 Peter 2:11), and so you learn to hate it. When that happens, sin has lost its seductive power over you. You are freed up to look to God as your life, and you find that He gives you the heart and strength to stand firm, resist sin, and walk with Him in grace.

Dead to Law

The other aspect of the work of the cross that many of us miss is this: Christ's death freed us from being controlled by the law because Jesus perfectly fulfilled the law through His perfect life, death, and resurrection!

When we, by faith, enter into a new relationship with God through Christ, we are taken out from under the law-system and placed under a grace-system. As Romans 7:1-6 declares,

> Do you not know, brethren (for I am speaking to those who know the law), that the law has jurisdiction over a person as long as he lives? For the married woman is bound by law to her husband while he is living; but if her husband dies, she is released from the law concerning the husband. So then, if while her husband is living she is joined to another man, she shall be called an adulteress; but if her husband dies, she is free from the law, so that she is not an adulteress though she is joined to another man.
>
> Therefore, my brethren, you also were made to die to the Law through the body of Christ, so that you might be joined to another, to Him who was raised from the dead, in order that we might bear fruit for God. For while we were in the flesh, the sinful passions, which were aroused by the Law, were at work in the members of our body to bear fruit for death. But now we have been released from the Law, having died to that by which we were bound, so that we serve in newness of the Spirit and not in oldness of the letter.

Our first husband, Mr. Law (as Juan Carlos Ortiz calls it), was perfect—absolutely perfect, holy, and good (Romans

7:12). Not a flaw in him, at least on the outside. But the problem was, he was perfectly horrid to live with because he demanded perfection of his bride. He was cold, hard, and unmerciful. No matter how hard we tried to please him, we would always fall short. We could just never measure up to his perfect demands. The harder we would try, the harder we would fall. And Mr. Law would make sure we knew it. So in this marriage, the honeymoon was over almost immediately, and rather than experiencing the joys of matrimony, all we knew was guilt. Guilt from knowing we were breaking God's laws, and guilt from wanting things that we knew our husband, Mr. Law, disapproved of.

Then our Knight in shining armor came and swept us away from that miserable marriage. But our deliverance did not come by way of a white horse. It came by means of a rugged cross—a cross on which we died to the law through our union with the death of the Lord Jesus. A death so powerful that it forever put us beyond the grasp of Mr. Law. We now serve Jesus through the newness and freshness of the Holy Spirit!

We Need a Funeral Service

How often, though, do we still listen to our old husband? How many times is Mr. Law even *welcomed* into our homes or churches? He is presented as our *defender*, the one who will keep us from sin. But in reality, he is a *pretender*, impotent to protect us. How many times do we feel compelled to fight temptation on our own strength by trying our hardest to obey the commands? And how many times do we futilely attempt to protect ourselves from sin by constructing a straw house made of our own religious rules? That is legalism.

We men make New Year's resolutions to exercise more consistently, eat fewer fatty foods, read more books, and spend more quality time with our wives and children. By the time the bowl games have started, we're already parked alone in front of the tube with a bowl of potato chips! We vow to pray more, memorize more Scripture, share our faith more, reach out to our neighbors or co-workers more, and be involved more at church. After a few weeks of trying harder, all we have to show for it is a load of guilt, a growing resentment toward God, and a disturbing attraction to the world.

It is only our new husband, the Lord Jesus, who is "able to keep you from stumbling" (Jude 24), "for since He Himself was tempted in that which He has suffered, He is able to come to the aid of those who are tempted" (Hebrews 2:18).

Isn't it time we held a funeral service for all our man-made rules and homemade efforts at living the Christian life? In fact, why don't you get out a piece of paper right now and list all the things you have felt you had to do or had to avoid in order to gain or maintain God's favor? Ask the Lord to bring to mind all of them. Write them all down—the rules, regulations, standards, expectations. They have all been whispers from Mr. Law or from the accuser of the brethren, producing guilt and robbing you of joy.

Then do yourself a favor. Burn that sheet of paper and watch your guilt be blown away like the smoke. As the smoke ascends, let it be an offering to God. Hear the Lord saying in response, "Grace to you. I accept you as you are. Stop trying to perform to win My favor. You already have it in Christ! Look to Me and I will give you the grace to stand in righteousness." The mountain of guilt in your life will crumble before His grace, as it says in Zechariah 4:6-7:

> This is the word of the LORD to Zerubbabel saying, "Not by might nor by power, but by My Spirit," says the LORD of hosts. "What are you, O great mountain? Before Zerubbabel you will become a plain; and he will bring forth the top stone with shouts of "Grace, grace to it!"

The Old Way Versus the New Way

Now is the time to enter into the newness of life in the Spirit so that you can bear fruit for God. Perhaps the following illustration will make things even clearer.

Consider two Greek myths. Two men. Two voyages. One danger—but two strategies for defeating it. A comparison of these two men, we believe, can be an education in how to fight...and how *not* to fight...sin.[2]

First, myth and man number one. Ulysses (Odysseus) was a great hero. Helen, wife of Menelaus, who was king of Greece, had gone off with Paris, prince of Troy. Whether she had been stolen or seduced, Menelaus was not taking the loss of his wife lying down. With Ulysses and a great army, the king invaded the city of Troy (via the famed Trojan horse), wiped out the town, and brought back Helen to Ithaca.

Helen's beauty was such that her "face launched a thousand ships." But for this lesson, we want to focus on just one—the ship on which Ulysses sailed during his return voyage.

External Shackles

At one point, Ulysses and his crew faced a terrible danger from the Sirens, gorgeous singing creatures whose song was irresistibly alluring to men. Many a ship's crew had been hypnotically seduced into drawing close...too close, only to be shipwrecked on the submerged rocks surrounding the Sirens' island. Unable to escape, the sailors would then find to their horror that the Sirens were actually savage cannibals.

As they approached the Sirens' island, Ulysses ordered all his crew members to stuff wax in their ears and row past the island as if their lives depended on it. Ulysses, on the other hand, wanted to have his cake and eat it, too. He wanted to hear the song and experience the thrill of temptation... without the unpleasant aftertaste. So Ulysses refused to put wax in his ears, but instead had his men bind him securely to the ship's mast.

Craving what the Sirens' song seemed to promise, Ulysses fought against the bonds that held him, pleading with his crew to let him go. Fortunately they did not.

In his book *Pleasures Evermore*, Sam Storms comments on Ulysses and how many of us are like him today:

Ulysses was utterly seduced by the songs of the Sirens. Were it not for the ropes that held him fast to the mast, Ulysses would have succumbed to their invitation. Although his hands were restrained, his heart was captivated by their beauty. Inwardly he said Yes, though outwardly the ropes prevented such indulgence. His "No" was not the fruit of a spontaneous revulsion but the product of an external shackle. Such is the way many live as Christian men and women. Their hearts pant for the passing pleasures of sin. They struggle through life saying No to sin, not because their hearts are so inclined but because their hands have been shackled by the laws, rules, taboos and prohibitions of their religious environment. *Their obedience is not the glad product of a transformed nature but a reluctant conformity born of fear and shame.* Is that the way you want to live?... Are you bound tightly to the mast of religious expectations, all the while wanting to do the opposite of what is done? Is there not a better way to say No to the sinful sounds of Sirens?[3]

Internal Rapture

Now for myth-man number two and strategy number two. On his sea journey, Jason the Argonaut also had to pass by the loathsome and seductive Sirens. But he refused the wax and the binding of himself to the ship's mast. Instead he had brought along Orpheus, a musician whose talents (especially upon the lyre and flute) were unsurpassed.

Before the Sirens came into earshot, Jason instructed Orpheus to play his most beautiful, rapturous songs. As he did so, the sailors totally ignored the Sirens' song and rowed safely by the treacherous island. None of them went *over*board because what was *on* board was too wonderful to give up.

We trust you get the point. The law can restrain our hands but it cannot transform our hearts. In fact, it actually arouses our sinful passions (Romans 7:5-8). Yet the grace of God and intimacy with Christ can provide such an alluring, magnetic attraction to that which is good, better, and best that the seducing power of sin is rendered old and impotent. Storms' comments are again insightful:

> My most satisfying spiritual pleasure is when I find myself drawn to those things that draw God and repelled by those things that repel Him. I want to be attuned to God's heart, to be of one mind, one spirit, one disposition with Him. If this occurs, it will only occur as the fruit of fascination with all that God is in Himself and all that He is for me in Jesus. That sinful habit you struggle with daily, that low-grade addiction that keeps you in the throes of guilt and shame, that inability to walk with consistency in the things you know please God, ultimately will only be overcome when your heart, soul, mind, spirit, and will are captivated by the majesty, mercy, splendor, beauty, and magnificence of who God is and what He has and will do for you in Jesus.[4]

The Devil's Smear Job

The problem with many who have lived under the yoke of a legalistic system is precisely this: *Deep down they are not convinced God wants them to enjoy life and experience pleasure.* So they are reluctant to pursue any kind of intimate relationship with Him.

Ever since the garden of Eden, the devil has been on a crusade to paint a picture of God as anti-pleasure. He has done a pretty good job of it (which is rather remarkable, when you consider that the word "Eden" *means* pleasure!) A recent Sunday cartoon pictures Moses coming down off Mt. Sinai with the tablets of the Ten Commandments. One of the Hebrews at the bottom of the mountain then calls out sarcastically, "That kind of rules out everything, doesn't it?"

The insinuation is clear: Once God comes on the scene, the party's over. That's how the writer of this brief testimony felt:

> Legalism is wrong and leaves scars that are deep. In the church where I grew up, I thought God was someone who stood over me with a whip and watched for me to break one of the many rules. No jewelry, no rings, no makeup, no shorts, pants, or bathing suits, no TV or going to movies, no attending kids' camps, no proms, no buying, sewing, or working on Sunday, no going away to college, no straight hair—had to have curls (in fact I was one year old when I had my first perm). Do I need to tell you how hard high school was with rules like these?

You might remember what the serpent said to Eve to open up their deadly conversation: "Indeed, has God said, 'You shall not eat from any tree of the garden?'" (Genesis 3:1). Translation: "You mean to tell me there are all these gorgeous trees around here just brimming with juicy, delicious fruit—and God won't allow you to eat from *any* of them? Man, what a party pooper!"

Despite the serpent's insinuations and slanderous attacks on God's goodness, in the garden of Eden there was only one tree that was forbidden. In fact, the Lord had said, "From any tree [except the tree of the knowledge of good and evil] you may eat *freely*" (Genesis 2:16). There were likely scores, maybe hundreds of trees that had, so to speak, signs all over them: "Welcome! Come here and enjoy! Eat to your heart's content!"

Human Evil Strengthens Satan's Lies

It was Eve, not God, who put restrictions on God's blessing. In answering the serpent's charge she replied, "From the fruit of the trees of the garden we may eat; but from the fruit of the tree which is in the middle of the garden, God has said, 'You shall not eat from it or touch it, or you will die' " (Genesis 3:3).

First, Eve *diminished* God's word from "eat freely" (2:16) to just "eat." The sense of joyful exuberance in celebrating God's goodness was reduced to a mere function of life. Isn't that exactly what legalism does? It just sucks the life out of life.

Second, she *changed* God's word from "the tree of the knowledge of good and evil" (2:17) to just "the tree which is in the middle of the garden." This does not appear to simply be an abbreviation or easier way to refer to the tree, since Eve's explanation is longer than God's! It appears, rather, to be a defense mechanism. By referring to the tree by its location, she was probably trying to remind herself to stay away from it. By not calling it by its descriptive, God-given name, maybe she hoped it would not have as much power to threaten or tempt her. Either way, a denial of reality and a refusal to look at things as they are have always been hallmarks of legalism... and have been completely futile in efforts to avoid sin.

Third, Eve *added to* God's word by tacking on her own man-made prohibition of *not touching* the tree. Sounds like good, sound practical advice, doesn't it? But it was the birth of human traditions being placed on an equal level with the pure Word of God—and the world has been crushed under that sort of legalistic yoke ever since.

The God Who Invented Pleasure

Many of God's people have been told "Don't do this! Don't do that!" so many times that they have come to think of God as a cosmic killjoy. But nothing could be further from the truth. God is not like the Santa Claus we learn about in the song: We'd better not shout, better not cry, better not pout, because he's coming to town. After making his list and checking it twice, he'll figure out who's been "naughty and nice." I'll bet you never thought of Santa Claus as a legalist, but he is! But it gets worse because this Santa Claus knows when you are sleeping and awake, and when you're "bad or good." Santa the legalist is bad enough, but Santa the stalker? Scary stuff!

God is not like Santa Claus at all. He is "compassionate and gracious" (Psalm 103:8). He is "good to all, and His mercies are over all His works" (Psalm 145:9). That means He is kind and generous and pours out the richness of that goodness upon all of us, even when we have not been particularly good. True, we can resist Him and deprive ourselves of the full expression of His bounty, but His heart is always one that "longs to be gracious to you, and therefore He waits on high to have compassion on you" (Isaiah 30:18).

God is a good God, who delights when we enjoy His creation in the manner for which He designed it. For example, God could have made human reproduction a sterile process of splitting in two, like amoebas. But God made sex *fun*. It is pleasurable, not painful, and it expresses and allows us to experience the intimacy, oneness, closeness, and affection that are some of our deepest human needs. Sure, God has placed limitations on sex—but only to multiply its pleasure, not diminish it. God's laws are protective, not restrictive.

God could have made eating an act in which we took off our shoes and dug our toes into the earth, extracting nutrients like trees. But God made eating *enjoyable*. He gave us taste buds, not roots—and He created the world with things like charcoal-grilled steaks, fresh-baked bread, chocolate, ice cream, and a thousand other delights!

God created pleasure and He "richly supplies us with all things to enjoy" (1 Timothy 6:17). Friendship, pets, food, clothing, sunsets, flowers, the smell of fresh-mown grass, snowfalls, fires in fireplaces, romance, beauty, children, the elderly...the list goes on. True, sin has tainted this fallen world, and there are numerous examples that could be cited to declare the perversity of life on the blue planet. But in the midst of a corrupt world, there is a strong, unquenchable whisper that says, "God is good. Enjoy life as He intended. The pleasures of life are from Him."

God's Gifts Are Good

Far too many of God's people have been hamstrung in their enjoyment of life's pleasures because of a faulty concept of God. To many, His countenance reflects the stern, scowling visage of parents and preachers who are constantly concerned that God's people might just be having too much fun and so they'd better knock it off right now! Philip Yancey speaks to this distortion:

> The churches I attended had stressed the dangers of pleasure so loudly that I missed any positive message. Guided by [G.K.] Chesterton, I came to see sex, money, power, and sensory pleasures as God's good gifts. Every Sunday I can turn on the radio or television and hear preachers decry the drugs, sexual looseness, greed, and crime that are "running rampant" in the streets of America. Rather than merely wag our fingers at such obvious abuses of God's good gifts, perhaps we should demonstrate to the world where good gifts actually come from, and why they are good. Evil's greatest triumph may be its success in portraying religion as an enemy of pleasure when, in fact, religion accounts for pleasure's source: Every good and enjoyable thing is the invention of a Creator who lavished gifts on the world.[5]

Have you been made to feel guilty for having fun? Have you believed the lie that life should be lived soberly (read: boringly) and that one should not enjoy things "too much"? Maybe you need to write out another list for burning—things you have been told should be avoided but which God has created for your enjoyment.

While you're at it, enjoy what God gives you. Really. It's okay. Actually, it's more than okay—it's honoring and pleasing to God! Eat heartily, sleep deeply, if married have sex passionately (with your spouse!), work hard, play hard, try being affectionate, spontaneous, and light-hearted for a while—and do it all to the glory of God. Have fun, and don't feel guilty for enjoying what God has given you! Be like Eric Liddell, the Scottish Olympian-turned-missionary, who said, "When I run, I feel His pleasure."

Maybe that's what the Lord had in mind when He inspired Malachi to write,

> For you who fear My name, the sun of righteousness will rise with healing in its wings; and you will go forth and skip about like calves from the stall (Malachi 4:2).

That sure sounds like freedom!

The Accuser Wants You to Forget

Jesus wasn't kidding when He said, "I came that they may have life, and have it abundantly" (John 10:10). Nor was He joking when He warned just before that, "the thief comes only to steal and kill and destroy" (same verse).

The enemy of our souls, the devil, is called the "accuser of the brethren" (Revelation 12:10). He is the proverbial wet blanket on true life and joy, like the Grinch that stole Christmas (without the softening heart at the end of the story). He is determined to rob Christians of the joy of their salvation, and one of his main strategies is to keep us under lock and key, bound in the chains of guilt.

Satan is a liar and the father of lies (John 8:44), and he does not want you to believe that anything in Scripture truly applies to you. He'll whisper sour nothings in your ear (though he'll make them sound true) like, "I've blown it too many times—God has given up on me." "You call yourself a

Christian?" "How could God love someone like me?" "I must not be saved if I'm struggling so much." "You can't do that—you're too weak." And so on. He masterfully masquerades as your own voice or the voice of God (or he speaks through significant people in your life), draining away your hope and your resistance, as the story of this brother in Christ describes:

> I have been struggling for years since my conversion to Christ. I cannot have complete peace, and every time I try to move to a higher level, there is always this accusing voice reminding me of the weakness I struggle with. So I keep on trying to drive away my guilt...to gain God's acceptance.

The psalmist experienced this relentless eroding of hope by the accuser and wrote this about it:

> All day long my dishonor is before me and my humiliation has overwhelmed me, because of the voice of him who reproaches and reviles, because of the presence of the enemy and the avenger (Psalm 44:15-16).

In the movie *Hook*, Robin Williams plays a grown-up Peter Pan (now named Peter Panning), a workaholic who neglects his family for the sake of his career. At first denying his true identity as Peter Pan, he then returns to Never-Never Land. With much difficulty, he finally regains his ability to fly and fight. Dustin Hoffman brilliantly portrays Captain Hook, an evil and cruel deceiver. In the final fight scene, Hook literally has Pan up against the wall, preparing to kill him. Hook's words are like those of the accuser:

> You know you're not really Peter Pan, don't you? This is only a dream. When you wake up, you'll just be Peter Panning—a cold, selfish man

who drinks too much, is obsessed with success, and runs and hides from his wife and children.

In the movie, you can see in Peter Pan's eyes that Hook's words are hooking his heart. Pan is losing his will and strength to fight...until one by one the Lost Boys speak to him: "I believe in you." "I believe in you." "I believe in you, Peter." Then his son, who earlier had rejected him as his dad, says with a big smile, "You are Peter Pan." Finally Tinker Bell (a miniature Julia Roberts) says, "I believe in you, Peter Pan." With renewed strength and zeal, Pan launches himself back into the battle with Hook, eventually defeating him.

It's Who You Are and Who You Know

If you let him, the enemy of our souls will relentlessly remind you of your failures, your weaknesses, and your sins. He will try to make you believe that you are still a slave to sin... and that religiously trying to keep rules, regulations, laws, and standards is the only way for you to live. He will use those laws to tempt you into sin—and once you have sinned, he will mercilessly accuse you and condemn you for your fall! We call this the "double whammy."

A former pastor of mine was once a missionary to Mexico. At that time many of the police officers there were corrupt and would extort money from innocent people. My pastor's friend owned a powder-blue minivan, a surefire tip-off that he was a Yankee—and Yankees meant money, and money meant *cerveza* (beer).

One day the two men were driving in that minivan, and they came to an intersection where the traffic light was stuck on red. On the other side of the intersection a police officer was waving traffic through, so they proceeded across. Once they did, the policeman pulled them over and ticketed them for running a red light!

My pastor friend told a friend of his, a high-ranking government official, about this abuse of authority. The official chuckled and gave him his business card. On it was his name (he was well-known) and his position: head over all media in Mexico. The people were afraid of him, for they knew him to be the chief spy in the whole nation. "If a police officer pulls you over illegally, just show him this business card and you'll be all right," he said.

My friend could hardly wait for the opportunity, and he didn't have to wait long. Soon he found himself face-to-face with a policeman demanding money in exchange for not ticketing him for a fraudulent charge.

"My friend who gave me this card said I should show it to you," he said, grinning. "He said you would get the message."

The police officer got a horrified look on his face and quickly waved my friend along, suddenly losing his lust for money and beer.

For too long, God's people have been brutally bullied around by Satan, the architect and builder of legalistic systems. We believe it is time for a little holy outrage. We believe it is time we pulled out our "I mean business" cards and reminded the accuser of who we are and Who we know!

Maybe you have forgotten who you really are. Perhaps you've never really known. In either case, we've got good news for you...the *new* you! In Jesus you are a child of God, a son of the Father, the precious bride of Christ, a wonderful new creation. God says, "I believe in you because you are in Me and I am in you." We eagerly invite you to plunge deep into the refreshing river of your identity in Christ. It is the antidote to shame—and is also the subject of our next chapter.

8

THE NEW YOU

The courtroom was packed and the atmosphere tense. A man was on trial for his life, accused of murder. The crime was spawned out of passion and revenge—another guy had stolen his girlfriend—and the defendant had the means, motive, and opportunity. According to police, he had chased "his girlfriend thief" by car for about 15 miles and then gunned him down at a local McDonald's. The prosecution had all the witnesses they needed.

His attorney was having trouble building a case, so he decided to try for a defense based on the man's excellent character. So I (Paul) was chosen to be a character witness.

I had spent some time with the man, trying to counsel him through a serious bout with depression. I would invite him to church, but he'd say, "I'm so miserable, why would I want to spread it around?" I had prayed with him and watched him weep like a child.

The newspaper had carried the story of this murder for days. It was big news in town, and as I got up on the witness stand I was nervous. Every face in the courtroom was deadly serious—and they were all focused on me. I took the oath to tell the whole truth "so help me God."

Immediately after I was introduced as a "Christian counselor," the prosecutor launched his attack against me.

"Christian counselor…Did you say, 'Christian counselor'?" the attorney sneered. "What kind of credential is *that*— 'Christian counselor'? You mean to tell me that you bring a man into this courtroom, calling him a Christian counselor, and expect me to be impressed? Why would I be impressed? What is a 'Christian counselor' *anyway?* Do you really think I'm impressed, or anyone else is? This is really meaningless. What kind of testimony could *you* give?"

The assault continued. The attorney questioned my qualifications, put me down, and tried to embarrass me. He was attempting to shame me in front of the whole crowd and didn't care what he said to do it.

At first I wanted to fall through the floor or run out of the courtroom. I didn't, though, because the Lord began to give me great courage. I silently asked myself two questions: *Who am I?* and *What is the truth?*

There on the witness stand I remembered: *I am a child of God, a joint heir with Jesus Christ. I am a temple of the Holy Spirit and a citizen of heaven!*

A burst of strength came to me. Then I recalled the truth. It came like lightning to my mind: *I have been forgiven of all my sins and am unconditionally accepted in Jesus Christ!*

I found myself genuinely concerned for the prosecuting attorney, seriously doubting that the man knew Christ. I truly pitied him, and I found myself praying for his salvation. Ultimately, however, my testimony was declared inadmissible, and though I said my piece, the jury was not permitted to hear it.

I can't remember a time when I felt the Lord with me more than that day. Instead of being shamed, I experienced His strength and peace. I was experiencing Jesus' promise of John 8:32: "You will know the truth, and the truth will make you free."

Speaking of freedom, the defendant didn't get it. He is now serving a life sentence for murder.

Who Are You? What Is the Truth?

That courtroom conflict with the prosecutor made such a lasting impression on me that now I always counsel people going through a challenge to ask themselves those very same questions: *Who am I?* and *What is the truth?*

The sad reality is that most of God's people don't know the truth of who they are in Christ—and so they are locked into a shame-based identity. Our desire and prayer in this chapter is that you would take a big drink of truth that would both satisfy you and make you thirsty for even more. An experience I (Rich) had with Jesus on the road to Roswell, Georgia, can provide the framework for this chapter's teaching.

I was right in the middle of a very intense two-week practicum, one of the requirements toward an MA degree in Christian counseling. All of us students were stretched, stressed, challenged, and fatigued. I felt I just had to get some exercise, so I left the house where I was staying and went for a walk around 5:30 in the morning. I was praying and trying to clear my muddled mind enough to commune with God.

Then the Lord showed up. That's the only way I can describe it. It was as if Jesus Himself caught up with me and started walking along with me. I remember clearly what we said, though there were no visions or audible voices.

Specially Chosen by God

"You have always trusted My Father to provide for you," I sensed the Lord saying as He opened our conversation.

"That's true, Lord," I replied. My mind went back to how good a provider my earthly dad had been, and how through 25-plus years of ministry I had seen God provide all my needs. Believing God to supply the material needs in my life has never been a problem. I waited for what the Lord would say next.

"But there are three other ways We want to reveal Ourself to you, if You desire it."

"What are those, Lord?"

"First, I want to be your friend, your very best friend."

That statement was filled with tremendous meaning for me. During my first years as a teenager I had become extremely tall, skinny, and uncoordinated. I had braces on my teeth and acne on my face. For a period of time it seemed like all I experienced from my peers was rejection. Nobody was excited about being my friend, and I always had to initiate getting together with others. I was lonely, and I even considered suicide. As a ninth-grader without Christ I wrote the following autobiographical poem in my rage and pain. It is called "The Lower Caste." It is not pleasant reading, but it accurately expresses the anguish of my rejection and shame. Maybe you or someone you know can relate.

> *Torn by words spouted at whim, scorned by looks
> that slash,*
> *Worn by days of ignorance from those who whip
> and lash.*
> *Those of shallow beauty wade in and out of hate,*
> *Scorching what is burned and black with flames of
> cruel fate.*
> *And those who cringe from fiery words are impris-
> oned by muted thoughts,*
> *Choked inside by pounded fears, bound by suspi-
> cion's knots.*
> *To venture past the tear-streaked skin, across the
> barren deserts*
> *Would show what bursts through clouded skies...*
> *A hidden, shackled treasure.*
> *A glowing beam within the storm of unimpris-
> oned fury*
> *Lights the way for truth and life where prejudices
> bury.*
> *The pity belongs to those who cling to biases of the
> past.*
> *Laugh at them, and spit at them, for they are the
> lower caste.*

Clothed and Given a New Name

Later on during the practicum, one of the leaders shared some Scriptures that spoke deeply to me. And if you have been scourged and beaten down by a legalistic system, they might just bring you some hope, too. Speaking of the people of God, Isaiah wrote,

> I will rejoice greatly in the LORD, my soul will exult in my God; for He has clothed me with garments of salvation, He has wrapped me with a robe of righteousness.
> ...You will be called by a new name which the mouth of the LORD will designate. You will also be a crown of beauty in the hand of the LORD, and a royal diadem in the hand of your God. It will no longer be said to you, "Forsaken," nor to your land will it any longer be said, "Desolate"; But you will be called, "My delight is in her" (Isaiah 61:10; 62:2-4).

Those words—especially the "robe of righteousness" and the "new name"—are so powerful, especially as an antidote to shame. Nakedness and shame go hand-in-hand in the Bible. Jesus advised the church in Laodicea to buy from Him "white garments so that you may clothe yourself, and that the shame of your nakedness will not be revealed" (Revelation 3:18).

Before sin came, Adam and Eve were "naked and were not ashamed" (Genesis 2:25). After the fall, mankind has felt intense shame and vulnerability (emotional and social nakedness). That's why the revelation that God has clothed us in a "robe of righteousness" so that we are now "the righteousness of God" in Christ (2 Corinthians 5:21) is such very good news.

The practicum leader also said that many of us live under a yoke of slavery, crushed under the burden of an "old name." Perhaps you can relate. Maybe you've lived life under a legalistic system, thinking you were *stupid, no good, not able to measure up, worthless, evil, unwanted, rejected, abandoned,* or *unloved.* Other people have proclaimed the message of your "old name" loud and clear to you. Maybe you have even thought that God knew you by that old name.

On that early-morning walk, I prayed and asked the Lord what my "old name" was. About a day later it became clear— the old name that I had worn in shame was *Outcast*.

Then I prayed, asking the Lord to reveal His *new name* for me. I wasn't really looking for a sneak peek at my "new name written on the [white] stone which no one knows but he who receives it [in heaven]" (Revelation 2:17). What I was asking God for was a revelation of my new *identity* in Christ.

After several more days, the answer formed in my mind. The new name is *Chosen Friend*. Take a big gulp of these Scriptures, for they are about you and for you too:

> You did not choose Me but *I chose you*, and appointed you that you would go and bear fruit, and that your fruit would remain, so that whatever you ask of the Father in My name He may give to you (John 15:16).

> He [Jesus] went up to the mountain and *summoned those whom He Himself wanted*, and they came to Him...so that they would be with Him and that He could send them out to preach, and to have authority to cast out the demons (Mark 3:13-14).

> No longer do I call you slaves, for the slave does not know what his master is doing; but *I have called you friends*, for all things that I have heard from My Father I have made known to you (John 15:15).

I remember the years when I was so tall and gangly that nobody would want me on their team during gym (PE) class. The two strong athletes picked by the teacher to be captains would show no interest in me until I was one of the only two left. Then I would be chosen...not because they wanted me, but because they had to take me.

Christian, Jesus chose you not because He *had* to, but because He *wanted* you. He wanted you so that you could be with Him! The God of the universe wants to hang out with you, to be your best friend. You are His chosen friend. Jesus is the friend who sticks closer than a brother (Proverbs 18:24), and He is not ashamed to call *you* His brother (or sister) either (Hebrews 2:11)!

Tenderly Fathered by God

As the Lord Jesus and I continued our walk to Roswell, He then told me the second way in which God wanted to reveal Himself to me.

"Just as you love your children and delight in them—playing with them, hugging them—so My Father wants to be that kind of Father to you."

I knew what the Lord was getting at. This was not an invitation to *salvation.* (At that time I had been a believer in Jesus for nearly 29 years.) It was an invitation to an *intimate relationship of safety, security, and joy.* To experience God on a deeper level—as a living reality—and not just as propositional truth in my head. That is what the Christian life is all about: not rules, not rituals, not routine, but relationship. Religion is a performance. Christianity is a relationship with a Person—not just knowledge *about* God, but *knowing* God.

For those caught in legalism, self-energized adherence to the law kills relationship and deadens even the *desire* for relationship. We come to accept as the norm (or as "the best we can hope for") a life of devotion-duty to Christ while never really knowing Him as a Person. It's kind of like the man who runs a Web-site fan club for his favorite athlete. He admires him and does all he can to honor and please him, but he doesn't *know* him. Not really. He may know more *about* him than almost anyone else, but it is all academic.

Reawakening the Relationship

In his book *The Journey of Desire,* John Eldredge writes,

> In the gospel of John, Jesus extends the offer to anyone who realizes his life just isn't touching his deep desire. "If you are thirsty, come to me! If you believe in me, come and drink! For the Scriptures declare that rivers of living water will flow out from within" (John 7:37-38 NLT). His message wasn't something new, but it confounded the religious leaders of the day. Surely, those scripturally learned Jews must have recalled God's long-standing invitation to them, spoken seven hundred years earlier through the prophet Isaiah [see Isaiah 55:1-2].
>
> ...Somehow the message had gotten lost by the time Jesus showed up on the scene. The Jews of his day were practicing a very soul-killing spirituality, a lifeless religion of duty and obligation. They had abandoned desire and replaced it with knowledge and performance as the key to life. The synagogue was the place to go to learn how to get with the program. Desire was out of the question, duty was the path that people must walk. No wonder they feared Jesus. He came along and started *appealing* to desire.[1]

Jesus is still appealing to desire today. Perhaps—in your heart—He needs to *awaken* it. In Christ it's never gone, you know. It's just asleep. With its voice drowned out by the demands of religion, it has gone into hibernation. But spring comes. The law has served its purpose—to lead you to Christ. Now its playing days are over. It has been retired, having been fulfilled by Christ Himself. That's what Paul was trying to convince the Galatians of, those who still wanted to listen to Mr. Law:

Before faith came, we were kept in custody under the law, being shut up to the faith which was later to be revealed. Therefore the Law has become our tutor to lead us to Christ, so that we may be justified by faith. But now that faith has come, we are no longer under a tutor. For you are all sons of God through faith in Christ Jesus. For all of you who were baptized into Christ have clothed yourself with Christ. There is neither Jew nor Greek, there is neither slave nor free man, there is neither male nor female; for you are all one in Christ Jesus. And if you belong to Christ, then you are Abraham's descendants, heirs according to promise (Galatians 3:23-29).

We're God's Kids, Safe in the Family

The problem with living under law is that you can't win. If you see yourself as a failure, ultimately you will be driven by guilt and crushed by shame. If you see yourself as a success in this world, ultimately you will be overcome with pride. But in Christ the playing field has been leveled! No one is higher than another—we are all sons and daughters of God through faith in Christ. "The Spirit Himself testifies with our spirit that we are children of God, and if children, heirs also, heirs of God and fellow heirs with Christ" (Romans 8:16-17).

We who were once merely God's creation have been born again. God has breathed the breath of spiritual life into us, and now we are living children of the living God! God's kids! We have an inheritance in Christ that is "imperishable and undefiled and will not fade away, reserved in heaven" for us (1 Peter 1:4)! "All things belong to you, whether...the world, or life or death or things present or things to come; all things belong to you, and you belong to Christ; and Christ belongs to God" (1 Corinthians 3:21-23).

In the story by Carlo Collodi, the wooden puppet Pinocchio, despite all his rebellion and lying and self-will, was finally transformed. He no longer was just a creation of his master, Gepetto, but a *new* creation—a living, breathing, fully alive son! A delight to his father! Like this, you and I also have a son-to-Father relationship, which will only grow stronger and deeper this side of heaven until the fullness of it is revealed in heaven. For now, "because you are sons, God has sent forth the Spirit of His Son into our hearts, crying, 'Abba, Father!' Therefore you are no longer a slave, but a son; and if a son, then an heir through God" (Galatians 4:6-7).

Children aren't expected to have all the answers. They aren't supposed to "have it all together." Children are weak, needy, dependent little people who know they need help and aren't ashamed to admit it or afraid to ask for it. When they are scared or hurt or lonely, they run to the loving arms of their parents because that's what moms and dads are for.

Child of God, you are safe in the arms of your heavenly Father. Why? Because you are *family*—in all the richness and goodness and wholeness that word is intended to contain. You are no longer an outsider, pounding at the door trying to get in or jumping at the window trying to get noticed.

In Christ, the door has swung wide open, and you have been warmly and cheerfully ushered into the light and warmth of God's house. Perhaps the chill of legalism still sends shivers through your body. You have spent so much time out in the cold. Come on in, warm yourself by the fire of God's grace. Look around. Relax. Let the Head of the house take off the old, wet, threadbare clothes of religious duty. Put on the warm, comfortable robe of acceptance, security, and significance in Christ.

In chapter 11 of this book, there is a list of scriptural truths about you *in Christ*. When you get there, we encourage you to spend some unhurried time at the spiritual banquet table, reading, drinking in and prayerfully savoring those realities. We firmly believe you'll sense the chill slowly leaving your bones.

Here's a sample hors d'oeuvre:

See how great a love the Father has bestowed on us, that we would be called children of God; and such we are. For this reason the world does not know us, because it did not know Him. Beloved, now we are children of God, and it has not appeared as yet what we will be. We know that when He appears, we will be like Him, because we will see Him just as He is (1 John 3:1-2).

Passionately Desired by God

The third invitation from the Lord was the newest and freshest to me. He said, "As a bridegroom passionately pursues his bride, would you allow Me to love you?" Immediately my thoughts went back to Shirley as she was on our wedding day. I recalled the deep love for her and delight in her beauty that I felt as she appeared at the door of the sanctuary dressed in her wedding gown. I wanted her and nobody else!

I replied to the Lord, "If that is how You want to love me, that is how I want to be loved."

In *The Sacred Romance*, John Eldredge and Brent Curtis take us through a series of metaphors picturing our relationship to God: clay to Potter. Sheep to Shepherd. Servant to Master. Children to heavenly Father. Friend to Friend. He concludes,

> But there is still a higher and deeper level of intimacy and partnership awaiting us at the top of this metaphorical ascent. We are lovers. The courtship that began with a honeymoon in the Garden culminates in the wedding feast of the Lamb. "I will take delight in you," he says to us, "as a bridegroom rejoices over his bride, so will I rejoice over you," so that we might say in return, "I am my beloved's and his desire is for me."[2]

As a man, I have to admit that my mind has to do some serious adjusting to grasp (and enjoy!) the concept of being

Christ's bride. I know that there is nothing sexual about Christ's relationship to us, but there *is* something *romantic*.

The consummation of our relationship with Jesus will be in heaven, as John records in Revelation 19:7-9:

> "Let us rejoice and be glad and give the glory to Him, for the marriage of the Lamb has come and His bride has made herself ready." It was given to her to clothe herself in fine linen, bright and clean; for the fine linen is the righteous acts of the saints.
>
> Then he said to me, "Write, 'Blessed are those who are invited to the marriage supper of the Lamb.' " And he said to me, "These are true words of God."

Breaking the Cycle of Shame and Rejection

As powerful and true as God's Word is, however, the truth often falls on ears deafened by a lifetime of shame and rejection. Scarring and hardening the outside, shame can also be a deep abscess in our hearts, one that is not quickly healed nor easily removed. After years of feeling like a failure and experiencing self-rejection and even self-loathing, we do not come to experience grace without a battle. Victims of legalistic homes and churches can be slow to believe the truth about their identity in Christ. We share a long portion of the testimony of a sister in the U.K. because it beautifully brings this problem to light:

A month ago I went through the Steps to Freedom in Christ. Since then my life has been changed. For as long as I can remember I have struggled with extremely low self-esteem and a crippling lack of self-confidence. As a teenager this was excruciating. I kept a diary, and I remember writing when I was 15 years old "I hate myself" on frequent occasions and "Why can't I be like…(anyone other than myself)." This entire time I was a born-again Christian and knew I had been saved by Christ at age seven. I was raised in a Bible-believing Christian family and church. I had a very bleak outlook on my future and just figured I would never change.

When going through the Steps, I finally stepped back and saw that one of the major root causes of my horrible sense of embarrassment and crippling regret and shame was the legalistic form of Christianity I was raised in. The difficult thing about legalism is that grace can appear to be preached…but what is acted out is judgmental, critical, perfectionistic, and appearance-based. Finally, I began to understand that my relationship with God was not based on how early I got up in the morning to pray or how well I knew my Bible or how sin-free I managed to keep myself or how committed I was to church activities.

I had grown up with no comprehension of how to feel accepted by God just as I was, without having to fulfill an impossible list of requirements first. The whole thing was one big guilt trip. I was racked by guilt for not being able to pray the way I knew I should, for not feeling like God was hearing me, and for not enjoying reading the Bible. I felt obliged to be at every service, and I eagerly wanted people to think of me as holy, spiritually minded, and a strong Christian, even though I wasn't any of these things.

My biggest source of guilt was my addiction to masturbation. I asked forgiveness from God every time I did it, and I tried not to do it again, but inevitably I would fall and then felt like I couldn't repent again. I felt weird, dirty, and insincere. The teaching I received as a teen convinced me that

God had abandoned me because of this sin. The verse "If I regard iniquity in my heart, the Lord will not hear me" rang in my ears every time I tried to pray. I had been addicted for so long and felt so unable to stop that I felt there was no way I could pray to God about anything until I found a way to stop. That left me in limbo-land: unable to pray, unable to stop!

As a girl brought up in legalism, I knew this was all my fault and only I could get myself out of it...except I couldn't. And because of the legalism around me, I felt like I couldn't tell anyone and feel understood. Everyone was keeping up the pretense of perfection and holiness. No one let on they were struggling with sin or experiencing any lack of closeness to God. Once a man confessed an inability to pray—and he was rebuked by an elderly man, who said that church wasn't the place for self-focus or repentance. He said, "You should have prepared yourself before you came!"

This dear saint's struggles with shame turn to victories in part two of her testimony (coming right up), but first we want to make some comments. Our hearts are deeply grieved by this woman's words, in part because a hurting man in her church had risked being real and had been rebuffed. We're sure that he and every other hurting person in that church made a vow at that moment to never let anyone else know their pain. What could have been and should have been the beginnings of a revival in that place was stifled, and it turned the church into a tomb. And that's exactly what the enemy of our souls wants.

The Bondage of Secrecy

I (Rich) remember an older college student who first discipled me at Penn State. This guy was a near-genius. He graduated first in the class of the College of Forestry. He memorized Scripture faster than most people could read it. He even memorized the punctuation marks! His rationale was that if he ever landed in a prison for his faith, he could write it out. We kidded him a lot but admired and respected him even more. But to be honest with you, I didn't feel close to him. He seemed to live life on a different spiritual plane. I was grappling with great emotional upheavals in my life, but wouldn't share any of them with him because he seemed so perfect. He was my leader, but he wasn't really my *friend*.

Then one day he came to our discipleship group really torn up. He showed anger, he displayed sorrow, he confessed that he didn't know what to do and that he had sinned. I wanted to applaud! I wasn't being sadistic, I was connecting! At that point we became friends because he had risked being real and honest.

But when we stuff our pain and deny our shame, we create a breeding ground in our souls (really, a cesspool) for sins of the flesh to incubate and spawn. Anger, bitterness, judgmentalism, pride, and a critical spirit are merely the ones you see in action. What you don't see are the addictions to alcohol, drugs, pornography, sexual perversions, and child abuse that have taken root behind the scenes, in the dark places, away from the bright lights of church services. Those areas of bondage are the secret sins that lock people into the futility of secret confession, a cycle that produces only secret failure, secret shame, and secret self-loathing.

God's Grace in Real People

This shame cycle can only be broken when a hurting person encounters God's irresistible grace—usually incarnated in another broken, wounded saint who cares more about being real and being healed than looking good. As Hebrews 5:1-2 tells us,

> Every high priest taken from among men is appointed on behalf of men in things pertaining to

God, in order to offer both gifts and sacrifices for sins; he can deal gently with the ignorant and misguided, since he himself also is beset with weakness.

That's how we are supposed to be with one another. The fruit of the Spirit is love, not rejection. It is joy, not a heavy burden. It is peace, not fear of discovery or embarrassment. It is patience, not a critical spirit. It is kindness, not judgmentalism. It is goodness, not shaming others. It is faithfulness, not skewering others behind their backs. It is gentleness, not haughty superiority. It is self-control, not denial and repression.

It is not clear from this woman's testimony whether her freedom came as the result of meeting a grace-filled Christian, but it is clear that she, at last, met Grace Himself:

One way in which grace was killed in my experience was the way every Christian I knew, most memorably my family and their friends, sat around and evaluated people, whether preachers and their strengths and weaknesses, singers on the quality of their voice, church members on their personalities, and on and on. The people who were approved and valued were outgoing, attractive, talented, genuinely spiritual, and had a great sense of humor. People who were not really valued were quiet, shy strugglers with no obvious talents. So I learned from an early age that it was very easy to be unvalued and rejected. That is what I have always feared—being thought of and spoken of like that. Therefore, in the rare times I got praise and compliments, I lived off them as a sign that I was okay.

Now, after going through the Steps, I have dealt with the bitterness and unforgiveness I had toward my church and my family for this indoctrinated lack of self-worth and value based on

> spiritual performance. I have also had to repent of and renounce the lies I have believed and announce the truth of WHO I AM IN CHRIST: a free child of God, not under law but under grace.
>
> The effect of this knowledge is incredibly liberating. I now feel the peace that passes understanding down in my heart…a peace I only sang about as a child. I know now that I am complete in Christ. He has done everything and I only have to stand in that freedom, for I cannot do anything to make myself free or His child or His friend! I just *am*.

That's true. We can never earn anything from God. We can only receive it. We can never say that we deserve any of God's blessings. We can only accept them as the free gifts they are. *We* try to *achieve; God* says to *believe* and *receive*.

God's Ardent Love Leaves No Place for Shame

When you are attacked by feelings of worthlessness and feel like no one (even God) would ever want you as a friend, remember John 15:13: "Greater love has no one than this, that one lay down his life for his friends." That's what Jesus did for you. He laid down His life for you. **You are Christ's friend**.

How do you estimate the value of an object? You look at what someone who knows that object would be willing to pay for it. If a little boy and a world-renowned art collector were gazing at the Mona Lisa in the Louvre in Paris, which one would have the better idea of the painting's value? One would be willing to give the change in his pocket—the other would pronounce the masterpiece "Priceless!" and know he could never afford such a beautiful thing.

When God the Father put a price tag on your soul, it was written in the precious blood of the Lord Jesus Christ. One drop of that blood is far more valuable than all the gold, silver, and precious jewels the world will ever produce.

Once we realize who we really are in Christ and understand all the provisions that God has made for us, how could we ever live in shame? When we comprehend that it is impossible for anyone to measure up (and that God never intended for us to try!), why would we ever burn ourselves out attempting to do it? Once we realize the supreme price paid for us at Calvary, how could we ever succumb to the enemy's lies accusing us of worthlessness again?

When you feel like a failure and shame tries to swallow up all the truth in your heart, just remember that **you are God's child:**

> The servant is accepted and appreciated on the basis of *what he does,* the child on the basis of *who he is.* A servant starts the day *anxious and worried,* wondering if his work will really please his master. The child *rests in the secure love* of his family. The servant is accepted because of his *workmanship,* the son or daughter because of his *relationship.* The servant is accepted because of his *productivity and performance.* The child belongs because of his *position as a person.*[3]

When you are tempted to wallow in the mire of self-pity, when you find yourself sinking in the quicksand of shame and rejection, then remember that you have been joined to Christ. He is the Head, and you are part of His body. **You are His precious bride.** Take a look in the mirror for a moment—the mirror of God's Word—and see how beautiful *you* are. We close with Scripture, praying that God will use it to be the lifter of your head:

> I saw the holy city, new Jerusalem, coming down out of heaven from God, made ready as a bride adorned for her husband. And I heard a loud voice from the throne, saying, "Behold, the tabernacle of God is among men, and He will dwell

among them, and they shall be His people, and God Himself will be among them, and He will wipe away every tear from their eyes; and there will no longer be any death; there will no longer be any mourning, or crying, or pain; the first things have passed away."

And He who sits on the throne said, "Behold, I am making all things new." And He said, "Write, for these words are faithful and true."

...One of the seven angels...came and spoke with me, saying, "Come here, I will show you the bride, the wife of the Lamb." And he carried me away in the Spirit to a great and high mountain, and showed me the holy city, Jerusalem, coming down out of heaven from God, having the glory of God. Her brilliance was like a very costly stone, as a stone of crystal-clear jasper.

...The material of the wall was jasper; and the city was pure gold, like clear glass. The foundation stones of the city wall were adorned with every kind of precious stone. The first foundation stone was jasper; the second, sapphire; the third, chalcedony; the fourth, emerald; the fifth, sardonyx; the sixth, sardius; the seventh, chrysolite; the eighth, beryl; the ninth, topaz; the tenth, chrysoprase; the eleventh, jacinth; the twelfth, amethyst. And the twelve gates were twelve pearls; each one of the gates was a single pearl. And the street of the city was pure gold, like transparent glass (Revelation 21:2-5,9-11,18-21).

"Arise, my darling, my beautiful one, and come with me. See! The winter is past; the rains are over and gone. Flowers appear on the earth; the season of singing has come...Arise, come, my darling; my beautiful one, come with me" (Song of Solomon 2:10-12,13 NIV).

9

LIVING LIKE JESUS

It was the greatest day in His earthly life to that point. Rising up out of the waters of the Jordan River, He beamed with joy as He shook the water from His hair. Gazing with love and admiration at His cousin, John the Baptist, Jesus suddenly shifted His vision upward. Shielding His eyes, He watched as the dove-incarnate Spirit of God fluttered down and perched on His shoulder.

Then the Voice boomed with exuberant joy from heaven. "You are My Son, whom I deeply love! I'm proud of You!"

The moment was historic. God the Father, speaking with a voice you could hear. God the Son, in a human form that you could behold. God the Holy Spirit, coming in the form of the gentlest of creatures, a bird you could have petted. Such Humility all together in space and time, meeting in a dirty river in the lonely countryside. A meeting filled with the purest and most potent Love the world had ever known.

Then the moment was over.

Jesus listened, waiting for the next word from the Father. The spellbound crowd waited, too. Heads were nodding in approval as people said to one another, "With a kickoff like that, I wonder what the first quarter will hold!"

"Yeah, it's gonna be incredible! Let's hang around and watch the game."

Suddenly Jesus acted. Though the people didn't know it, the Voice outside was also the Whisper inside. The Power lodged inside the bird had become the Power inside the Word Himself.

The Three had met as One. The decision had been made. The crowd would be disappointed, but that didn't matter. This great day in Jesus' life would serve to usher in a great *test* in His life.

While the crowd stared in stunned disbelief, Jesus just left. No goodbyes. No more voices from heaven. Just silence—and the back of this God–man disappearing over the ridge into...of all places!...the wilderness.

The Father said, "Go now, Son." The Spirit said, "I'll show You where." Jesus simply said, "Yes, Sir." So it began.

Forty days with no food and water—with only the Father, the Spirit, and the desert animals to keep Him company. It was enough. Jesus loved people, more than any man had ever loved, but His greatest delight was to be with the Father.

The Ancient Lies

True, there was one other, the serpent of old. He was there, too. During the whole 40 days he fired his missiles, and Jesus deftly deflected each one. Undoubtedly the barrage intensified as the days dragged on and His hunger grew. How odd that time *slows* so dramatically during a *fast*.

The snake's relentless needlings all had a similar theme. *Well, just look at this! You take the plunge into ministry, say "I do"— and this is the honeymoon? Forty days with not even a small bite of stale bread, let alone fresh, hot bread out of the oven? So this is how God treats his kids? You can do better than this, Jesus.*

After all, you ARE the Son of God, aren't you? You are God, the Almighty, the Creator who made all things...You can do whatever you want. What harm could there possibly be in just zapping one of these worthless stones and turning it into a loaf of bread? After all, that's what you want, isn't it? I know you are hungry...aren't you? Don't forget, you're also a man! Don't you think you've fasted long enough? You need to eat or you're going to die!

The counterpunch from Jesus was swift and hard. "The Scriptures say this, Satan: 'Man does not live on bread alone, but on every word that comes out of the mouth of God.'"

The quote from Deuteronomy stung like a hard right jab. Jesus had made Himself clear. The way to His heart was not through His stomach. The first man had fallen by eating forbidden food. Jesus would not make the same mistake. He would eat only when the Father gave Him the green light. The 40-day red light had not yet changed. Until it did, Jesus would find deeper nourishment from the delicious words of His Father.

Okay, okay—fair enough, Jesus. Would you mind coming with me for a minute?...The view from up on this mountain is spectacular, wouldn't you say? Well...you ain't seen nothin' yet! Now, look at that! All these glorious kingdoms can be yours today for the low, low price of just one teeny, weeny act of worship...of me! This is mine, you know, all mine! And I can give it all to any man I choose. And I choose you!

Revealing His utter disgust at such a vile proposition, Jesus countered, "The Scriptures say this, 'You shall worship the Lord alone, and He is the One you should serve.'"

Crunch! The blow to Satan's pride was brutal in its truth. For the devil's violation of that very command, and his subsequent rebellion, had led to his own judgment. Jesus would not fall into the same pride trap. He would not let His eyes be His guide. He would wait. The Father had already promised Him all the nations as His inheritance. That time would come, but a cross would come first, complete with its own painful crown.

All right, Jesus. If you are determined to go through with this silly ministry of yours, I'll join you. It's clear I'm no match for you. But you've obviously got a lot to learn about how to get the crowd on your side. You need a PR man big-time. I'm the guy for the job. By the way, walking off and leaving everyone after your baptism was very poor marketing. You had them in the palm of your hand

and you blew it. Here's a chance to redeem yourself. Now, just go up there on top of the temple...that's right. Good! Now launch yourself off. Do a swan dive, and you won't get hurt. The crowd will love it. Remember, the Scriptures say that "God will command the angels to take care of you and they will hold you up in their hands so that even your foot won't get hurt." That's in Psalm 91, in case you forgot.

The knockout blow from Jesus came like lightning. "The Scriptures also say, 'You shall not put the Lord your God to the test.'"

End of conversation. Jesus had drawn a line in the sand, a line that He would never cross. He would surrender His life to the Father's plans and not cave in to the seductive allure of popularity. He would follow God. Yes, God would lead Him into miraculous works that would touch and heal the wounded. But Jesus would not pander to the fallen human lust for the spectacular and flashy. He had come to seek and save the lost, not run a religious sideshow. So the devil left.

The Lure of Independence

When we look at how Satan tempted Jesus in the wilderness, one thing stands out clearly: Though he was defeated in his attacks, the devil knew exactly how and where to attack. He struck at Jesus' commitment to live a life of dependence upon the Father. That is how he had attacked the first man and woman, and he used the same strategy on Jesus. With Adam and Eve, he succeeded. With Jesus, he failed.

At its core, every temptation is an enticement to take life into our own hands. To not wait for the Father. To be our own god and follow our own desires. To give in to our fears. In the case of legalism, it's the enticement to create our own religious system (or buy into someone else's)—a system we erroneously believe we can follow and thus please God in our own strength and resources.

Legalism, at its roots, is a system designed by the devil and developed by man to keep people from truly walking in dependence upon the Father. A rule becomes our Ruler. A law becomes our Lord. Our flesh-driven performance becomes a substitute for a personal relationship of surrender and dependence upon God.

In this chapter, we want to look at three elements of Jesus' teaching and life that provide a model for us of how to walk *with God* and walk *away from fear*. If we want to truly live like Jesus, we must first understand how Jesus lived—in complete union with the Father, in continual communication with Him in prayer, and under the guidance of and in the power of the Holy Spirit.

We Are United with Christ

Perhaps the greatest sermon Jesus ever preached was not to the crowds, but to the disciples. Even Judas was gone during the "Upper Room Discourse" recorded in John 13–17. One of the key elements of Jesus' message was what Paul called "the riches of the glory of this mystery among the Gentiles, which is *Christ in you*, the hope of glory" (Colossians 1:27). But there was another element to this mystery as well. In his next statement after the above, Paul wrote, "We proclaim Him, admonishing every man and teaching every man with all wisdom, so that we may present every man complete *in Christ*" (verse 28).

Christ in us, and we in Christ. That is the mystery (hidden truth) that Jesus began to unfold to His disciples. Its unfolding required further revelation through the apostle Paul, who wrote, "This mystery is great; but I am speaking with reference to Christ and the church" (Ephesians 5:32). The context of Paul's discussion in that chapter was marriage. He had reminded his readers that "a man shall leave [his parents] and shall be joined to his wife, and the two shall become one flesh" (verse 31). The union of husband and wife, therefore, provides a glimpse on earth of this remarkable union that has taken place between Jesus Christ and His church...which is you and me!

In the "Upper Room Discourse," Jesus spoke prophetically, saying, "In that day [once the Spirit of truth would have come] you will know that I am in My Father, and you in Me, and I in you" (John 14:20). This unity between God and His people, Christ and His church, was to display the unity and love of the Godhead so that the world would stand up and take notice! Jesus later prayed in John 17:20-23,

> I do not ask on behalf of these alone, but for those also who believe in Me through their word; that they may all be one; even as You, Father, are in Me and I in You, that they also may be in Us, so that the world may believe that You sent Me.
>
> The glory which You have given to Me I have given to them, that they may be one, just as We are one; I in them and You in Me, that they may be perfected in unity, so that the world may know that You sent Me, and loved them, even as You have loved Me.

No wonder Paul called it a "mystery"! It is beyond our greatest imagination or our wildest dream that our connection, our union, our oneness with Christ would be mentioned in the same sentence as the unity between the Father and Son. But there it is.

A Cosmic Difference

Do you see how this union between us and God elevates the Christian life light-years above our mere human efforts— even our best ones—at keeping God's commands? It is the difference between, on the one hand, a child who can barely read music trying desperately to learn a complicated piano concerto and, on the other hand, that same child sitting in the lap of a concert pianist, resting her hands on the master's hands as he plays that same piece. The first results in a lot of noise, the second in a work of art.

This union is the antidote to our fear of failure. Rather than muddling along, vainly trying to "imitate Jesus" or keep the commandments on our own, we are in union with Christ Himself. The same resources that enabled Him to live in the Father can enable us to live in Him—*in Christ.*

Jesus described our union with Him this way:

> You are already clean because of the word which I have spoken to you. Abide in Me, and I in you. As the branch cannot bear fruit of itself unless it abides in the vine, so neither can you unless you abide in Me. I am the vine, you are the branches; he who abides in Me and I in him, he bears much fruit, for apart from Me you can do nothing (John 15:3-5).

Just as a branch's only responsibility is to stay close and connected to the vine, so we are to abide in, or *make our home in,* Christ. As we see His great love for us, His profound wisdom to guide us, and His awesome strength to empower us to live, we grow to trust Him more. We learn to draw on His resources rather than our own. Remarkably, we find that we are actually supernaturally obeying the very commands in Scripture that once seemed an unbearable burden.

Included in God

Further, can you sense the delight God has in opening His heart to us and watching us respond in return? Can you pick up the excitement in Jesus' voice as He announces to us that we are included in God and in all He is doing? There is no closed door to heaven. No exclusive club open only to God and angels. In fact, the truth of *our being in Christ* and *Christ being in us* is an honor afforded only to fallen but redeemed man!

In the classic 1986 film *Hoosiers,* Gene Hackman plays small-town-Indiana Hickory High School's new basketball coach, Norman Dale. As Dale tries to whip the undisciplined

Hickory High Huskers into a team, he loses the services of his assistant coach because of a heart condition.

In a touch of genius, Coach Dale decides to approach one of his players' dads, the notorious town drunk, with an offer. "Shooter" (Dennis Hopper) greets Dale at his property line with a warning shot...and then an offer to drink with him. Dale avoids the first and declines the second.

As they settle down by the fireplace in Shooter's ramshackle dwelling, Coach Dale makes his offer:

"I've got a proposition for you. [The old assistant coach] is going to be laid up for a while. I want you to give me a hand," he begins as Shooter drinks away.

"Well, I can tell you anything that you need to know," Shooter replies, the drink providing a little bottled bravado.

"No, you don't understand. I want you to be my assistant...Come to the practices and sit on the bench with me during the games."

Shooter is stunned and looks it. Then a big smile creases his face as he says, "Me? You want me?"

Coach Dale does want him, but lets him know he expects Shooter to clean himself up, shave, and show up in a dress shirt and tie. Shooter is excited about the offer until Dale tells him the drinking must stop (at least around the kids) because it's not good role modeling, plus he's embarrassing his son.

Fearful of life without his liquid courage, and unwilling to face his own pain as well as the pain he's causing others, Shooter tells Dale to leave. It appears like the offer to join the team is refused...until Shooter shows up—cleaned up, dressed up, and sober—to help coach the next game. He's tense and nervous, but he comes anyway.

Warmly welcoming him, Coach Dale announces to his shocked team members, "Shooter here is going to be one of our assistants."

Even though Shooter screws up and ends up in detox at a hospital, he is a changed man. No longer is his self-esteem in the mud. He contributes to the team effort, gets his son's respect back, and enters into the joy of the team's final victory.

That's what Jesus does for us. He recruits us out of the muck and mire of our sinful misery. He personally cleans us up through His shed blood, putting on us the new garments of His righteousness. Even when we mess up, Jesus never gives up on us. He welcomes us in as an integral part of His kingdom "team" and gives us significant work to do through Him.

Abiding

But how do we actually do that? How do we, practically speaking, *abide in Christ?* After all, living according to the law appears safe and secure, manageable and measurable. It may be hard, but at least we think we know how we're doing. This thought of living out of a relationship with Someone we don't see and certainly can't control is, well...a bit scary. How can we be sure we're doing it right?

The dependence we are to live out in Christ is the same dependence that Jesus modeled in His relationship with the Father. So when we take a good, hard look at how Jesus lived by abiding in the Father, we'll see how we, in turn, are to abide in Christ.

Numerous times Jesus made it clear that He was not operating out of His own "God-ness," but was letting God the Father call all the shots. The following Scriptures give a taste of the life of surrender and trust Jesus had in the Father:

> Truly, truly, I say to you, the Son can do nothing of Himself, unless it is something He sees the Father doing; for whatever the Father does, these things the Son also does in like manner. For the Father loves the Son, and shows Him all things that He Himself is doing; and the Father will show Him greater works than these, so that you will marvel (John 5:19-20).

> I can do nothing on My own initiative. As I
> hear, I judge; and My judgment is just, because I
> do not seek My own will, but the will of Him who
> sent Me (John 5:30).

> When you lift up the Son of Man, then you will
> know that I am He, and I do nothing on My own
> initiative, but I speak these things as the Father
> taught Me. And He who sent Me is with Me; He
> has not left Me alone, for I always do the things
> that are pleasing to Him (John 8:28-29).

We think you get the idea. The first step in Christ's life in
the Father was His choice and commitment to do only the
Father's will. In other words, Jesus had no agenda but the
Father's. The severest test of this was in the garden of Geth-
semane. Jesus was honest about His desire not to go to the
cross, but three times He declared to the Father, "Not My
will, but Yours be done" (see Matthew 26:36-44).

This same choice and commitment to do our Father's will
is crucial for us as well. Will we truly trust that our Father
knows best? Do we believe that He is wise enough to always
know the right way? Are we convinced that He loves us
enough to show us that way? Do we have the confidence that
He will supply all the strength we need to do what He calls us
to do?

This walk of faith takes time to grow into. But as we get
to know Him through His Word and watch Him act on our
behalf through our life experiences, our faith grows.

We Are Invited to Know God Intimately

Jesus' walk of faith was not only characterized by His emp-
tying Himself of His own agenda, it was also enabled by His
life of *prayer*. Prayer was the lifeline between our Lord and the
Father, the means by which they spent time together enjoying
each other's presence. It was also the avenue by which Jesus

learned of the Father's directions for His life. For us, as for Jesus, *knowing God's will* comes on the heels of *knowing God*—spending time with Him in prayer.

Jesus prayed all the time. It was His lifestyle. Before He made His first tour of Galilee, *Jesus prayed* (Mark 1:33-35). At one time the crowd was going to take Him by force and make Him king, but before He sent them away *He prayed* (Matthew 14:22-23; Mark 6:45-46). Before Jesus raised Lazarus from the dead, *He prayed* (John 11:41-42). Before His great message of revelation given in the upper room, *He prayed* (John 12:27-28).

Of the four Gospel writers, Luke most often mentions Jesus praying. *He prayed* at His baptism (Luke 3:21). *He prayed* in the desert after withdrawing from the enthusiastic crowds (5:15-16). *He prayed* all night before choosing the 12 disciples (6:12-13). *He prayed* at the Transfiguration (9:29). These examples are just scratching the surface of Jesus' prayer life.

In fact, it was Jesus' prayer life that prompted the disciples to request of Him, "Lord, teach us to pray just as John also taught his disciples" (Luke 11:1).

In the garden, in the desert, in a crowd, by Himself, and even on the cross, Jesus' life of dependence upon the Father was characterized by prayer. It was these frequent times of communion with the Father that gave Him wisdom to know what to do, as well as the strength to do it...even when the future meant suffering. Christ is our example for life, as Peter explained:

> You have been called for this purpose, since Christ also suffered for you, leaving you an example for you to follow in His steps, Who committed no sin, nor was any deceit found in His mouth; and while being reviled, He did not revile in return; while suffering, He uttered no threats, but kept entrusting Himself to Him who judges righteously (1 Peter 2:21-22).

He Wants Us

What is obvious from the pages of Scripture is the intimate love relationship that existed between Father and Son, Son and Father. Jesus spent time with His Father, not because He was *supposed to,* but because He *wanted to.* I (Rich) do not need to convince my daughter Emily to spend time with me. She is always ready to sit in my lap or jump into my arms or show me something she has made. In fact, we call her our "lap cat." When I go to pray with her and her sister, Michelle, at bedtime, she doesn't want that time to end. She'll ask me to make one of her stuffed animals talk. Or she'll ask me about things in my day. Anything to prolong our time together! Sometimes we'll even talk about things (usually bugs!) that frighten her, and as we talk and pray, she finds the peace to sleep.

Fear can easily overwhelm us when we feel like "we're in this alone." Fear can control our lives when we are trying to escape from legalistic systems. We're used to the "safe confines" of religion and its security blanket of measurable rules and regulations. So we wonder, *Can I really stay away from sin and do what's right? Will God come through for me? Can I truly trust Him to be all I need? Is it possible for me to learn to abide in Christ? Does He really love me even when I mess up? Won't He get mad at me if I'm not perfect? How can I be sure He won't change the rules on me?*

The answers lie in knowing God as the infinite, personal, unchanging, unconditionally loving and accepting, strong, gracious, faithful, and caring One who is on our side. "If God is for us, who is against us?" (Romans 8:31).

He Is Eager for Us to Know Him

Paul declared, after renouncing all that he was and had tried to be in legalistic, self-righteous religion,

> But whatever things were gain to me, those things I have counted as loss for the sake of Christ.

More than that, I count all things to be loss in view of the surpassing value of knowing Christ Jesus my Lord, for whom I have suffered the loss of all things, and count them but rubbish so that I may gain Christ, and may be found in Him, not having a righteousness of my own derived from the Law, but that which is through faith in Christ, the righteousness which comes from God on the basis of faith, that I may know Him and the power of His resurrection and the fellowship of His sufferings (Philippians 3:7-10).

That's what it all boils down to, *knowing Christ.* You don't get to know someone, especially God, through rules, regulations, standards, and performance. You get to know someone by spending time with him or her. In *Grace Walk*, author Steve McVey writes about this experience:

> Grace changes our concept of the nature of prayer. It stimulates a continuing prayer *relationship* as opposed to a daily prayer routine. Before I understood grace, my prayer life could be characterized as something I *did*, an action...but it is much more than that. It is an *attitude*.
>
> ...Sometimes words are necessary; at other times they aren't...You will find yourself talking to your Father dozens of times a day, not just during a designated prayer time...There's no way to say how He may speak to you, but He *will* speak as you learn to relate to Him through grace.
>
> ...God's desire is to fellowship with His children in an ongoing dialogue. Grace opens a person's ears to hear God in a way that legalism will never allow. As a legalist, I focused on knowing what God wanted me to do. In the grace walk, I have experienced a growing desire to know God.[1]

Maybe your times with God have been characterized by reading a certain number of chapters of Scripture a day. That's great if you do it for the right reasons. But you might want to try breaking the pattern for a while, adding some variety. Read a devotional. Sing some hymns. Put on the headphones and worship along with some praise music you enjoy.

Maybe you have felt like you have to pray for a certain amount of time a day or that you had to make it through a list in order to have a "good" prayer time. Break the mold for a time. Try taking a prayer walk with nothing but an ear to hear God and a heart to be honest with Him. If you have always prayed silently, try praying out loud. Try praying through a passage of Scripture, asking the Spirit to empower you and help you formulate prayers based on what the verses are saying.

The key is to relax and know that you're already the delight of God's heart. You are the apple of His eye. He has great plans for your times together, as 1 Corinthians 2:9 reveals: "Things which eye has not seen and ear has not heard, and which have not entered the heart of man, all that God has prepared for those who love Him." And these things are revealed through the Holy Spirit within us.

We Are Given the Spirit of Adoption

That brings us to our third and final characteristic of Jesus' life: His *dependence upon the Holy Spirit*. When Jesus went into the wilderness to be tempted by the devil, Luke 4:1 says He was "full of the Holy Spirit," and consequently, He "was led around by the Spirit." To be guided, directed, and empowered by the Spirit of God is the privilege of every child of God, as the apostle Paul explained in Romans 8:14-16:

> All who are being led by the Spirit of God, these are sons of God. For you have not received a spirit of slavery leading to fear again [which is legalism], but you have received a spirit of adoption as sons by which we cry out, "Abba! Father!" The

Spirit Himself testifies with our spirit that we are children of God.

Legalism enslaves us and makes us fear that we are not doing enough to please God. Being led by the Spirit (as we are filled with the Spirit) gives us the assurance that we are part of God's family, privileged to walk in intimacy with our heavenly Father, guided into the things that please His heart. The difference is like night and day. We ran across this short meditation on "guidance" on the Internet:

> When I meditated on the word "guidance," I kept seeing the word "dance" at the end of it. I remember reading that doing God's will is a lot like dancing.
>
> When two people try to lead, nothing feels right. The movement doesn't flow with the music, and everything is quite uncomfortable and jerky. When one person relaxes and lets the other lead, both bodies begin to flow with the music. One gives gentle cues, perhaps with a nudge to the back or by pressing lightly in one direction or another. It's as if two become one body, moving beautifully. The dance takes surrender, willingness, and attentiveness from one person and gentle guidance and skill from the other.
>
> When I saw "G" in guidance, I thought of God, followed by "u" and "i." And it hit me: God, let's u (you), and I dance. This statement is what guidance means to me. As I lowered my head, I became willing to trust that I would get guidance about my life. Once again, I became willing to let God lead.[a]

Connecting with the Spirit of Life

What paves the way for being filled with the Spirit (see Ephesians 5:18) is making the choice, like Jesus did, to lay aside one's own agenda and accept God's instead. Once we are *emptied* like this, we can then by faith receive the Spirit's *filling*.

A lamp that is plugged in is connected to the same vast power source as the entire community. But that lamp will not shine unless the old, burned-out bulb is removed and a new, fresh one replaces it.

The plumbing system of a house is connected via the water main to the overflowing resources of the city water system. But water will not flow through the faucet if the faucet handle is rusted and unyielding.

Each one of us, in Christ, is connected to the infinite wisdom, power, and love of Almighty God. We must come to the further realization that we cannot make the Christian life happen in our own strength or with our own ingenuity. Our flesh is a burned-out lightbulb, a rusted-shut faucet handle. We need the Holy Spirit to take over so we can shine out the light of Jesus. We need the Spirit's lubricating, liberating anointing so that God, the fountain of living waters (Jeremiah 2:13), can flow in and through our lives.

Frustrated, no doubt, by the sheer futility of depending on religious rules and rituals to truly give life and spiritual power, Jesus rose to His feet on the last day of the Feast of Booths and cried out, "If anyone is thirsty, let him come to Me and drink. He who believes in Me, as the Scripture said, 'From his innermost being will flow rivers of living water.' " John tells us that Jesus was speaking of the Spirit, whom believers were to receive after Jesus' glorification (John 7:37-39).

Life by the Spirit, Not Death by Law

Laws cannot quench spiritual thirst, nor can they bring life to others. The Holy Spirit does both in and through us, just as He did both in and through Jesus.

Luke provides a couple interesting comments in his account of the temptation in the wilderness. He reveals that Jesus entered the temptation *"full* of the Holy Spirit," but "returned to Galilee in the *power* of the Spirit" (4:14). There is encouragement in knowing that even greater spiritual strength will be ours as we fight and win the spiritual battles that we encounter!

The following testimony is helpful in understanding the distinction between walking by the Spirit versus living according to laws. It is written by a mom who worked hard to protect her children from harmful influences from the media while also trying to teach them to be "constructive critics" of what they did watch. The parents knew that simply slamming the door on secular culture would not cut it. They were trying to teach *discernment*. At one point, however, this woman's teenage daughter came to realize that she was not doing a good job of critiquing popular culture, and as a result she had suffered. We pick up the story there:

> After class one day, our daughter happened to be talking to another student about critiquing culture. This person told her about a camp she had gone to that expressly taught the campers how to assess worldviews and evaluate things in the culture. A lightbulb turned on, and that night Rebeccah [not her real name] called me with this thought. She said that, although she now realized what her father and I had been trying to do, she was embarrassed to admit that all along she had simply been making a checklist of do's and don'ts. She would make a mental list of "Rules from Mom and Dad": *They don't like this show. I can't listen to this music. I shouldn't read that book.*
>
> For me this was such a clear example of how legalism can creep in so innocently. I had been frustrated for the last few years that, while we were preparing to let Rebeccah leave the nest, she would still come to us and ask if it was okay to watch certain shows or listen to certain things. I

couldn't understand why all that we were trying to instill in her was falling to the side unlearned. It all started with a happy, well-adjusted child trying to please Mom and Dad. It started with the (wrong) perception that a checklist would keep her safe. But what happens when someone else isn't there to make the decision?

I am happy to say that the Holy Spirit led Rebeccah to a recognition of exactly how important it is to understand *why* she does what she does, rather than relying on other people to make rules for her. I will try to use this experience to help our three other children before they leave the nest. I want them to understand that it is not their parents they need to please, but Christ. I really want them to learn how to listen to the leading of the Spirit, read and understand God's Word for themselves, and apply *it* to their daily life with joy—not *checklists!* Fifteen years from now, I would be very sad to find that they are trying to please Jesus through legalistic rules instead of glorifying Christ through appreciation and love for all He has done for them.

There is both a *science* and an *art* to most things. The science can be taught and understood in a class, or read from a book. The art comes from within, from the heart, and it seeks expression outwardly, maturing through life experiences. So it is with being filled with the Holy Spirit. You can read this chapter and gain an academic knowledge of what it means to be filled with the Spirit. It is the Spirit within us, however, that gives life—and He leads us as we live out that life. And it is as we walk through the experiences of life that we learn to lean on Him more and more. It ought to encourage us to know, however, that even Jesus, "although He was a Son...*learned obedience* from the things which He suffered" (Hebrews 5:8).

You will find, as Jesus did, that the Father is a very willing and able Teacher!

Living Life Like Jesus Did

As you realize the union that has taken place between you and Jesus—*Christ in you* and *you in Christ*—as you develop your intimate relationship with the Father in prayer, and as you learn to lean on the presence and power of the Holy Spirit, you will begin to live like Jesus. You will find that it is not trying to keep laws, but trusting in the Lord, that keeps you from sin and enables you to walk in righteousness. You will never achieve perfect performance this side of heaven, but any failure is meant to bring you back to the light of the cross, where "the blood of Jesus His Son cleanses us from all sin" (1 John 1:7). That's where faith lives. Don't let failure drive you back to the darkness of living under the law. That's where fear lurks in its quest to control us.

We conclude this chapter with a testimony of hope. Let it speak to your heart, no matter how long the road to freedom seems to stretch out in front of you.

> I was born again at age 11. Our little evangelical church won people to Christ, but the discipling process consisted of teaching us to read our Bibles daily, witness, obey the Word, and pray. "Use 1 John 1:9 a lot and do your best at being a good Christian. Don't question anything and stay out of trouble." I wanted to be the best Christian I could be, so I worked very hard...and very unsuccessfully...at all of these things.
>
> I met my husband in that church, and we both had the same desire: Since we were both schoolteachers, we decided that what would please God most would be for us to become missionary teachers and houseparents, which we did. We kept our four-year commitment abroad, but we were

very unhappy. We both had many unhealed childhood hurts. When all the comforts of home were
removed, we realized we had very little internally
to sustain us. So we kept reading and praying and
trying very hard to please God. We knew we
should be happy and should love being missionaries, but we weren't and we didn't.

After our return to the States, I realized that I
didn't really like being a Christian. It was joyless
because I could never really measure up or do
enough. Miraculously, though, the Lord led us to
some books from your ministry that brought hope.
Then Neil Anderson came to our church and conducted a conference. As my husband and I listened
to Neil, the Lord grabbed our hearts. God wanted
to heal some wounds in our own hearts that had
been there for years. When Neil said he was sorry
for the pain some of us were feeling, I started to
weep. No one had ever apologized to me before,
and this melted my heart.

We were both so impacted by this conference
and the "Steps to Freedom" and the truths of our
identity in Christ that we took training classes and
became the leaders of this ministry in our church.
Our hearts were overjoyed as we saw the Lord
using us to help others get freed in their own
hearts.

I have found that this legalism is something
that I need to fight daily with the truth of God's
Word. It is so easy and natural for me to entertain
condemning thoughts about my performance.
What has helped me the most with daily victory is
the knowledge of the Person of the Holy Spirit,
who will live the Christian life through me as I
yield totally to Him and choose to worship and
praise God in spirit and truth. The Spirit alone is
my power to live the Christian life! It is a daily

surrender to Him that is necessary. On my own I can't die to that independent, proud, fleshly part of me that thinks I'm really pretty good and can live out the Christian life myself. He bids me to present my body as a living sacrifice, and then He does the rest as I walk by faith in Him.

The Christian life is a relationship with God day by day. Some days are great, and some are not so great, but His love for me never changes. I can still struggle at times, feeling bad about my performance. I am learning, however, that even on the great days I still need to come to Him solely on the basis of Christ's shed blood for me. When I remember that, it is easier to draw near on the not-so-great days. His acceptance of me is never based on my performance, which is often poor. It is based on His! And His is perfect!

10

BITTERSWEET PAIN

Shirley and I (Rich) had been married about three months when the letter came. It was an invitation to open up a new ministry to youth in the Philippines. Shirley's first reaction was to cry. She had just made a major cultural shift from life in the South to an apartment in Philadelphia, and her reaction was, "But I just put up the drapes!" I threw the letter in the trash.

I felt I had already paid my dues to tropical ministry back in 1980, and I was looking more for an invitation to serve in some place like Switzerland. With a body thermostat more suited to the Arctic than to equatorial Asia, I was convinced God could not be behind a move to Manila.

I was wrong.

Despite my cries to Him to leave me in the U.S. to help see revival come to our nation, God had other plans. As it turned out, He was interested in seeing revival come to *me*, and His operating table happened to be in the Philippines.

The Breaking Begins

After several months of a major evangelistic thrust to metropolitan Manila high schools (with the help of scores of short-term missionaries), Shirley and I were left with no more American manpower, a few inexperienced Filipino workers—and 52,000 youth to follow up and help in their spiritual growth.

Those turned out to be the ingredients for this sweating director to become a stressed-out dictator. I mobilized volunteers to address by hand (this was before small-office computer technology), stuff, seal, and mail follow-up material to all 52,000. That was accomplished in a few months. Meanwhile, I was mobilizing a team of youth workers to revisit high schools all over the city to establish ongoing ministries.

I drove myself hard, and I expected my staff to keep up with me. Some just couldn't, and I was often impatient and demanding with them. Shirley reminded me that we had decided to take a half-day a week to pray, but I angrily informed her that we were too busy to pray. She was saddened…but I kept on pushing.

Little did I realize the hard feelings I was creating in some of my staff. One of them wrote me a letter telling me that I was much like his authoritarian father, and that he strongly resented my attitude toward and treatment of others. This letter came out of the blue—and I was stunned. This was to be the first of a series of much-needed blows to my "full speed ahead" ego.

The Lord's Mercy Appears

While I was reading 1 Corinthians 13 one day, blow number two came. I was considering the verse, "Now these three remain: faith, hope and love. But the greatest of these is love" (verse 13 NIV), and the Lord spoke immediately and distinctly. He said, "Rich, if someone looked at your life, they would say that you believed 'the greatest of these is faith.' "

I knew what the Lord was saying. Without minimizing the crucial nature of faith (for salvation, for life, for growth), the Lord was pointing out a major flaw in my heart. I was placing the accomplishing of goals for the kingdom of God above people, and He reminded me that without love I am nothing.

Without love what I do counts for nothing (see 1 Corinthians 13:1-3).

The Lord wasn't done, however.

Shirley and I had to move into an upstairs room of a house where there was no air conditioning. One day while listening to a Christian radio station in that home, I heard a song that irritated me. The chorus repeated over and over again, "Lord, have mercy—Lord, have mercy." Being full of myself, I remember disdaining the song and thinking, *What a cheesy, weak song for wimps.*

In the room where we were staying, it was over 90 degrees at night and eventually I became ill. I contracted the Philippine version of Montezuma's revenge and became dehydrated. While in the hospital I came down with double pneumonia.

The antibiotics helped knock out the pneumonia, but because of the damage to my lungs, I developed serious asthma. Neither the doctor nor I recognized it. One night around 2 A.M., I was up, desperately trying to breathe. Using the nebulizer the doctor had given me didn't help. I was lying on the floor, gasping for air, helpless. I found myself from the depths of my heart crying out, "Lord, have mercy! Lord, have mercy!"

He did! He saved my life, and He also broke my pride and fleshly self-sufficiency. I discovered that the very thing I had disdained in the song was the very thing I desperately needed in my life—God's mercy.

Brokenness Hurts

After my wife's sudden death, I (Paul) was really hurting. I tried to keep it all under control, but many times I burst into tears, especially on weekends. It seemed like the bottom had fallen out of my life, and I was at a standstill, not knowing what to do.

I'm not much of a cook, so I would eat out on Friday evenings. Many times I would arrive at the restaurant and have to wait a while in my car for the tears to stop. I didn't want people to see me crying. I never wanted people to see me out of control. That was the one thing I always wanted to maintain—control. And that was the one thing the Lord set His sights on to break in my life.

I had to learn the hard way that in order to be free, I had to be broken...and brokenness hurts.

During my studies at Grace Fellowship, Atlanta (now Grace Ministries International), I began to know Christ as my Life, not just as my Savior and Lord. What a shock it was to learn that the objective of the discipleship counselor training I was undergoing was not to give advice or tell people what to do, but to gently lead them into truth! This turned out to be God's avenue for brokenness in my life.

I spent a whole week allowing counselors to take me through a process in which the Lord shined His spotlight on my life. This was very personal and very humbling, tracing through the hurts and rejections I had experienced in life. The walls of "control" were beginning to crumble, but the battering ram was yet to come.

Later in the internship we were asked to write a response to a letter from a woman who was asking for help. She was really hurting and desperate, and she had a number of crippling problems we were supposed to address in our reply to her. We were expected to draw thoroughly on all our training up to that point.

The Humbling of the Lord

There was tremendous tension and a hush in the room as all the interns prepared to write. Nobody moved at first. Finally, we all plunged in, working very hard to do it right. We took great pains to describe to her the real, root problems in her life and what she needed to know and do to resolve these problems. We made sure we addressed everything that she had mentioned in her letter. We were thorough!

Then we were thoroughly humiliated. Our leader brought us to tears. He demolished our egos by basically tearing apart everything we had written—and rightfully so! He showed us how insensitive we had been and how devastated this woman would have been to read what we had written. Our letters would have come across as rejection and all our fine advice would have been wasted.

What we should have done was simply share our compassion and concern for her. Instead we had just blasted her with all our training and "expertise." The answers we had given were well-thought-out and well-documented, but they were cold. We really did care for her, but you would not have known it from what we had written.

When the leader finished with us, we felt as though we'd been run over by a train. We felt crushed. The Lord knows that it is only those whose pride has been crushed who are ready to receive His love down deep and share it with others. That humbling process is called *brokenness*. It is the bittersweet pain of the Christian life, and every one of God's followers must undergo it if they want to be like Christ.

King David was under deep conviction because he had abused his authority in order to have sex with Bathsheba. To cover up his sin he had masterminded a plot to have her husband, Uriah, killed. Nathan the prophet had confronted David about his sin, and the "man after God's heart" had repented deeply. David's words show us what God is looking for in our repentance:

> You do not delight in sacrifice, or I would bring it; you do not take pleasure in burnt offerings. The sacrifices of God are a broken spirit; a broken and contrite heart, O God, you will not despise (Psalm 51:16-17 NIV).

The Futility of Prideful Self-Sufficiency

When people caught in the grip of legalism mess up their lives or someone else's, their tendency is to try to "make up for it" by performing better, so they can "show God" how sorry they are. They'll work harder or try to make some great sacrifice—but God is looking for a change of heart inwardly before a change of behavior outwardly.

The pride, arrogance, and self-sufficient spirit of those ensnared in legalism must be broken if the life of Jesus is to be fully released in them. The apostle Paul recognized the need for this to be an ongoing process in his own life:

> We have this treasure in jars of clay to show that this all-surpassing power is from God and not from us. We are hard pressed on every side, but not crushed; perplexed, but not in despair; persecuted, but not abandoned; struck down, but not destroyed. We always carry around in our body the death of Jesus, so that the life of Jesus may also be revealed in our body. For we who are alive are always being given over to death for Jesus' sake, so that his life may be revealed in our mortal body (2 Corinthians 4:7-11 NIV).

James says, "God is opposed to the proud, but gives grace to the humble" (4:6). Humility is drawing near to God, recognizing our complete and utter need for Him as well as our need for our brothers and sisters in Christ. The proud, independent, self-reliant spirit in us must die—and since God is opposed to it, He unleashes a barrage of events in our life to kill it.

God wants us to come to the place where we joyfully acknowledge that apart from Christ, we can do nothing (John 15:5), but that we can do all things through Him who strengthens us (Philippians 4:13).

More often than not, however, we give only lip service to the truth that we are spiritually bankrupt without Christ. When the heat is on, we tend to rely on our own strengths, experience, giftedness, problem-solving abilities, persuasiveness, powerful personality, finances, networking, and so on. We dig deep into our fleshly bag of tricks to try and get ourselves out of jams, accomplish our goals, or shield ourselves from pain.

Somewhere along the line we must come to the painful realization that nothing good dwells in our flesh (Romans 7:18) and that legalism is the flesh trying to live the Christian life. Though others may applaud our efforts, and though even we may be impressed with ourselves, fleshly living is a total failure in God's eyes. It is rubbish, as Paul the apostle wrote in Philippians 3:7-8. It is wood, hay, and stubble that will burn up at the judgment of the works of believers (see 1 Corinthians 3:11-15).

Coming face-to-face with the futility of relying on our own fleshly resources to live the Christian life will be a painful experience. But it opens the door wide to the kingdom of God in our lives. That was what Jesus was driving at in the Beatitudes:

> You're blessed when you're at the end of your rope. With less of you there is more of God and his rule.
>
> You're blessed when you feel you've lost what is most dear to you. Only then can you be embraced by the One most dear to you.
>
> You're blessed when you're content with just who you are—no more, no less. That's the moment you find yourselves proud owners of everything that can't be bought.
>
> You're blessed when you've worked up a good appetite for God. He's food and drink in the best meal you'll ever eat.
>
> You're blessed when you care. At the moment of being "care-full," you'll find yourselves cared for.
>
> You're blessed when you get your inside world—your mind and heart—put right. Then you can see God in the outside world.
>
> You're blessed when you can show people how to cooperate instead of compete or fight. That's when you discover who you really are, and your

place in God's family (Matthew 5:3-9 The message).

His Relentless Love

God is not out to make our lives miserable. He wants us to
live life to the full in Jesus (John 10:10). But when we lock ourselves into the coffin of legalism, thinking that life is found
there, would it be the loving thing for God to allow us to
remain there and rot spiritually? Our merciful God is willing
to sacrifice our temporary comfort and pleasure in order to
put us into the place where we can experience love and life as
it was intended…in Jesus, not in the law.

In the film *The Horse Whisperer*, Robert Redford plays the
part of a gentle and firm horse-healer, Tom Booker. A desperate mom (Kristin Scott Thomas) calls Booker for help
when her daughter and her horse are seriously injured in a
riding accident. The girl's name is "Grace" and the horse's
name is "Pilgrim." Once they're out on Booker's Montana
ranch, healing begins to take place both in the horse's and the
girl's lives.

Finally, it is time for Grace to try and ride her horse again.
The horse is very wary, and he rears and whinnies in fear
when she comes near. Booker realizes that Pilgrim needs to be
loved into trusting again—so he places the loop of a rope
around his left foreleg, pulling it off the ground so he can only
use three legs.

"What are you doing?" the concerned girl calls out to
Booker.

"We're going to have to do something different…" he
replies.

"It's not going to hurt him…right?" Grace asks, fighting off
tears.

"Nothing we've done has hurt him. Grace, this is Pilgrim's
chance…and it's yours, too."

She agrees and watches the painful scene as Booker forces
the horse to go around and around the pen. Pilgrim struggles

along, trying desperately to keep going on three legs. At one point the horse begins to bow his head, but then he rears up again, fighting hard in a renewed burst of energy and will.

Grace can't bear to watch her animal suffer and cries out, "That's enough! Stop!" But Booker won't stop.

Pilgrim's eyes are full of fear as he continues fighting Booker's efforts to bring him to his knees. The horse is scared because he is no longer in control. Someone stronger than himself is in control, and he cannot get away. Gradually, the horse begins to tire. You see a change from fright to resignation in his brown eyes. At last, the horse gives up, hangs his head, and flops on his side, moaning softly. Booker reaches down and tenderly strokes him, caressing the fear out of him.

Turning to the girl, he says, "Grace, this is where you come in."

She hesitates, wondering whether Pilgrim will trust her.

Booker responds, "Grace, look at him. Look at him. He's okay. And you never did anything to let him down…Trust me just one more time."

As Grace bends down to stroke Pilgrim, the rope is removed from his leg. The horse is free. He turns his head and looks into Grace's eyes. The fear is gone, replaced by trust.

Pilgrim again allows Grace up on his back. At first they walk together, then they run. The scene ends with the rightful rider joyfully celebrating on the back of the one born to run. Pilgrim needed to be broken so he could be healed.

So do we. God is at work in each of our lives to break us of self-sufficiency, and He is relentlessly loving. "My son, do not regard lightly the discipline of the Lord, nor faint when you are reproved by Him; for those whom the Lord loves He disciplines, and He scourges every son whom He receives" (Hebrews 12:5-6). Those are strong words describing a painful process.

God's discipline does not seem joyful but sorrowful—but once we have surrendered to Him, peace and righteousness reign in us (Hebrews 12:11).

Merciful Sovereignty

What areas is the Lord putting His finger on in your life? Usually it is areas of *control.* God is the sovereign Lord, and He resists all of our efforts to usurp that control from Him.

Do you always have to have your way? Are you engaged in a proud power struggle at home, at church, or at work? Have you become "territorial," believing that something (a place, a role, a position, a ministry) is yours? Do you think you are always right, and do you work hard at convincing others of that "fact"? Are you engaged in a power struggle with God? Is He exposing a critical, judgmental spirit—and have you been resisting His grace? Have you become proud of your ministry "successes" and feel self-confident and self-assured? Do you like being "in charge" a bit too much? Have you become convinced that God *needs* your service for His kingdom?

If any of these things are true of your life, don't be surprised if God slips a rope around your leg and hobbles you. He will wear you out until you finally bow your knee to Him and give up. It is at that time you will experience—maybe for the first time in your life—another aspect of His love. Then it will be time for *grace* to come in. God will mercifully and gently bring you His tender healing touch. He will *make you* lie down in green pastures and lead you beside the quiet waters because that's what you need. God wants to restore your soul (Psalm 23:1-3). Usually He has to slow us down or shut us down in order to do so.

You see, everyone of us is a Pilgrim, journeying through life. The question is, will we stop fighting and allow God's Grace to be our master?

He Woos Us in the Desert

In Hosea 2 the Lord likens the unfaithfulness of Hosea's wife, Gomer, to the nation of Israel's unfaithfulness to Him. Israel's sin was following after Baal, a foreign god. God informs Hosea what He is about to do because of His great love for His people:

> I will hedge up her way with thorns, and I will build a wall against her so that she cannot find her paths. She will pursue her lovers, but she will not overtake them; and she will seek them, but will not find them (Hosea 2:6-7).

Just about anything in life can become more important to us than God. These "lovers" of ours are rivals to God's love for us and our ability to experience it. Following after *any* other master—even the law—instead of walking in dependence upon the Lord is spiritual adultery. Thus, at its core, legalism is spiritual adultery. But God always sets out to woo us back to Himself. The ways that God does this in our lives are innumerable. Loss of respect, loss of reputation, loss of a job, financial or legal difficulties, ruined relationships, and ruined health are just some of God's breaking instruments. Whatever instrument He uses, be assured that God is tailor-making it in order to bore down to the core of our pride and control issues...and in order to rescue us and restore the intimacy of our relationship to Him.

The passage in Hosea goes on to show us God's planned result:

> Then she will say, "I will go back to my first husband [God], for it was better for me then than now!" (Hosea 2:7).

In the dark time of God's breaking, we find that He intentionally strips away from us many of the things that used to bring us joy and a sense of well-being. Not everything that God takes away is evil in itself, but if something has become more our god than God Himself, then He will attack that idol. Idols choke out an intimate relationship with God—and that deeply disturbs Him because what He is always after with us is *us*...because He loves us!

> The greatest enemy of our hunger for God is
> not poison but apple pie. It is not the banquet of
> the wicked that dulls our appetite for heaven, but
> endless nibbling at the table of the world. It is not
> the X-rated video, but the prime-time dribble of
> triviality we drink in every night. For all the ill that
> Satan can do, when God describes what keeps us
> from the banquet table of his love, it is a piece of
> land, a yoke of oxen, and a wife (Luke 14:18-20).
> The greatest adversary of love to God is not his
> enemies but his gifts.[1]

Tragically, even some of God's greatest gifts—the Scriptures, the gifts of the Spirit, church life and its services and programs, ministry opportunities, Christian books and music, and so on, can be substitutes for God Himself.

Hosea 2:14-17 shows the tender side of God as He reaches out to us in the desert experience of brokenness. Why, you may ask, does God have to take us into the desert? Simply because there is nothing there to attract us. Most important, He starts to look pretty good to us in the desert!

> I am now going to allure her; I will lead her into
> the desert and speak tenderly to her. There I will
> give her back her vineyards, and will make the
> Valley of Achor [trouble] a door of hope. There
> she will sing as in the days of her youth, as in the
> day she came up out of Egypt.
> "In that day," declares the LORD, "you will call
> me 'my husband'; you will no longer call me 'my
> master' " (NIV).

Once God ends the period of discipline and the breaking has accomplished its work, the joy of our salvation returns (Psalm 51:12). He puts a new song in our mouths, a hymn of praise to our God (Psalm 40:3). In some ways it is like when we were first saved, for we are truly free again!

You're in Good Company

If, by God's providence, you are reading this book while going through just such a breaking process, don't despair. You're in good company.

The apostle Peter boasted to Jesus that even if everyone else fell away, he would never do so (Matthew 26:33). It was pure bravado, an expression of the self-sufficiency and pride that needed to be carved out of Peter's soul. Peter was a natural leader, but he needed to be broken so that he could become a *supernatural* leader.

Within hours after his boast, Peter found himself denying the Lord Jesus three times, even frightened so much by a slave girl that he swore, "I do not know the man" (Matthew 26:72). Then the cock crowed, Jesus gazed with sorrow at Peter, and the hero-turned-zero went out and wept bitterly.

> That was the beginning of true greatness in Peter! Now he began to see himself as God saw him. He began to see his weakness, his pride, his false strength, his bullheadedness and his outspokenness. He was rocked by the realization that he was everything his given name "Simon" implied. Simon means "weak or fickle." Jesus had called Simon a "rock" (Peter). The thing he needed to learn, however, was that only Jesus could make a Peter out of a Simon. Only Jesus can make a rock out of a fickle, vacillating and boastful man. True greatness comes this way—by the road of brokenness! No man is really great who has not been broken before God.[2]

After this process that the late Dr. Richard Halverson so profoundly described above, Jesus graciously did not leave Peter in a crumpled spiritual heap on the ground. After His resurrection, the Lord appeared to Simon (Luke 24:34), and then later restored him to the ministry of "feeding the sheep,"

God's people (see John 21:15-17). Filled with the Spirit, the apostle Peter became a powerful preacher, seeing thousands come to Christ through his ministry (Acts 2:41). But first he had to be broken.

Other scriptural examples of broken people are numerous. Moses had to spend 40 years on the backside of the desert before God was ready to use him to deliver a nation from bondage. In his own strength, Moses had killed one Egyptian man—and then fled for his life. Years later, in the strength of Jehovah, Moses watched God wipe out the entire Egyptian army—and he escaped with much of the wealth of Egypt! But he wasn't ready to lead the millions of Israelites through the wilderness until he had first met God there himself.

A Broken Man Sees the "Face of God"

Jacob lived 147 years. The first 75 years of his life are a picture of the *natural man* (the man without God). Then he experienced God's presence at Bethel (the "house of God") in Genesis 28:16-22. Jacob made a vow to serve God, but it was conditional and self-serving. The next 20 years of Jacob's life, as he worked for his uncle Laban, are a picture of the *carnal, or fleshly, Christian*—one who knows the Lord, but when the heat is on still depends upon the flesh and its ability to scheme and scramble.

It wasn't until God broke Jacob at Peniel (the "face of God") that Jacob began to walk in dependence upon Him. Jacob's experience alone with the angel that night is a classic story of brokenness. Let's set the stage.

Jacob, his wives, his children, and his livestock were on their way back to the land of Canaan. But Jacob was afraid that Esau (his twin brother) was still angry with him for taking his birthright and stealing their father Isaac's blessing. So Jacob swung into action.

First he divided his family and possessions into two groups, hoping that at least one company would escape Esau's wrath. To his credit, Jacob then calls upon God to deliver him, asking God to fulfill His promise to bring him safely back to Canaan.

Still unsure of God's trustworthiness—and trusting in his own cleverness to manipulate and control—Jacob devises a cunning plan to butter Esau up. He sends out wave upon wave of gifts (goats, sheep, camels, cows, and donkeys) to go before him and his family.

Finally, Jacob sends all his family and other possessions on ahead, and he is left alone to wrestle with his fears. That's where we'll pick up the story:

> Then Jacob was left alone, and a man wrestled with him until daybreak. When he saw that he had not prevailed against him, he touched the socket of his thigh; so the socket of Jacob's thigh was dislocated while he wrestled with him. Then he said, "Let me go, for the dawn is breaking." But he [Jacob] said, "I will not let you go unless you bless me." So he said to him, "What is your name?" And he said, "Jacob." He said, "Your name shall no longer be Jacob, but Israel; for you have striven with God and with men and have prevailed." Then Jacob asked him and said, "Please tell me your name." But he said, "Why is it that you ask my name?" And he blessed him there. So Jacob named the place Peniel, for he said, "I have seen God face to face, yet my life has been preserved." Now the sun rose upon him just as he crossed over Penuel, and he was limping on his thigh (Genesis 32:24-31).

Notice that once Jacob was broken (by a physical infirmity), he would not let the presence of the Lord go until He had blessed him. Up until this time he had tricked and manipulated people. He had tried to do it his way. Now he was clinging to the Lord and relying upon Him. There was much pain later in Jacob's life, especially when he was separated from his precious son Joseph for 20 years, but at Peniel—the "face of God"—he became a new man. No longer was he called "Jacob" (which means "deceiver")—God had changed his name to "Israel" (which means "God fights").

"God, I Trust You"

There is a theme running throughout God's creation and the Scriptures, and this is that *there can be no making without breaking.* Before a house can be built, there has to be the breaking of the tree. Before grain can be grown, the soil must be broken up. There is death before life, weeping before joy.

When Gideon was fighting the Midianites, God used broken pitchers (Judges 7:18-20) to shine light. Jesus fed the 5000, but not until the bread and fish were broken. In Mark chapter 14, Mary anointed the head of Jesus with a very precious ointment, but not until the container had been broken.

Jesus said, "Truly, truly, I say to you, unless a grain of wheat falls into the earth and dies, it remains alone; but if it dies, it bears much fruit. He who loves his life loses it, and he who hates his life in this world will keep it to life eternal" (John 12:24-25).

Brokenness brings a person to the place of total surrender or total commitment. Many times invitations are given in church for people to go forward and say, "I'll go wherever you want me to go and say whatever you want me to say." That is good as far as it goes, but there is much more. Are we willing to say to the Lord, "I will allow You to put me through any experience that You want me to go through. I want You to do in and through me whatever You wish, Lord, for I belong to You and I fully trust You to have my best interest at heart"?

When John Collinson was asked what brokenness meant, he responded this way:

> Brokenness is not easy to define but can be clearly seen
> in the reactions of Jesus, especially as He approached the

cross and in His crucifixion. I think it can be applied personally this way:

WHEN to do the will of God means that even my Christian brethren will not understand, and I remember that *"Neither did His brethren believe in him"* (*John 7:5*), and I bow my head to obey and accept the misunderstanding, THIS IS BROKENNESS.

WHEN I am misrepresented or deliberately misinterpreted, and I remember that Jesus was falsely accused but He *"held His peace,"* and I bow my head to accept the accusation without trying to justify myself, THIS IS BROKENNESS.

WHEN another is preferred before me and I am deliberately passed over, and I remember that they cried, *"Away with this man, and release unto us Barabbas"* (*Luke 23:18*), and I bow my head and accept rejection, THIS IS BROKENNESS.

WHEN my plans are brushed aside and I see the work of years brought to ruins by ambitions of others, and I remember that Jesus allowed them to lead Him away to crucify Him (*Matthew 27:31*) and He accepted that place of failure, and I bow my head and accept the injustice without bitterness, THIS IS BROKENNESS.

WHEN in order to be right with my God it is necessary to take the humbling path of confession and restitution, and I remember that Jesus *"made Himself of no reputation"* and *"humbled Himself... unto death, even the death of the cross"* (*Philippians 2:7,8*), and I bow my head and am ready to accept the shame of exposure, THIS IS BROKENNESS.[3]

He Will Give You the Desire of Your Heart

There is a great difference between the man or woman walking in freedom and the one walking in legalism. We pray and hope that the Lord has brought you to the point in your life where you are longing to be free. (The next chapter will guide you through a process that can help you break the chains and throw off the yoke of legalism in your life.)

Consider the following chart that contrasts life as a liberated child of God versus the lifeless way of legalism. It's like the difference between day and night. For your sake and the glory of God, we pray you choose the light.

The Way of Liberty *The Christian...*	The Way of Legalism *The Christian...*
hungers for God's Word and listens with eagerness	critiques the sermon
lives a life focused on and centered around God	lives a life focused and centered around self
fears God in a healthy way	fears people
gets angry at sin	is angry or bitter toward God, others, or self
attends church services as an overflow of relationships	attends church services out of tradition and with a sense of duty
serves God out of love and delight	serves God out of drivenness and duty
receives truth from God and is humbled	accumulates head knowledge and information, and becomes proud
rejoices with those who rejoice and weeps with those who weep	is stifled in experiencing appropriate emotions
rests in being accepted by God	performs in order to gain acceptance and approval
surrenders control	has to be in control

yields the "right to be right"	has to be right
treats others with grace	puts others under the law
is secure in Christ, even in the midst of trial	is filled with anxiety and complaining
is accepting and compassionate	is self-righteous, judgmental, and critical
is willing to change and grow	resists change and clings to traditions of men
is willing to be of no reputation	is very concerned about image and reputation
walks in the light and is honest about sin	hides or denies sin
is willing to admit when wrong	struggles with saying, "I was wrong"
is led by the Spirit of God	is driven by the flesh
lives by Christ's life flowing from within	lives by rules imposed by self or others
is dependent upon the Holy Spirit	relies on the resources of religious tradition
bears fruit and glorifies God	lives a defeated life

The following brief letter (used by permission) is from a friend of mine (Rich's) who is seeking to reestablish a relationship with an old friend of his. It is, in part, a testimony of life viewed from the "after" side of some painful breaking.

Have you seen the movie *Signs*? We saw it in the theater and then rented it this weekend. I enjoy Mel Gibson and tend to believe the many faces of the actor are facets of the man. *Signs* is no exception. The whole crop circle/ET aspect fades into the background as I view this film. The underlying conflict is that Mel's character, a former priest, lost his wife tragically, became angry with God, and tried to walk away from his faith. The reality confronting him is that a man cannot oppose God without also being in opposition to himself. This is because we are made in God's image and each of us has a purpose for which He created us. Fulfillment and contentment only come from learning to live in harmony with Him. And that kind of living tends to demand a certain amount of dying.

I found myself identifying strongly with the character. At least twice I have gone through prolonged periods of being bitter and angry toward God. I didn't abandon my beliefs and disciplines or ditch church, but in many ways I checked out of life. I fathomed depths of depression that were horrible. Both times, in the end, I had to allow God the right to do with me, my family, and my career precisely as He pleased. It meant forever surrendering the control of certain things we might deem natural "rights." That can be awfully tough, but in many ways that is what faith is all about. We can't know Jesus for long without tasting death, but the quality of life beyond the "tomb" (not just in the hereafter, but here as well) is a treasure without price.

Jesus Is There

When we are faced with a brick wall—placed there by God to break us of self-reliance—it is a common mistake to just keep trying to climb it, maintaining a brave face even as we fail. In reality, what we need to do is collapse into the arms of Jesus and let Him take us to the other side.

We conclude this chapter with a song by the Christian artist Gersh (Mark Gersmehl) that expresses that theme. He explains why he wrote it. "I have a friend whom I love dearly, a father of three. He was caught in a divorce not of his choosing. Day after day, I watched him put on his brave face, the face that could not possibly hide the sorrow in his broken heart. Although I admired his courage, I came to believe that the very best thing he could do was to fall apart, to fall into the loving arms of Jesus. So I wrote this song in honor of my friend." The song is entitled *Breakdown*.

> *I've been watching you*
> *And this is hard to see*
> *Brave, brave player in your tragedy*
> *You think if you're strong enough*
> *And tough enough*
> *You'll forget what you've been through*
> *Just last long enough*
> *Well, that's not enough*
> *To calm the storm in you*
>
> *Breakdown, my friend*
> *You don't even realize*
> *How hurt you've been*
> *Breakdown to this*
> *The best thing you could ever do*
> *Is fall to pieces*
> *Fall into the loving arms of Jesus*
> *And breakdown*
>
> *Well, this hurts so much*
> *We all love you so*
> *Can we tell you something*
> *You already know?*
> *He is strong enough*

And tough enough
You've told others that before
You've held out long enough
This time you're the one He's reaching for

Breakdown, my friend
It's time for you to realize
How hurt you've been
Breakdown to this
The best thing you could ever do
Is fall to pieces
Fall into the loving arms of Jesus
And breakdown, breakdown

There is really no shame at all
To say you've got so much pain
You can't hold it all
So just let your tears just fall and fall
It's gonna be all right
It's the only way you'll be all right

Breakdown, my friend
He is gonna rock you
'Til the sorrow ends
Breakdown to this
Lovingly He'll gather up
The broken pieces
So you just go and fall
In the arms of Jesus
And breakdown, breakdown
It's okay now
We're gonna stick around
You just go ahead and...breakdown[4]

11

BREAKING THE CHAINS

Real change is tough, even agonizing at times. It requires a radical change in our thinking—what the Bible calls repentance—which results in a real change of behavior. Repentance is a requirement for Christian growth, but it is a continuing process, not just a one-time experience. We are "transformed by the renewing of [our] mind" (Romans 12:2), and that takes time.

Indoctrination Versus Truth

Legalistic religious systems tend to indoctrinate their followers, rather than challenge their thinking. Further, some people are content simply to let others do their thinking for them. That kind of complacency stunts growth and brings stagnation.

We often stiffly resist facing the reality that what we have believed for so long may not be true. This is because we don't like to admit we're wrong. It goes against our pride. Yet we must be willing to rethink what we believe if we want to grow. Spiritual renewal takes place when our minds are enlightened by truth.

In his book *The Road Less Traveled and Beyond*, Dr. M. Scott Peck concurs with this:

Thinking is difficult. Thinking is complex. And thinking is—more than anything else—a process, with a course or direction, a lapse of time, and a series of steps or stages that lead to some result. To think well is a laborious, often painstaking process until one becomes accustomed to being "thoughtful."

Various institutions of society, in their failure to teach or demonstrate how to think well, set people up for thinking simplistically. Typically, this failure is found among the most immensely influential institutions of society including, more often than not, the family, the church, and the mass media. Given that they have the greatest impact on our lives, the deceptive messages they [may] impart to us about what's important in life cannot be taken lightly.

Because they are our cultural leaders in portraying certain ways of thinking and living as truth, these institutions have the power to fool and manipulate us. They often unwittingly promote half-truths—sometimes even blatant lies—under the guise of cultural ideas that we've taken for granted to be "normal." On the basis of cultural norms, we usually assume that if everyone is thinking this or doing that, it must be normal and correct.[1]

By default, we tend to adopt the cultural mores (morally binding customs) of the significant people around us. The peer pressure to conform to those standards can be as intense for an adult in church as it is for an adolescent in middle school. In addition, strongholds of wrong thinking and acting are difficult to recognize in our lives and are even harder to tear down, especially when they represent years (or even decades) of mental programming received through family and church indoctrination.

The Mental Rut of Legalism

Mental strongholds are like deep ruts in a dirt road in the country. If you drive a pickup truck along that road after a drenching downpour, this will produce a shallow indentation in the mud. Repeated over and over again, the combination of raining, driving, and baking in the hot summer sun will make deep and lasting impressions in the road.

After a time you will not even need to steer the truck once it gets into the ruts. You can put it on "autopilot," so to speak—just hit the gas and the wheels will stay right in the grooves. In fact, it will take a considerable amount of effort and determination to steer the pickup out of the ruts.

The problem with ruts is that they force you to go in only one rigid, restricted direction, robbing you of enjoying an abundant life outside of that narrow "dirt road" experience. (In fact, someone once used the phrase "a rut with ends on it" to describe...a grave.)

Legalism is a spiritual rut. Seeking to gain or maintain acceptance from God and people on the basis of "performance" is a mental stronghold, one that is difficult to steer out of. To remain stuck in such a "rut" is dulling at best and deadening at worst. To steer out of that rut will require a strong conviction that extricating yourself is the right thing to do, even when everyone around you is contentedly driving in the same rut and is maligning you for trying to do otherwise.

To make things more difficult, the rut of legalism is actually reinforced by the world system which operates entirely on "performance-based acceptance" and not grace. Even those who are blessed to attend grace-based churches find themselves accepted and affirmed on Sunday only to be criticized or rejected at the office or school on Monday.

The apostle Paul instructed us to tear down all mental strongholds that keep us from experiencing the grace of God:

> Though we live in the world, we do not wage
> war as the world does. The weapons we fight with

are not the weapons of the world. On the contrary, they have divine power to demolish strongholds. We demolish arguments and every pretension that sets itself up against the knowledge of God, and we take captive every thought to make it obedient to Christ (2 Corinthians 10:3-5 NIV).

Truth Brings Freedom, Even from Legalism

The spiritual war is primarily a battle between truth and error. It is fought against the world's philosophies (even religious ones) that raise themselves up against the true knowledge of God. It is fought primarily on the battlefield of the human mind. This is a winnable war because Jesus Christ has already won the victory for us through His death and resurrection, and He has given us weapons infused with and energized by the power of God.

The following testimony is a powerful reminder that the truth does indeed set us free (John 8:32) and that nothing is too difficult for the Lord (Jeremiah 32:17). The change from legalism to grace—no matter how tough it might be—is well worth the effort.

In February 1995, into a clear, starry night I cried out in utter helplessness, "Lord, I can't do it!" Those were to be my last words before ending my life with the rope I had brought to work that night. A beam high above my bench, a noose, one step...and an end to this misery at last. Twenty years of striving to keep the rules, trying to guide my family "in the law" as a member of one of the most legalistic Christian cults, had ended in failure...failure at every turn. In the end, even the veneer of "living the moral and godly life" had cracked and splintered as I resorted to escaping the pain of failure through addiction to pornography, while my wife suffered from depression and an anxiety disorder. My children had turned to the world. A son and daughter chose the "gay" lifestyle; my other two sons simply found more "life" in the world than in the church.

So why am I alive, writing these words? A miracle…grace…Jesus. In response to my cry that night, like a whisper I clearly heard the words, "No, Rob—but I can." My imagination? Maybe, but I think not.

An amazing thing had been happening in the four months preceding that night. The leadership of our little "sect" of about 150,000 members had been confessing that the treasured doctrines of our church were simply not necessary for salvation. They were things like keeping the Sabbath, strict tithing (first, second, and even third tithes), abstaining from "unclean" foods, keeping Jewish holy days, and many more. In announcement after announcement, these false foundation stones were cast aside. The word GRACE was being talked about in a whole new way. Though I had been perplexed at this sudden about-face that was shattering our church around the world, something was now penetrating this confused and very desperate mind. (By the way, more than half of our members have left our fellowship, forming new, equally or even more legalistic denominations of their own!) Two words summed up the process of freedom for me: *surrender* and *abide*.

That starry night I surrendered. There was simply no question of going back to the law once I had felt that weight lift off my shoulders. The rest was simply learning to abide in Christ. I began reading the entire Bible, drinking great draughts of grace as I read whole New Testament books. What joy! I began meeting with Christian men, being purposefully open about my former moral failures, and I was even more relieved of the burden. I talked a friend into going through the Steps to Freedom together. More freedom! I began a men's group at church, encouraging other men that there was a way out of the performance trap. I gained brothers who both shared their burdens and helped carry mine. Each step has been gently prepared by the Lord. Not once have I had to strive, but I am learning to *abide* in Christ and take the steps He ordains.

Over the past three years the Lord has led me into ministry to others in bondage, now counseling sex addicts and homosexuals seeking freedom in Christ. And in a divine irony, I was ordained to the ministry last year, sanctioned and free to preach grace—unadulterated grace—within the same body that once had added such heavy burdens that grace was lost and hope nearly gone.

Starting Out Toward Real Change

Our prayer and desire as we have been writing this book is to provide real hope for real change. This is possible because "nothing will be impossible with God" (Luke 1:37). If Saul of Tarsus (later the apostle Paul) could be transformed from an ultraorthodox Jewish legalist into the greatest grace-author the world has ever known, then you and I can change, too.

In this chapter we will provide guidance for lasting change. The agent of change is the Spirit of truth. We can try to *reform our behavior,* but only the Holy Spirit can *transform a life.* That same Paul wrote, "Now the Lord is the Spirit, and where the Spirit of the Lord is, there is liberty. But we all, with unveiled face, beholding as in a mirror the glory of the Lord, are being transformed into the same image from glory to glory, just as from the Lord, the Spirit" (2 Corinthians 3:17-18). Freedom and transformation come *only* through the presence and power of the Holy Spirit sent by Jesus Christ.

As you work through the process in this chapter, we encourage you to enlist others to pray for you. They can pray for protection for your mind (so that you are not besieged by thoughts of doubt, fears, guilt, shame, confusion, and so on), and they can pray for protection over your body as well. They can also pray that you would be willing and able to face the issues the Lord brings to your mind with courage and humility and that you would persevere to the end.

If you have a friend (preferably of the same sex) who cares about you and your spiritual health, is trustworthy, and is walking in grace and freedom, you ought to consider having that person sit with you while you work through the process. They can be bathing the whole time in prayer and can be there to talk things through with you when that is needed. There may be places where some very real pain in your life surfaces, and it will be healing to share those painful memories with a trusted brother or sister in Christ.*

We believe you will find this to be a much more powerful exercise if you pray the prayers and proclaim the declarations out loud and from your heart. The reason for that admonition is this: When Jesus Christ, our example, resisted the devil, He did so verbally (see Matthew 4:1-11; Luke 4:1-13). Satan is under no obligation to obey your thoughts. Of course, there is nothing magical in the words themselves. Feel free to make *our* prayers *your* prayers, and *our* declarations *your* declarations.

Now we are ready to begin with the process we call...

---

* There are other issues in our life—in addition to legalism—that significantly block our spiritual freedom and hinder our spiritual growth. For an even more thorough "spiritual housecleaning," we encourage you to obtain a copy of the "Steps to Freedom in Christ" and work through that entire process. The Steps have been a guide by which the Lord Jesus has set many captives free all over the world. You can find them in my (Neil's) book *The Bondage Breaker.* They are also available separately in Christian bookstores under the title *The Steps to Freedom in Christ*, a book that you can also order on-line at www.ficm.org.

Breaking the Bondage of Legalism

Opening Prayer

Dear heavenly Father, I thank You that You love me and that Your Son died and rose again so that I could have a close personal relationship with You. I have spent too much of my life trying to gain *Your acceptance when I already* have *it. I have tended to relate to You more on the basis of head knowledge rather than heart experience, laws rather than love.*

Your Word says "it was for freedom that Christ set us free," and that is what I really want…freedom. There are many ways in which I have not stood firm in your new covenant of grace but instead have allowed a yoke of slavery to legalism to weigh me down and wear me out. Please deliver me from all bondage in my life and bring to my mind all the ways legalism has trapped me. I ask that Your truth would set me free to love, worship, know, obey, and serve You in the love and acceptance that You have graciously extended to me in Christ. In Jesus' name I pray, amen.

(See Galatians 5:1.)

Declaration

In the name and authority of the risen Lord Jesus Christ, who has all authority in heaven and on earth, I take my stand against all demonic opposition to my quest for freedom. I refuse all fear, anxiety, doubt, confusion, deception, distraction, or any other form of harassment that comes from the enemies of the Lord Jesus. I choose to take my place in Christ, and I declare that all His foes have been disarmed and that Jesus Himself came to destroy the devil's works in my life. I declare that the chains of legalism have already been broken by Christ and that I am in Him. Therefore, His victory is my victory.

Step 1: Renouncing Lies and Choosing Truth

Truth sets us free (John 8:32), and lies keep us in bondage. Lies are the fuel that keep legalism alive and in control of our lives. Deception is Satan's primary strategy, so we need the Spirit of truth to reveal the ways we are being deceived.

The following prayer is an invitation for the Holy Spirit to lead you into all truth and show you the areas of deception that have kept you in bondage. It is also a confession of your desire to renounce (verbally reject) those lies. Following the prayer is a list of some of the more common lies of legalism. Be sensitive to the leading of the Spirit—there may be other deceptions He will reveal to you in addition to the ones below.

> *Dear heavenly Father, Your Word is truth, and Jesus Himself is truth. The Holy Spirit is the Spirit of truth, and it is the truth that will set me free. I want to know the truth, believe the truth, and live in accordance with the truth. Please reveal to my mind all the ways that the lies of legalism have kept me in bondage. I want to renounce all those lies and walk in the truth of Your grace and Your acceptance of me in Christ. In Jesus' name I pray, amen.*
> (See John 17:17; 14:6; 16:13; 8:32.)

In order to be freed from the bondage of legalism, we need to realize that we are totally accepted *by* God and totally acceptable *to* God *in Christ*. To be *in Christ* means that our souls are in union with God. Christians are described throughout the New Testament as being alive *in Christ*. Everything that we are and everything that we have as Christians comes because we are *in Christ*. God's Word says that "He made us accepted *in the Beloved* [Christ]" (Ephesians 1:6 NKJV).

We have listed below some of the lies that those trapped in legalism often believe. We have also listed some of the possible reasons (causes) why you have believed those lies, as well as some of the probable results in your life. Later in this process you will have the opportunity to confess any sinful results in your life, as well as forgive people who contributed to your being trapped in legalism.

Lies, Their Causes, and Their Results

Lie: "I can't do anything right, and my best is not good enough."
Cause: continual criticism and put-downs
Results: instability, indecision, vacillation, irresponsibility, critical or judgmental spirit

Lie: "I must measure up to a certain standard to be a valuable person."
Cause: living under a system of "performance-based acceptance"
Results: perfectionism, drivenness, anxiety, insecurity

Lie: "I'm unlovable and have no worth. I'm unattractive and unwanted."
Cause: receiving little or no affection or healthy physical touch
Results: withdrawing from people, or using my body to get attention and affection

Lie: "I am guilty, evil, or dirty."
Cause: physical, verbal, emotional, sexual abuse
Results: trying desperately to alleviate guilt, or living in accordance with the lie (sexual promiscuity, substance abuse, criminal or deviant behavior)

Lie: "I am not important or wanted."
Cause: being ignored or rejected
Results: trying hard to please, dropping out, acting out to gain attention; anger, rage, bitterness, depression

Lie: "I am incompetent, inadequate, weak, or untrustworthy."
Cause: overprotection or smothering
Results: perfectionism, fear, feelings of inadequacy

Lie: "I *am* (the negative names) they are calling me
or I call myself."
Cause: cursing and name-calling
Results: self-hatred, inferiority, attacking others

Lie: "I am (we are) better than others."
Cause: repeatedly hearing others "different from us"
being put down
Results: boasting, arrogance, putting others down, separatism, self-righteousness

Below is a suggested prayer to renounce the lies that you
have believed about yourself as a result of being under a legalistic system. Again, we want you to feel the freedom to pray
from your heart about these issues. Take as much time as you
need. As you come to grips with how these lies have governed
so much of your life for so long, it may be very emotional for
you. Don't feel like you have to maintain emotional control
during this time. Allow the emotions and feelings to surface,
expressing and releasing them to the Lord in prayer. The Lord
is a safe place for you.

Following the prayer is a list of truth affirmations for you
to verbally announce. Accompanying those truths are Scripture references for you to study further, so that over time you
will no longer be conformed to the world's lies but transformed through the renewing of the mind (Romans 12:2). We
pray, and we trust God, that this will be a healing time for you.

Prayer to Renounce Lies

*Dear heavenly Father, I thank You for showing me the
lies I have believed about myself and my life. I can see how
devastating they have been to me, and I can see the harmful
behaviors that have resulted in my life. I renounce the lie
that (state the lie or lies you have believed). I confess I have
believed all these things that are contrary to Your truth, and
I thank You for Your total forgiveness and cleansing
according to 1 John 1:9. In Jesus' name I pray, amen.*

Affirmations of Truth: Who I Am in Christ

I am deeply loved by God the Father:

John 17:23 *The Father loves me as much as He loves Jesus*

Ephesians 1:6 *The Father accepts me in Christ, just as I am*

Ephesians 1:7-8 *The Father has lavished His grace upon me*

1 Corinthians 6:20 *The Father purchased me with the blood of His Son*

1 John 3:1 *The Father has poured out His love on me*

Ephesians 2:10 *I am my Father's workmanship, His "poem"*

Zechariah 2:8 *I am the apple of my Father's eye*

I am safe and secure in Christ:

John 15:5 *I am connected to Jesus like a branch to the vine*

John 10:27-30 *I am protected, held in Jesus' and the Father's hands*

2 Corinthians 5:21 *I am the righteousness of God in Christ, therefore in Him I do measure up!*

Romans 15:7 *I am accepted in Christ to the glory of God*

Romans 6:3-4 *I died with Christ to the rule of sin and have been raised up to live a new life*

Romans 7:4 *I died to the law through the body of Christ*

Hebrews 13:5 *I will never be deserted or forsaken by Christ*

I am indwelt by the Holy Spirit, who is my strength:

1 Corinthians 6:19 *I am the temple of the Holy Spirit, who was given to me by my Father*

Ephesians 1:13   *I am sealed by the Spirit, who was given to me as a pledge of my full inheritance in Christ*

Romans 8:14-15   *I am led by the Spirit of adoption and am no longer a slave to fear; He enables me to cry out "Abba! Father!"*

1 Corinthians 12:13   *I have been baptized by the Holy Spirit and placed into the body of Christ as a full member*

1 Corinthians 12:4   *I have been given spiritual gift(s) by the Holy Spirit*

Ephesians 5:18   *I can be filled with the Holy Spirit instead of leaning on substances to empower me*

Galatians 5:16-18   *I can walk by the Spirit instead of giving in to the lusts of my flesh*

The Truth About God Our Father

When we are bound up in legalism, it is inevitable that we develop a distorted view of who God is, especially in His relationship with us. The following exercise is designed so that you can renounce *out loud* the lies you may have believed about Him, as well as affirm the truth about His character. Next to the truths there are Scripture references for you to look up. We heartily encourage you to do so, especially for those aspects of God's character that are hard for you to believe are true. Meditation upon the truths of who God is can be one of the most important aspects of your freedom and healing in Christ.

We encourage you to work down the columns from left to right, prefacing each phrase on the left with "I renounce the lie that God my Father is…" and prefacing each phrase on the right with "I receive the truth that God my Father is…"

I renounce the lie that God my Father is...	I receive the truth that God my Father is...
distant and disinterested	intimate and involved (Psalm 139:1-18)
insensitive and uncaring	kind and compassionate (Psalm 103:8-14)
stern and demanding, like a taskmaster	accepting and filled with joy and love for me (Romans 15:7; Zephaniah 3:17)
passive and cold	warm and affectionate (Isaiah 40:11; Hosea 11:3-4)
absent or too busy for me	always with me and delighted to be with me (Hebrews 13:5; Jeremiah 31:20; Ezekiel 34:11-16)
never satisfied with what I do, impatient, or angry	patient and slow to anger (Exodus 34:6; 2 Peter 3:9)
mean, cruel, or abusive	loving, gentle, and protective of me (Jeremiah 31:3; Isaiah 42:3; Psalm 18:2)
trying to take all the fun out of life	trustworthy, and wants to give me a full life; His will is good, acceptable, and perfect for me (Lamentations 3:22-23; John 10:10; Romans 12:1-2)

controlling or manipulative	full of grace and mercy, giving me freedom to fail (Hebrews 4:15-16; Luke 15:11-16)
condemning or unforgiving	tenderhearted and forgiving, with His heart and arms always open to me (Psalm 130:1-4; Luke 15:17-24)
nit-picking, exacting, or perfectionistic	committed to my growth, and proud of me as His growing child (Romans 8:28-29; Hebrews 12:5-11; 2 Corinthians 7:4)

I am the apple of God's eye! (Deuteronomy 32:9-10)

As you work through this chart, you may become aware of some deep-seated misperceptions of God. You may find it helpful to take plenty of time and unhurriedly pray through those issues. The following testimony was written by a godly woman who did just that:

> This exercise made an enormous impact on my life. The renunciations and affirmations about God my Father were such a precious, priceless, and powerful process to refocus and empower my life. It certainly clarified my thinking and cleared out the cobwebs. Burdens were lifted, and I felt like I could just "cut my suspenders and float away." When I initially went through the first four sets of statements I was impressed to go back and start again at the top and do some serious "heart work." While I was going back over the list, I found that it reached my emotional and intellectual core. I started sobbing

with gratitude and praise to the Lord for such a
healing process. It is an enormously practical tool
that can provide deep, healing medicine—because
it's the truth that sets us free.

The following prayer may help you process these truths at
a deeper level. Let it be a springboard into your own time of
opening your heart honestly to the Lord. It is not the words,
but the heart behind the words, that is most important.

*Dear heavenly Father, I confess and repent of believing the
lie(s) that You are (list the specific lies you have believed). I
thank You for Your gracious and merciful forgiveness. I choose
to believe the truth(s) that You are (list the corresponding
truths). In light of those truths, please change the way I worship, pray, live, and serve, empowering me now by the fullness of the Holy Spirit. In Jesus' name I pray, amen.*

Step 2: Confessing Sins

When we believe lies about ourselves, God, and others, it
is inevitable that we commit sin. Sin is "missing the mark," or
falling short of God's glory in our lives (Romans 3:23).
Though the wages of sin is death, "the free gift of God is
eternal life in Christ Jesus our Lord" (Romans 6:23)! For
believers, there is no condemnation (Romans 8:1). We are to
confess our sins (agree with God concerning them)—and as
we do, we experience His forgiveness and cleansing (1 John
1:9).

Below we have categorized some sins into areas of fleshly
weakness that are typical of people caught in legalism. (There
are many other sins of the flesh—see, for example, Galatians
5:19-21; Ephesians 4:25-32; Mark 7:20-23—and you may
want to consult these Scriptures in order to experience a fuller
cleansing.) Following the opening prayer and lists of sins,

there is a model prayer of confession that we encourage you to pray out loud from your heart.

To ask the Lord to reveal to you the sins you need to confess, begin by praying the following prayer:

> *Dear heavenly Father, You have told me to "put on the Lord Jesus Christ, and make no provision for the flesh in regard to its lusts." I confess that I have often given in to fleshly lusts that wage war against my soul. I thank You that in Christ my sins are already forgiven, but I acknowledge that I have broken Your holy law and given the devil a chance to wage war in my body. I come to You now to confess and renounce these sins of the flesh so that I might be cleansed and set free from the bondage of sin. Please reveal to my mind the sins of the flesh I have committed and the ways I have grieved the Holy Spirit. In Jesus' holy name I pray, amen.*
> (See Romans 13:14; 1 Peter 2:11; Romans 6:12-13; James 4:1; 1 Peter 5:8; Proverbs 28:13 NIV; 2 Corinthians 4:2.)

Categories of Sin

Performance:

❏ Trying to keep God's commands in order to earn His acceptance or favor

❏ Trying to keep God's commands in my own strength

❏ Trying to measure up to the standards of others in order to be accepted

❏ Being driven to work harder and harder in order to succeed

❏ Feeling like achievement is the means of gaining personal happiness and a sense of worth

❏ Centering my life around keeping laws rather than knowing the Lord

Perfectionism:

❑ Living in the fear of failure

❑ Being afraid of going to hell because I have not kept God's laws perfectly

❑ Being unable to accept God's grace because I think I need to be punished (even though Jesus said my sins were "paid in full" on the cross!)

❑ Being obsessed with doing everything perfectly and keeping things in exact order

❑ Sweating the small stuff

❑ Having unreasonable expectations of perfection in others

❑ Being angry at others when they disrupt my neatly controlled world

❑ Punishing others when they are not perfect

❑ Being unable to experience joy and satisfaction in life unless something I do is absolutely perfect

Pride and Prejudice:

❑ Thinking that I am more spiritual, devoted, humble, or devout than others

❑ Thinking that my church, denomination, or group is better than others

❑ Not being willing to associate with others who are different (having an independent, separatist, or isolationist spirit)

❑ Elevating religious opinions (for example, which translation of the Bible to use) to the level of inflexible convictions

❑ Not being willing to soften religious opinions in order to promote love, peace, and unity among true brothers and sisters in Christ

❑ Finding it hard to admit that I am wrong, and feeling that I always have to be right and prove to others I am right

❑ Bigotry against those of other races and other economic and social groups

Picking Apart (Judgmentalism):

❑ Having a critical spirit toward worship styles, music, sermons, other people's clothes, and so on; always being quick to criticize and critique

❑ Judging others (impugning their motives and character)

❑ Demeaning ministers and other Christian leaders (either my own or those of other churches and organizations)

❑ Intolerance of anyone who differs (unwillingness to listen to them on the radio or TV, unwillingness to read their books, and so on)

❑ Guilt-by-association thinking

❑ Labeling of others, placing them into religious categories, and writing them off

Persistence (Unhealthy):

❑ Being rigid in beliefs in which sincere Christians disagree

❑ Clinging to traditions in church that are not Bible-based and that are not conducive toward reaching the current generation with the gospel

❑ Stubbornness and resistance to innovation by church leaders

❑ Close-mindedness; being unwilling to even listen to new ideas

Power and Domination:

❑ Using guilt and shame tactics to get others to do what I want

❑ Expecting or demanding that others attend every church service, be at every church function, and so on

❑ Controlling others by means of strong personality, overbearing persuasion, fear, or intimidation

❑ Experiencing strong anxiety when I am not able to be in control

❑ Finding security in rules, regulations, and standards rather than in the Lord

❑ Being more concerned about controlling others than developing self-control

❑ Being driven to attain powerful positions in order to gain control and accomplish my agenda

❑ Feeling unhealthy responsibility for the lives and well-being of others

Pleasureless Living:

❑ Living a joyless life of duty and obligation

❑ Feeling guilty for experiencing pleasure or being secretive in pursuing it

❑ Being unable to rest and relax

❑ Suffering from workaholism

❑ Being strongly attracted to (or giving in to) illegal substances, illicit sex, pornography, and so on in order to escape or find some gratification

❑ Feeling and living as if pain, suffering, deprivation, and self-abusement were more spiritual than enjoying the good things God has given me

As the Spirit of God reveals these (and any other) sins of the flesh to you, confess and renounce them by praying the following prayer out loud from your heart:

> *Dear heavenly Father, I confess that I have sinned by (name the sins of the flesh). I agree that these attitudes and actions are not proper for a child of Yours, therefore I renounce them all. I thank You for Your forgiveness, and I now yield myself to the Holy Spirit's filling so that I might become more like Christ. I choose to allow You to develop the fruit of the Spirit in my life, which is "love, joy, peace, patience, kindness, goodness, faithfulness, gentleness, self-control." In Jesus' holy name I pray, amen.*
>
> (See Galatians 5:22-23.)

Step 3: Forgiveness

It is a very human thing to experience anger toward those who have caused us pain. This is especially true when those people we expected and needed to model and teach us love, grace, and acceptance did not do so. The hurt we feel in our lives because of the physical, verbal, emotional, sexual, and spiritual abuse we have suffered can be devastating.

Though we cannot turn the clock back and reverse the wrongs done to us, we can be free from their hold over our lives. Jesus Christ can enter those wounded places and begin to heal the damage done to our souls. That healing begins when we make a choice to forgive from our hearts.

The apostle Paul writes, "Let all bitterness and wrath and anger and clamor and slander be put away from you, along with all malice. Be kind to one another, tender-hearted, forgiving each other, just as God in Christ also has forgiven you" (Ephesians 4:31-32).

Christ forgave us when He took the *eternal* consequences of our sins upon Himself. When we forgive others, we are agreeing to live with the *temporary* consequences of their sin. It seems unfair, but the only real choice we have is between the bondage of bitterness or the freedom of forgiveness.

To forgive means to choose not to hold someone's sin against them any more. It means canceling the debt and letting them off your hook, though knowing they are not off God's hook. It is choosing to release the person and what they did into God's hands, trusting Him to deal with that person justly—something you are simply not able to do. It is believing that Jesus died for the sin of the person who sinned against you. And it is relinquishing the right to seek revenge.

Forgiveness means you accept that what was done to you by the offender is an unalterable fact of life, one that comes from living in a fallen world. It involves recognizing that holding on to your anger hurts *you* the most, so forgiveness is necessary for your freedom.

Forgiving from the Heart

Don't you want to stop the pain? Don't you want Jesus' healing touch in your life? Then you need to forgive from the heart. To forgive from the heart means you mean what you say and mean what you pray. How do you come to that point of sincerity? By acknowledging the hurt and the hate you feel. Then remember that you were not deserving of God's forgiveness either, but He freely gave it to you through Christ. It is experiencing God's forgiveness in your own life that frees you to forgive others.

Forgiving someone from the heart means that you are honest with God and yourself about how the offense(s) made you feel. You allow Jesus to bring to surface the feelings that you have held inside so that He can begin to heal you.

If you have lived all or part of your life under a legalistic system, there are people associated with that whom you need to forgive. In addition, there may be others who have hurt you as well. Begin this crucial step by praying the following prayer from your heart:

> *Dear heavenly Father, I thank You for the riches of Your kindness, forbearance, and patience toward me, knowing that Your kindness has led me to repentance. I confess that I have not shown that same kindness and patience toward those who have hurt me. Instead I have held on to my anger, bitterness, and resentment toward them. I realize, too, that at times I have been hard on myself, being unwilling to forgive myself and living with a burden of regret. Please bring to my mind all the people I need to forgive in order that I may do so now. In Jesus' name I pray, amen.*
>
> (See Romans 2:4.)

Making the Choice

The need to forgive others is huge—but for some people, the need to forgive themselves can be even bigger. To forgive yourself means simply that you accept once and for all God's forgiveness—the forgiveness that is already yours in Christ. It is realizing that beating yourself up for past sins, mistakes, and imperfections only makes things worse. Only Christ's shed blood can cleanse us. By punishing ourselves we are trying to add to that which Christ already suffered for us—but that is futile. How can we possibly add anything to that which Christ declared complete ("finished") when He died on the cross?

Jesus paid the penalty so that we ourselves, as well as others, don't have to pay it. That is grace.

You may wish that others would come and apologize to you before you forgive them. That would be nice. However, many—perhaps most—won't. Some may not be able to, having passed out of your life by now. But your freedom simply cannot be dependent upon what others do or don't do.

Freedom comes through forgiveness, and forgiveness is a choice that you can make today. Don't wait till you feel like forgiving—you may never get there. Forgiveness is the right thing to do, regardless of how you feel. Once you make the choice to forgive, however, your emotions can begin to heal. *Freedom* is what you will gain today—not necessarily an immediate change in feelings.

A Process for Forgiveness

We encourage you to make a complete list (by name, whenever possible) of all the people the Lord brings to your mind whom you need to forgive. To guide you, here are some suggestions:

❑ Parents and other family members who abused me in any way, or who caused me to believe I was worthless, unlovable, or valuable only when I "performed well"

❑ Ministers and other church leaders who hurt me by fostering a law-based rather than grace-based church environment

❑ Schoolteachers or school officials who were harsh, critical, or legalistic

❑ People who stifled the free expression of grace or spiritual liberty in my life and who forced me to conform to legalistic standards

❑ Others whom the Lord is bringing to mind: ones who were used by the enemy to rob me of joy and freedom, including any perpetrators of abuse or neglect

❑ Myself: for leading my family into legalism; for leading my church into or influencing my church toward legalism; for attacking those teaching freedom and grace; for being hurtful, hateful, critical, or judgmental toward family, friends, others; for robbing others of freedom and joy by my attitudes, words, and actions

As you are giving the Lord free rein to bring the hurt in your heart to the surface, we encourage you to use the prayer below as a beginning point in choosing to forgive those on your list. Don't rush through this process. Some of your memories may be very painful. You may need to talk things out with the Lord for a while. You may even be angry with Him. If so, tell Him how you feel, but make the choice to release your anger, knowing that He truly does all things well (Mark 7:37). You may not understand why He has allowed certain things in your life. In fact, it may be impossible to fully understand all the reasons this side of heaven, but you can make the choice to trust Him today because He "is good to all, and His mercies are over all His works" (Psalm 145:9).

Start with the first person on your list, forgiving him or her for all the painful memories the Lord brings to your mind. Once you can't think of anything else to forgive that person for, move on to the next person, and so on down your list. Take as much time as you need.

Prayer for Granting Forgiveness

> *Dear heavenly Father, I choose to forgive (say the person's name) for (be specific in what the person did), which made me feel (be honest in expressing how you felt or still feel).*

Once you have forgiven someone on your list (and if they are still alive), pray the prayer of blessing (see below) over them. Jesus said, "I say to you who hear, love your enemies, do good to those who hate you, bless those who curse you, pray for those who mistreat you" (Luke 6:27-28). When you can pray for someone to be blessed and mean it from your heart, you have truly forgiven.

Prayer for Blessing

Dear heavenly Father, I choose not to hold any of these things against (name) any longer. I thank You for setting me free from the bondage of my bitterness toward (name). I now ask You to bless (name). In Jesus' name I pray, amen.

A Final Word About Forgiveness

Perhaps the Lord has reminded you of some people that *you* have hurt. Perhaps these people have held a grudge against you because of the suffering you have caused in their lives. According to Matthew 5:23-24 you need to approach those people humbly and gently and ask them to forgive you for what you have done to them. As you go, be specific in spelling out your wrongs and say something like, "Will you please forgive me? I am so sorry." Then wait for them to respond. If they have hurt you as well, make sure you have forgiven them before you go to them, but do not go expecting any apology on their part. If they refuse to forgive you, you are still free because the Scripture says, "If possible, so far as it depends on you, be at peace with all men" (Romans 12:18). Sometimes being at peace doesn't depend on you. If, however, reconciliation takes place, then God be praised!

Step 4: Fearing People Versus Fearing God

Proverbs 29:25 says, "The fear of man brings a snare, but he who trusts in the LORD will be exalted." *Fearing* man ultimately leads to *pleasing* people—and that indeed is a trap. People-pleasers find themselves more and more concerned about what others around them think, because they erroneously believe that their personal worth and happiness are dependent upon the acceptance or approval of others.

Paul wrote, "Am I now seeking the favor of men, or of God? Or am I striving to please men? If I were still trying to please men, I would not be a bond-servant of Christ" (Galatians 1:10). When we make it our goal to keep people happy, we end up becoming enslaved to them, and we remove ourselves from the safety and security of serving Christ alone.

Ultimately, we all must make the choice: *Will I fear people and thus try to please them, or will I fear (stand in awe of) God and seek to please Him?* If we choose to be people-pleasers, we will inevitably displease God. If we seek to please God, we will not please *all* people, but we *will* please the right ones.

In 2 Timothy 1:7, the apostle Paul admonished his disciple, Timothy: "God has not given us a spirit of fear ["timidity" NASB], but of power and of love and of a sound mind" (NKJV). Fear weakens us, it causes us to become self-centered, and it robs us of clear thinking. Fear can so overwhelm the "computer screen" of our mind that all we can focus on is the person or thing that frightens us. The fear of God is the fear that dispels all other fears. When we fear Him, He becomes a sanctuary (Isaiah 8:11-14).

To allow the Lord to examine your heart in this area, begin by praying this:

> *Dear heavenly Father, I know that I have not always walked by faith, but have allowed the fear of people to control me. I have been too concerned about gaining approval from others, and I have been led astray from a simple, pure devotion to Christ. I want to walk in a healthy fear and awe of You, Lord, and not of people. Thank You for Your forgiveness. I now ask You to bring to my mind the specific ways that I have allowed the fear of other people to control me. In Jesus' name I pray, amen.*

The Fear of People

❑ I have been afraid to say what I really think or feel for fear of being reprimanded, ridiculed, or rejected

❑ I have changed the clothes I wear, the makeup I put on, or the way I wear my hair to prevent people at church from scolding me

❑ I am afraid to say "no" when asked to do something, for fear of experiencing disapproval or anger

❑ I am often tired and on the verge of burnout because of my inability to say "no"

❑ I resent feeling "used," but I can't seem to bring myself to set healthy boundaries in my life

❑ I find myself easily intimidated by strong personalities who tell me I must do certain things in order to be pleasing to God

❑ I constantly need the affirmation of other people in order to feel happy or significant

❑ If I don't get the affirmation I feel I need from people, I can easily become discouraged or depressed

❑ I do not handle criticism well; it makes me feel like a failure

❑ I will do almost anything to gain the approval of important people in my life

❑ I make sure others know about the good things I have accomplished

❑ I have found myself lying in order to cover up things in my life that might result in disapproval from others

❑ I have been more concerned with following man-made traditions in our church than with obeying Scripture

❑ Other ways I have allowed the fear of others to control me:

Prayer of Confession

> *Dear heavenly Father, I realize now that much of my life has been lived in the fear of people, seeking to please them— rather than discerning and doing Your will. I realize that is sin. I specifically confess now the sins of (<u>list sins the Lord has revealed to you</u>). Thank You for Your gracious forgiveness. I ask You to strengthen me so that I will fear no one but You. Empower me by Your Spirit to learn what pleases You and to do it, regardless of what others might think. I thank You that You already love, accept, and approve of me so that I don't have to go looking for those things from people. It is nice when I get them, but let them be by-products of having pleased You first. In Jesus' name I pray, amen.*

Step 5: Surrendering Rights

It is a scary thing to think about surrendering all our "rights" and putting ourselves unreservedly into the hands of another—even God. For instance, if we are going to undergo surgery, we are required to sign a "consent form" before the procedure is done. This form gives the surgeon permission to do whatever he sees fit, regardless of the possible consequences. Such a total commitment requires serious thought.

When we are dealing with the Lord, we are being asked to commit to One who has already committed Himself to us— He has shown His love for us by giving His Beloved Son to die on the cross on our behalf. Do we truly believe that "He who did not spare His own Son, but delivered Him over for us all" will likewise freely give us all things (Romans 8:32)? To trust Him means to put our life, reputation, future, health, ministry, family, and everything else into His hands.

Paul urged the Roman believers to present their bodies as living and holy sacrifices to the Lord. He said that this was our "reasonable service" of worship in light of His great mercies (Romans 12:1 NKJV). Are you willing to do that?

In our nation, we are so focused on our "rights"—and we have made the "right to choose" a god. A bond-servant, however, surrenders all rights in order to serve his master. We are bond-servants of Christ, but we are also children of God—and He has promised that "all things belong to [us], and [we] belong to Christ; and Christ belongs to God" (1 Corinthians 3:22-23). When we lose (surrender) who we are in the natural order of this world, we find who we really are in Christ (Matthew 10:39).

In truth, we have only one right, and we *need* only one right: "As many as received Him, to them *He gave the right to become children of God,* even to those who believe in His name" (John 1:12).

To fully surrender ourselves into the hands of our loving, heavenly Father puts us in the place of complete security. The following exercise and prayer are designed to make this commitment real and personal for you.

Things to Surrender

I surrender "my rights" to...

❏ live life in my own strength

❏ rely on my own resources

❏ say what I want to say when I want to say it

❏ go where I want to go whenever I please

❏ live wherever I want to live

❏ have the kind of job I want to have

❏ have the kind of financial security I desire

❏ be single or be married

❏ have the number (and sex) of children I want to have

❏ have all of my children grow up and love the Lord

❑ be right all the time

❑ be always loved, accepted, and understood by people

❑ have the friends I want

❑ be used by God

❑ be in control or in charge

❑ have a good reputation

❑ know the will of God all the time

❑ be able to fix people and circumstances around me

❑ have good health

❑ be free from pain and suffering

❑ have the respect and support of people around me

❑ be always shielded from the abuse and neglect of others

❑ receive forgiveness from those I have hurt

❑ be spared heartache, crisis, and tragedy

❑ engage in sinful practices out of anger toward or in rebellion against those who have hurt me

❑ these other things the Lord is laying on my heart to surrender to Him:

Prayer of Surrender

Dear heavenly Father, in the past I have claimed all these "rights" as mine, but now I present myself to You as having been purchased by the precious blood of the Lord Jesus Christ. I am no longer my own. I appreciate Your giving me a choice to surrender these things to You. I choose to surrender all my selfish rights to You, the One who has loved me and given up

Your Son for me. While I accept my responsibility to follow Your good, acceptable, and perfect will for me by the power of the Holy Spirit, I also give You permission to do in me and through me whatever You desire and whatever will glorify You. In Jesus' name I pray, amen.

NAME _____ DATE _____

Final Affirmation

- *I affirm that it was for freedom that Christ set me free. I therefore choose to keep standing firm and to no longer be subject to the yoke of slavery to legalism.* (See Galatians 5:1.)

- *I affirm that, having begun by the Spirit, I am not being perfected by the flesh, but through the transforming power of the Spirit of liberty.* (See Galatians 3:3; 2 Corinthians 3:17-18.)

- *I affirm that, though the law served as my tutor to bring me to Christ, now that faith has come I am no longer under that tutor.* (See Galatians 3:24-25.)

- *I affirm that I am now an unconditionally loved, accepted, and secure child of God in Christ.* (See Galatians 3:26; Ephesians 1:6.)

- *I affirm that I am now dead to the law through the body of Christ and that I have been joined to the risen Christ in order to bear fruit for God.* (See Romans 7:4.)

- *I affirm that I am a bond-servant of Jesus Christ and that my life's purpose is to please Him, not others.* (See Galatians 1:10.)

- *I affirm that the Lord's word to me is now "grace to you and peace from God our Father and the Lord Jesus Christ."* (See Galatians 1:3.)

- *I affirm that God's strength is made perfect in my weakness and that His grace is sufficient for me.* (See 2 Corinthians 12:9.)

- *Therefore, I affirm that by the grace of God I am what I am and that by His grace I stand.* (See 1 Corinthians 15:10; Romans 5:2.)

...All to the praise of His glorious grace, which He freely bestowed on me in Christ. (See Ephesians 1:6.)

We trust the Holy Spirit that going through this chapter was, for you, a powerful experience of connecting with the Living God. In order to maintain your freedom, we encourage you to meditate often and joyfully upon the Scriptures mentioned in this chapter. Enjoy your relationship with God—He enjoys you! When the Spirit of God points out times when you are not living according to your new relationship with the Father, quickly confess your sin and enter again into the joy of your salvation.

Our final chapter will bring this journey to a close, as we find out how to relate to the commands in Scripture in a new way—as new creations in Christ living under the new covenant of grace in the new kingdom of God. What good news it is to know that "this is the love of God, that we keep His commandments; and His commandments are not burdensome" (1 John 5:3)!

12

NEW-KINGDOM LIVING

Jesus knew His time was short. The clock was already ticking toward the time when the darkness would have its opportunity, and there would be no more occasion to teach His disciples. He had spent three years with them, and yet there was still so much He wished to say, so much they needed to learn.

They were eager to serve in His kingdom, and they were full of questions.

In the upper room, Jesus poured out His heart—the Father's heart—to them about His second coming, His relationship with the Father, the Holy Spirit, and prayer. John—faithful John—leaned against Him drinking in every word, not missing a drop. Little did he know that one day he would share Jesus' words with the world, and that for thousands of years those words would bring supreme comfort and guidance to God's people.

But His disciples still hadn't really understood what the kingdom was all about, so before He taught with His lips, Jesus had a message to preach with His hands.

He looked at them with the deepest, purest love. It was the Father's love that had sent Him to earth in the first place, and it was the Father's love that was drawing Him back to heaven again. The Father had placed the future of those men and the future of all creation into Jesus' hands. The Father loved Him and trusted Him, and was ready for Him to finish His work and come home. Those joyful realities would be the food and drink that would sustain Jesus during the dreadful hours ahead.

The Last Supper was over. It was time for a sermon the twelve would never forget. It was to be a message they *must* never forget.

The Way of the Kingdom

As Jesus rose from the table, the men looked up, eagerly anticipating the words that would pour from their Lord's lips. But anticipation changed to confusion as Jesus removed His outer garments, stripped to a loincloth like a slave, and wrapped a long towel around His waist. The confusion turned to whispering disbelief as the Lord poured water into a basin and began to wash the dusty feet of the twelve.

Jesus knew from the stunned looks on the disciples' faces that this was a very hard thing for them to watch. Most of them were too numb to protest as He went from person to person, washing their feet and drying them with the ends of the towel that encircled His waist. Then He came to Peter.

Lord, what are You doing? This is not right. You should not be doing the work of a common slave!

"Peter, you can't understand right now what I'm doing to you, but one day you will" (John 13:7, paraphrased).

No, Lord! I forbid it. I will simply not allow You to wash my feet, ever! Peter quickly shifted his position, pulling his feet away from the hands of Jesus and tucking them safely against his body. The air was thick with tension as the others stared at the scene playing out in front of them.

The Lord answered quietly, gazing into the anguished eyes of Peter. "If I do not wash you, you have no part with Me" (John 13:8).

Peter's eyes widened, and then his face softened as he looked into the welcoming face of the Lord. There was nothing he wanted more than to be with Jesus and be a part of all He was doing. Before Jesus could pass him by, he blurted out, *Lord, then wash all of me! Bathe my hands and my head as well as my feet!* Jesus smiled with joy, and the whole room breathed a sigh of relief. The tension was broken. Peter shifted his position again and let the strong, gentle hands of the Master wash away the filth of the world from his feet.

Serving in Love

It is hard for us today to grasp the impact of this moment when Jesus showed His disciples the way of the kingdom, the way of serving others in love. He would soon show them the ultimate expression of love by laying down His life for them, His friends (John 15:13), something He would call all of His disciples to do as well (1 John 3:16). Jesus' kingdom way is the way of lowliness and humility that will stoop to everything and stop at nothing to meet the needs of others. That is what it means to follow our Lord. Jesus said, "You call Me Teacher and Lord; and you are right, for so I am. If I then, the Lord and the Teacher, washed your feet, you also ought to wash one another's feet" (John 13:14).

Jesus was ushering in a new kingdom, and before He went back to the Father, He was teaching His kingdom friends how they should live. In this new kingdom there would be a *new commandment,* a *new covenant,* and a *new commission*—all lived out by *new creations* in Christ! These three areas will be our final focus as we conclude our journey from legalism into liberty in Christ.

The New Commandment from Jesus

In the upper room, after Judas Iscariot had left to do his dirty work, Jesus again spoke of the disciples' relationship with "one another":

> A new commandment I give to you, that you
> love one another, even as I have loved you, that you
> also love one another. By this all men will know

that you are My disciples, if you have love for one
another (John 13:34-35).

This life of love was so crucial to kingdom living that Jesus
repeated this teaching a little while later:

> This is my commandment, that you love one
> another, just as I have loved you. Greater love has
> no one than this, that one lay down his life for his
> friends. You are my friends if you do what I com-
> mand you (John 15:12-14).

Jesus had said that He was giving us a *new commandment*.
What was the old commandment—and what made this one
new? An expert in the Law of Moses once asked the Lord,
"Teacher, which is the great commandment in the Law?"
Jesus replied,

> "You shall love the Lord your God with all
> your heart, and with all your soul, and with all your
> mind." This is the great and foremost command-
> ment. The second is like it, "You shall love your
> neighbor as yourself." On these two command-
> ments depend the whole Law and the Prophets
> (Matthew 22:36-40).

Jesus had gathered up all the hundreds of old-covenant
rules, regulations, and prophetic exhortations, tied them up in
a neat bundle, and summed them up by declaring that we are
to love God and people with all we have and all we are.

It's Impossible in the Flesh

When Jesus proclaimed a new commandment, He did not
change the first and greatest one. It remains. We are still to love
the Lord our God with all our heart and soul and mind. What
has changed is us! We have been given a new heart (Ezekiel
36:20). Our soul *(psuche*—also translated *spirit)* is new as well,
joined to God's Spirit (36:26-27). And we now have the mind

of Christ (1 Corinthians 2:16). Therefore, our capacity to love God is deeper and purer now that we are *in Christ.*

The second commandment, however, *has* changed. Jesus has raised the bar—He has moved this commandment totally out of the possibility of our fulfilling it in our own strength: "A new commandment I give to you, that you love one another, even as I have loved you, that you also love one another" (John 13:34).

The old commandment of loving your neighbor as yourself is still important. In fact, James writes, "If...you are fulfilling the royal law according to the Scripture, 'You shall love your neighbor as yourself,' you are doing well" (James 2:8). To show the same concern and to demonstrate the same care toward others that we do toward ourselves is a monumental leap out of selfishness and into godliness. It is a truly noble accomplishment, and it is very hard to do.

But to love others as Christ does? That is not simply hard—it's *impossible* for any of us to accomplish on our own. The level of Christ's love for us far exceeds the love we have even for ourselves. So, in order for us to fulfill this commandment, a new source of supernatural strength must be provided to us. That point is exactly what Jesus was trying to communicate in John 13–17. In his first epistle, John reinforces this:

> By this we know that we are in Him: the one who says he abides in Him ought himself to walk in the same manner as He walked.
>
> Beloved, I am not writing a new commandment to you, but an old commandment which you have had from the beginning; the old commandment is the word which you have heard. On the other hand, I am writing a new commandment to you, which is true *in Him and in you,* because the darkness is passing away and the true Light is already shining (1 John 2:5-8).

It's Possible in Him

The context of John's writing is loving our brothers. That we do so has always been the will of God, but now the *degree* of loving has changed, as has the *means* of doing so—as John indicated above: "I am writing a new commandment to you, which is true *in Him and in you.*" Now that we are new creations *in Christ,* we can love as Jesus loved. We can walk in the same manner as He walked...in the pure *agape* love of the Father. It is all possible because we who are believers are now alive *in Christ.*

When Jesus spoke about the vine and the branches (see John 15), He was not giving a horticultural lesson. He was illustrating the intimate connection that would exist between Himself and His people. "I am the vine, you are the branches; he who abides in Me and I in him, he bears much fruit, for apart from Me you can do nothing" (John 15:5). The fruit of the Spirit is, first and foremost, love (Galatians 5:22)!

In John 15:17 Jesus said again, "This I command you, that you love one another." How was He expecting the disciples to do this? By trying to keep the law in their own strength? By huffing and puffing their way into acceptable spiritual performance? Absolutely not! He was commanding them to do that which would only be possible through the supernatural union that would be theirs *in Christ.* It is His life, His love, and His character that abide within us.

Through this abiding relationship with Christ, like branches connected to the nourishing vine, we can ask whatever we wish and it will be done for us (John 15:7)—and that includes loving hard-to-love people.

The Supernatural Life of Love

While I (Rich) was ministering in the Philippines, I got to know a fellow Campus Crusade staff member named Tom Roxas (pronounced Ró-hahs). Tom was mature in Christ beyond his years, possessing a kindness, gentleness, and yet firm authority that I greatly admired. Such maturity had come at a painful price to him.

Tom's older brother, Ino, his childhood idol and mentor, had been brutally stabbed to death by the head of a ruthless crime syndicate in Manila. Ino had been monitoring the syndicate's operations and was about to go public with his knowledge. When the syndicate boss and his son fatally stabbed him in the abdomen and neck, it was broad daylight, with a stunned, paralyzed crowd looking on.

Ino left behind a wife and six young children, which was difficult enough, but the nightmare wasn't over. Syndicate members hurled death threats at another family member over the phone, in an effort to frighten the entire family into silence. For three months, Tom tried to win justice for his brother, only to find himself facing closed doors and a labyrinth of red tape.

At the funeral, however, God had begun to unfold His redemptive plan. Tom had the opportunity to preach the gospel of hope to an overflow crowd at a Baptist church. When the invitation was given, almost the entire group rose to receive Christ. A few weeks later, an even more amazing picture of the love of God took place:

> By an unexpected twist of Providence, the syndicate boss was arrested and detained, not for Ino's murder, but for some lesser charge. Tom, deeply burdened to share Christ with the man, found a Christian military officer who accompanied him to the killer's detention area. For some tense moments, before the military officer rejoined them, Tom sat alone face-to-face with the man who had slit his brother's throat. A wild thought occurred to Tom— what if the man should grab him and hold him hostage? The man in turn presumed Tom and his friend were police agents aiming to lynch him right there. Looking depressed and defeated, he confessed to his bone-weariness with his life and his

desire to die. He was in fact looking for a priest so he could make things right with his Creator. The Lord used the moment. Tom's defenses melted, and there was no bitterness, but rather a transcending compassion from God as he touched the man briefly, comfortingly, on the shoulder.[1]

Knowing that the syndicate boss had been deeply steeped in the occult, Tom's friend, the military officer, had fasted in preparation for their visit. As the two men shared the gospel, they sensed a thick oppression in the jail cell. While one would preach, the other would sing praises or rebuke the enemy. As the killer knelt to receive the Lord, he was flung back into a grotesque convulsion. The furniture in the room shook. But the prayers and preaching broke through:

> Suddenly the man gasped, "Jesus...save me!" With those words, his body was released and his countenance began to change and soften. He was free! Tom and his friend assured him that his sins were forgiven and evil spirits could no longer hold him. Gripped by the reality and new sensation of freedom, he jumped to his feet, prancing and clapping for joy like a child, praising God and commanding the spirits to leave him forever in the Name of Jesus.
>
> As they prepared to leave, the man asked for their names. The military officer introduced himself, then Tom Roxas. *"Roxas?!!"* the man gasped at the familiar family name, reeling back. "Yes, he's the brother of the man you killed," Tom's friend confirmed. Suddenly the man fell prostrate to the ground, his face to Tom's feet, sobbing, "Forgive me, forgive me!" Tom knelt, lifted him up, hugged him, saying, "Christ has forgiven me, and I also have forgiven you." In a rush of emotion, they hugged, sobbed for joy, praising God loudly.

Days later, Tom and his friend visited their new brother to assure him again of his salvation. "I couldn't look into your eyes previously," the man confessed of the upheaval in his conscience. "If I were in your place, my blood would boil with hate. Christ surely must be in you, for no man could forgive me as you have."[2]

Truly we can now do all things *through Christ* who strengthens us (Philippians 4:13)! Because Jesus fulfilled all the commandments of God (Matthew 5:17), *in Him* we can too! A life of love is the supernatural outflow and overflow of abiding in Christ and walking by the Spirit:

> The law of the Spirit of life in Christ Jesus has set you free from the law of sin and death. For what the Law could not do, weak as it was through the flesh, God did: sending His own Son in the likeness of sinful flesh and as an offering for sin, He condemned sin in the flesh, *so that the requirement of the Law might be fulfilled in us, who do not walk according to the flesh, but according to the Spirit* (Romans 8:1-4).

Scripture makes it clear that trying hard to obey God's commands in the energy of the flesh is futile. All that God requires of us in His Word happens in and through us supernaturally as we yield to the Holy Spirit's leading and filling.

A New Motivation for Obedience

In this new kingdom with the new commandment (of living in Jesus' love), there comes a whole new motivation for obedience. Rather than trying to obey God in our own strength to earn God's acceptance (which is legalism), we obey God in response to the acceptance and love we already have (which is liberty)!

Jesus said in John 14:15, "If you love me, you will obey what I command" (NIV). How does that sound to you? In what tone of voice do you hear Jesus saying that to you? How you answer those questions is a strong indicator of how much you understand or don't understand grace.

There are two basic ways you can picture Jesus saying those words. The first would be in a firm voice and with a stern expression—as a warning, almost a threat. It would be in the demeanor and tone of voice of an angry principal, parent, or teacher.

The second way you could picture Jesus would be with a smile on His face and joy in His voice. He would merely be stating the way things are—in the form of a basic "cause and effect" statement: "If you love Me...well, then you will just naturally obey what I command." One follows the other. Obedience is not a duty demanded by an angry master, but a delight birthed in the heart of a devoted follower!

Try saying John 14:15 both ways. Knowing Jesus, which way do you think He spoke those words?

Isn't it true that when you love and respect someone in authority over you, you delight to please them and follow their directions? Perhaps you can think of a parent or teacher or coach that you adored as a child or teen. Wasn't it almost unthinkable to disobey them, because they believed in you so much and were so committed to you?

That's how it is with Jesus—only a lot more so. Our obedience to the commands we find in the Scriptures becomes an expression of love back to Jesus. Having been touched by and filled with His love for us, we simply respond—our deep love is demonstrated by our obedience. And the fulfilling of those commands is now possible because we are in Christ and He is in us. It is *our decision* but *His strength* that makes obedience possible.

Grace Opens the Way

Are we saying then that we should obey God only when we *feel* love toward Him? Not at all. Ideally, we would always experience His love with our emotions, but realistically there are many times when we lose focus and fail to grasp "the breadth and length and height and depth" of the love of Christ (Ephesians 3:18-19). We question His love and balk at the prospect of doing what He says. In cases like that, John Piper offers sound advice:

> It is true that our hearts are often sluggish. We do not feel the depth or intensity of affections appropriate for God or his cause. It is true that at those times we must, inasmuch as it lies within us, exert our wills and make decisions that we hope will rekindle our joy. Though joyless love is not our aim ("God loves a cheerful giver!"), nevertheless it is better to do a joyless duty than not to do it, provided there is a spirit of repentance for the deadness of our hearts.
>
> I am often asked what a Christian should do if the cheerfulness of obedience is not there. It is a good question. My answer is not to simply get on with your duty because feelings are irrelevant! My answer has three steps. First, confess the sin of joylessness. Acknowledge the culpable coldness of your heart. Don't say it doesn't matter how you feel. Second, pray earnestly that God would restore the joy of obedience. Third, go ahead and do the outward dimension of your duty in the hope that the doing will rekindle the [inner] delight.[3]

This kind of obedience to the commands in God's Word is not legalism, it is an integral part of what it means to be a believer in Christ. Paul writes the following in his greeting to the Roman believers:

> Paul, a bond-servant of Christ Jesus...who was declared the Son of God with power by the resurrection from the dead, according to the Spirit of

> holiness, Jesus Christ our Lord, through whom we
> have received grace and apostleship to bring about
> the *obedience of faith* among all the Gentiles for
> His name's sake, among whom you also are the
> called of Jesus Christ; to all who are beloved of
> God in Rome, called as saints: Grace to you and
> peace from God our Father and the Lord Jesus
> Christ (Romans 1:1,4-7).

Obedience to God is not an abdication of grace. It is not "falling from grace." Grace *opens the way* for obedience because we are already accepted in Christ and beloved of God. Obedience flows from us, not as a means of gaining favor with Him, but as a means of expressing our gratitude for the favor we already have!

His Loving Protection

In addition, God's commands are not *restrictive,* they are *protective.* As John declared, "This is the love of God, that we keep His commandments; and His commandments are not burdensome" (1 John 5:3). The rules, regulations, standards, and expectations of a legalistic system *are* burdensome—because they carry with them guilt, shame, fear, and a drivenness to perform for or try to be accepted by God and people. It was just such a crushing religious system in Jesus' day that moved Him to cry out,

> Come to Me, all who are weary and heavy-
> laden, and I will give you rest. Take My yoke upon
> you and learn from Me, for I am gentle and
> humble in heart, and you will find rest for your
> souls. For My yoke is easy and My burden is light
> (Matthew 11:28-30).

Notice that Jesus did not say there was no yoke, just that His yoke was easy. As Bob Dylan sang years ago, "You gotta serve somebody." For 2000 years now Jesus has been offering a refreshing alternative to the heavy load of laboring under a yoke of slavery to the law. He, the gentle and humble One, is inviting us to walk with Him, learn from Him, and grow in obedience to Him. The yoke of slavery brings only exhaustion of spirit—Jesus' yoke brings rest to our souls.

His Love Makes Our Liberty Possible

We are inviting you to look at the Word of God with new eyes...to see the Scriptures as coming from the heart of our holy, loving heavenly Father, not from a hard-to-please task-master. They are designed to provide for us and protect us, not unfairly restrict our freedom. The distinction is vast—it is the difference between liberty and legalism.

A number of years ago I (Rich) bought a Siberian husky pup. Because he was a purebred and came with papers (not just newspapers!) I decided to name him Graywolf of the Brandy-wine. The AKC sent back word that he would be officially named Graywolf VIII. Well, within a few weeks he was just "Wolfie."

When Wolfie was really young, he was a lot of fun and pretty much stayed in the yard, where I was. As he grew toward adulthood, he decided that the entire subdivision was his yard and would not stay home.

In order to teach him that safety was near home, we put in an invisible fence around the yard. The system was controlled by a radio transmitter in our basement, which would send a signal to a wire buried at the property line. Wolfie wore a small battery-operated radio receiver on his collar. When he approached the edge of our property, his collar would receive the radio signal, and he would hear a beeping sound for two seconds. If he did not back off from the wire that was sending the radio signal, he would then receive a mild electrical jolt in the throat. It was nothing harmful—but it was definitely a shocking experience!

At first, Wolfie would think the beeping noise was an animal in the grass and would pounce with his paws, trying to catch it. Then he *would* "catch it" with a jolt and come yipping back toward the house. It made me sad to see him in pain, but I knew it was worth it to keep him safe.

After a while, he became so afraid of what was "out there" at the edge of the yard that he was fearful of venturing out from the house. We would open the door for him to go out and play...and he would slink around fearfully a foot or two away from the wall! I had to throw a ball out into the middle of the yard for him to chase so he could see that there was a lot of room for freedom! The invisible fence around the house was not restrictive, but protective. Even though Wolfie was mildly hurt when he strayed too close to the edge, he wasn't harmed. On the other side of the fence, however, there was something far more dangerous, even deadly—a street where cars could kill him.

God's commands are placed there by His love because He wants to protect us from the evils that await us in a fallen world ruled by a fallen angel. We may experience some mild pain by not getting to do something we think will be fun, but it is nothing compared to the harm that might come to us were we given no protective boundaries at all!

The apostle James, Jesus' brother, captured the heart of God's desire to bring liberty and blessing to our lives through obedience to His Word:

> The one who looks intently at the perfect law, the law of liberty, and abides by it, not having become a forgetful hearer but an effectual doer, this man will be blessed in what he does (James 1:25).

The New Covenant in Jesus

One of the amazing things about life in this new kingdom is that God has done more than just hand us a tablet with commands on it. He has placed His laws inside us, upon our hearts and minds. That is part of the *new covenant* that we have *in Christ.*

About 600 years before the birth of Jesus, the Lord spoke a revolutionary revelation through the mouth of the prophet Jeremiah:

> "Behold, days are coming," declares the LORD, "when I will make a new covenant with the house of Israel and with the house of Judah, not like the covenant which I made with their fathers in the day I took them by the hand to bring them out of the land of Egypt, My covenant which they broke, although I was a husband to them," declares the LORD. "But this is the covenant which I will make with the house of Israel after those days," declares the LORD, "I will put My law within them and on their heart I will write it; and I will be their God, and they shall be My people. They will not teach again, each man his neighbor and each man his brother, saying, 'Know the LORD,' for they will all know Me, from the least of them to the greatest of them," declares the LORD, "for I will forgive their iniquity, and their sin I will remember no more" (Jeremiah 31:31-34).

As the book of Hebrews points out, the old covenant of the Law of Moses was just a "shadow of the good things to come and not the very form of things" (10:1). The Law had come through Moses, but grace and truth came through Jesus Christ (John 1:17).

The Purpose of Law

What was the purpose of the Law under Moses? It was not designed by God to produce righteousness in its followers, but to *point out unrighteousness*. Paul points this out:

> While we were in the flesh, the sinful passions, which were aroused by the Law, were at work in the members of our body to bear fruit for death. But

> now we have been released from the Law, having died to that by which we were bound, so that we serve in newness of the Spirit and not in oldness of the letter.
>
> What shall we say then? Is the Law sin? May it never be! On the contrary, I would not have come to know sin except through the Law (Romans 7:5-7).

He also writes,

> We know that whatever the Law says, it speaks to those who are under the Law, so that every mouth may be closed and all the world may become accountable to God; because by the works of the Law no flesh will be justified in His sight; for through the Law comes the knowledge of sin (Romans 3:19-20).

That is the purpose of law, whether it is the Law of Moses or the laws of the land. Law shows you what the boundaries are—and going beyond those boundaries is sin (in the case of the law of God) or a crime or civil offense (in the case of human laws).

The Problem with Law

The problem with the law of God is not the law itself, for "the Law is holy, and the commandment is holy and righteous and good" (Romans 7:12). The problem lies with the weakness of human flesh (8:3). Because of the reality of sin within us, the law ends up arousing sinful desires so that we commit sin (7:8-11).

We have all seen that principle in action. How often do we have no interest in something until we are categorically forbidden to have it! Our daughter Emily recently received three stuffed animals as presents: a German shepherd, a Jack Russell terrier, and a rottweiler. But almost immediately after we informed her brother Luke that they were not his, but hers, he wanted them. When Emily climbed into bed, we would find them missing. Luke would have them in bed with him. We tried locking Emily's door, and that worked for a while...until Luke figured out how to unlock the door. Almost nightly Emily troops upstairs and reports, "Luke has one [or two, or all] of my stuffed animals." What are we going to do about this petty thievery? In order to catch Luke in the act (he doesn't understand discipline that is not immediately connected to the crime!), we may have to put some kind of alarm system in Emily's room.

Does the problem lie with our rule against theft? No, the problem lies with Luke's controlling flesh and his inability to resist temptation. It will be much easier when he enters into the new covenant in Christ and the law of God is written on his heart!

God's New Plan

Because of the futility of the first covenant, the covenant of law, to bring about righteousness, God declared that He would make a whole new covenant with His people. He would not just add something on top of the old way of relating to Him—He would do away with the old and replace it with something new and better. Speaking of the Lord Jesus, the author of Hebrews wrote,

> He has obtained a more excellent ministry, by as much as He is also the mediator of a better covenant, which has been enacted on better promises. For if that first covenant had been faultless, there would have been no occasion sought for a second.
> ...When He said, "A new covenant," He has made the first obsolete. But whatever is becoming obsolete and growing old is ready to disappear (Hebrews 8:7-8,13).

The main distinction between the old covenant and the new is that the old primarily involved the external *performance* of people under the law, while the new is grounded in people's inner *transformation* in Christ by grace through faith. It is the difference between what we do "for God"—and what God has already done for us. In his introduction to the book of Hebrews, Eugene Peterson wrote,

> It seems odd to have to say so, but too much religion is a bad thing. We can't get too much of God, can't get too much faith and obedience, can't get too much love and worship. But *religion*—the well-intentioned efforts we make to "get it all together" for God—can very well get in the way of what God is doing for us. The main and central action is everywhere and always *what God has done, is doing, and will do for us.* Jesus is the revelation of that action. Our main and central task is to live in responsive obedience to God's action revealed in Jesus. Our part in the action is the act of faith. But more often than not we become impatiently self-important along the way and decide to [try to] improve matters with our two cents' worth. We add on, we supplement, we embellish. But instead of improving on the purity and simplicity of Jesus, we dilute the purity, clutter the simplicity. We become fussily religious, or anxiously religious. We get in the way.[4]

It's All About Him

It may sound simplistic, but it is profoundly true that life in the new covenant is *Jesus*. He is the "Alpha and Omega" (Revelation 1:8), the "first and the last" (1:17). It is Jesus who is the mediator of a better covenant (Hebrews 8:6). It is Jesus who always lives to make intercession for us (7:25). It is Jesus who is able to save forever those who draw near to God through Him (7:25). It is Jesus who offered Himself as a sacrifice for sins once for all time (10:12). It is Jesus who has sanctified us to God through the offering of His body (10:10). It is Jesus who has opened up a new and living way into the presence of God so that we have confidence to enter the most holy place through His blood (10:19-20).

It is Jesus!

What a difference Jesus makes! Instead of cowering among the bushes of the Garden in guilt, we can draw near to the throne of grace with great confidence (Hebrews 4:16)! No longer do we need to try desperately to keep rules, regulations, laws, and commandments to gain God's favor—He has already accepted us as we are in Christ and has imprinted His word and will on our minds and hearts (10:16). Instead of having to wait once a year for the high priest to enter the Holy of Holies (9:7), we *are* the Holy of Holies in Christ (1 Corinthians 6:19-20).

In light of this life we have under the new covenant, we encourage you to do what Scripture exhorts you to do. *Draw near.* "We can draw near with a sincere heart in full assurance of faith, having our hearts sprinkled clean from an evil conscience and our bodies washed with pure water" (Hebrews 10:22). *Draw near.* "Draw near to God and He will draw near to you" (James 4:8).

Fix your eyes on Jesus (Hebrews 12:2). Seek His face (Psalm 27:8). Make your aim like King David's: "One thing I have asked from the LORD, that I shall seek: that I may dwell in the house of the LORD all the days of my life, to behold the beauty of the LORD, and to meditate in His temple" (Psalm 27:4).

Don't worry about what to do while spending time with the Lord. Let Him lead you. Don't be concerned about things like "how much I should read" or "how long I should pray." Remember "g–u–i–dance"? Let Jesus lead the dance.

The Spirit of Jesus Brings Freedom

It may take a little time to overcome some old habits and awkwardness, but relax, and don't give up. Sometimes you'll feel like you're making progress—other times you won't. But that's okay—we're no longer under law, but under grace (Romans 6:14). The following testimony will encourage you that new-kingdom living *is* a journey.

I've had great struggles (and continue to do so) with "quiet times." I love God, and once knew a time where to take time out to pray and be with the Lord was such a delight. I have been very sensitive, and if I hear a preacher saying "Come on, pray more," I immediately feel guilty. More recently, I have become so tense when praying, feeling that I ought to be doing things better. Sometimes this leads into such times of striving...an hour can pass of fruitless prayer, and I feel guilty. This impacts my relationship with my wife. Also, if my prayer time is too late or not focused on praying for others enough, then I feel very low. Then the precious time is ruined. The problem is that sometimes when I decide to try to relax a bit and find time later or tomorrow to pray, the day is awful!

It's not always like this. I still have times when it's just me and God, heart to heart. I'm slowly learning that my relationship with God is unique and that I have a *24-hour* relationship with Him where I can pray. It's not just in the "quiet time." Jesus went up into the hills, led a busy life, yet His relationship wasn't "between 7 and 8 A.M." Oh, how I'd love to know how to break out of this! Sometimes I get stuck between legalism and license (though I fear I walk more in legalism, out of fear of falling). But what I need is the freedom of the Spirit!

This man is right. That's what we all need: the freedom of the Holy Spirit. "Where the Spirit of the Lord is, there is liberty" (2 Corinthians 3:17). Do not be afraid of the Spirit of God. He is the Spirit of Jesus, God's Son "sent forth...into our hearts, crying, 'Abba! Father!'" (Galatians 4:6). The Holy Spirit is "another Helper," a Helper just like Jesus (John 14:16). He is the Spirit of truth, who has come to "guide you into all the truth" (John 16:13).

Moving from a life of legalism (which is just our own "spin" on living life under the old covenant) to life in the new covenant is like leaving a calm but stagnant harbor and venturing out to sea. It may seem scary—however, ships were not made to lie at dock, but to sail. Even though the wind blows hard out on the open water, Jesus is at the helm, and so there is no need to fear. The wind is the Spirit, and the Spirit of Christ and Christ Himself always work in perfect harmony.

In fact, the Spirit alone is the source of all fruitful ministry, as Paul made clear in 2 Corinthians 3:5-6:

> Not that we are adequate in ourselves to consider anything as coming from ourselves, but our adequacy is from God, who also made us adequate as servants of a new covenant, not of the letter but of the Spirit; for the letter kills, but the Spirit gives life.

Freedom was never meant to be hoarded. It should be *heralded!* Jesus Himself said, "You will receive power when the Holy Spirit has come upon you; and you shall be My witnesses both in Jerusalem, and in all Judea and Samaria, and even to the remotest part of the earth" (Acts 1:8).

The New Commission from Jesus

Living in the light of the *new covenant* and keeping the *new commandment* opens the doors for us to fulfill the *new commission* (which many have called the "Great Commission"):

> All authority has been given to Me in heaven and on earth. Go therefore and make disciples of

all the nations, baptizing them in the name of the
Father and the Son and the Holy Spirit, teaching
them to observe all that I commanded you; and lo,
I am with you always, even to the end of the age"
(Jesus, in Matthew 28:18-20).

The doors of heaven have been flung wide open to everyone. The four living creatures and the twenty-four elders,
falling down before the Lamb, sang a new song about this
new commission:

Worthy are You to take the book and to break
its seals; for You were slain, and purchased for God
with Your blood men from every tribe and tongue
and people and nation. You have made them to be
a kingdom and priests to our God; and they will
reign upon the earth (Revelation 5:9-10).

God is no "respecter of persons" (Acts 10:34 KJV), "but in
every nation the man who fears Him, and does what is right
is welcome to Him" (10:35). Native American, African-
American, Hispanic, Slavic, Asian, Caucasian, rich, poor,
male, female, old, young, single, divorced, married, widowed,
orphaned, unemployed, on welfare, in prison, homeless, drug
addict, alcoholic, homosexual, abused, abuser, and legalist—
Jesus loves them *all*, and all need to hear His gospel.

Every Part of Christ's Body Has a Role

In the kingdom of God there is no place for isolationism,
separatism, or favoritism. There is no room for prejudice or
bigotry. Jesus died for all, and we are commanded to go to all
for His sake:

If anyone is in Christ, he is a new creature; the
old things passed away; behold, new things have
come. Now all these things are from God, who
reconciled us to Himself through Christ and gave

us the ministry of reconciliation, namely that God was in Christ reconciling the world to Himself, not counting their trespasses against them, and He has committed to us the word of reconciliation.

Therefore, we are ambassadors for Christ, as though God were making an appeal through us; we beg you on behalf of Christ, be reconciled to God. He made Him who knew no sin to be sin on our behalf, so that we might become the righteousness of God in Him (2 Corinthians 5:17-21).

Billions stand this day outside of the kingdom of God, with no hope apart from Jesus. The task is too great, the call is too urgent, and the stakes are too high for true believers in Christ to be separate from one another anymore. We're not calling for a dissolving of denominations, but a unity of diversity. This has nothing to do with a liberal agenda of ecumenism—rather, it has everything to do with biblical unity in Christ.

Every part of the body of Christ has something uniquely significant to contribute to the proper functioning of the whole. A divided body of Christ, however, is tragically crippled in its efforts to see His new commission fulfilled in this or any generation. We need each other! Whatever your doctrinal or denominational preference, we are one body in Christ. We are family—brothers and sisters in Christ. Isn't it time to stop fighting the wrong war? There have already been far too many casualties from religious "friendly fire." Didn't Paul write that our struggle is *not* against flesh and blood (Ephesians 6:12)? So long as we continue our family feuds, the god of this world will continue to blind the "minds of the unbelieving so that they might not see the light of the gospel of the glory of Christ, who is the image of God" (2 Corinthians 4:4).

The Glory of Our Unity in the Spirit

All born-again followers of Christ, whether they be Pentecostal, Reformed, dispensational, Orthodox, fundamentalist, socially active, charismatic, Catholic, evangelical, mainline, liturgical, and so on, are already one in Him. We are not called to *create* unity but to "*preserve* the unity of the Spirit in the bond of peace" (Ephesians 4:3). The world has yet to see what would happen if the body of Christ laid aside all hostility, bitterness, resentment, suspicion, mistrust, and competitive-spiritedness for the sake of the gospel. But Jesus told us what would happen:

> I do not ask on behalf of these alone, but for those also who believe in Me through their word; that they may all be one; even as You, Father, are in Me and I in You, that they also may be in Us, so that the world may believe that You sent Me (John 17:20-21).

What would happen? A flooding of souls into the kingdom of God such as the church has never seen before. We're certainly not there yet, but there are places where this *is* beginning to happen. The trickle of living water from the throne of God will become ankle-deep, then knee-deep, then waist-deep. Then we will all be caught up in its current as the good news flows like a flood around the world, bringing the fresh water of life to thirsty souls (Ezekiel 47:1-10).

And everywhere the water flows, there will be life (47:9).

A Love Story of His Grace

We could be one immense step closer to fulfilling the new commission if each of us made the decision today to follow the new commandment...as a new creation living under the new covenant.

We close with these thoughts:

> *When I am dying, how glad I shall be,*
> *That the lamp of my life has been blazed out for*
> *Thee.*
> *I shall not mind in whatever I gain,*
> *Labor or money, some sinner to save!*
> *I shall not mind that the way has been rough,*
> *That Thy dear feet led the way was enough.*[5]

Let us make our lives count. Some of us who have made the poorest start could, by the grace of God, make the best finish.

Lord, make our lives to be a good Love story—the story of Your grace—that will be worth telling and well worth reading. Through Jesus we pray, amen.

Grow in the grace and knowledge of our Lord and Savior Jesus Christ. To Him be the glory, both now and to the day of eternity. Amen (2 Peter 3:18).

He who testifies to these things says, "Yes, I am coming quickly." Amen. Come, Lord Jesus. The grace of the Lord Jesus be with all. Amen (Revelation 22:20-21).

ABOUT THE SURVEY "CHRISTIAN BELIEFS ABOUT SPIRITUAL LIFE AND THE CHURCH"

During this Barna OmniPoll[SM] phone survey, two levels of screening the respondents were used. The first level of screening identified those who considered themselves to be Christian and who said that a Christian denomination was the type of church they attended most often. Those who identified themselves as atheist, agnostic, Hindu, Muslim, Buddhist, Jewish and so on, and those who had no church, were ineligible to participate.

The second level of screening was to determine the frequency with which respondents attended church. Only those who said they had attended a church for worship services during the past month were eligible. As a result of the screening process, the base of respondents included 529 Christian churchgoers. The sampling error for OmniPoll is plus or minus three percentage points at a 95 percent confidence level.

Our segment (529 respondents) was a portion of the total OmniPoll, which included 1007 telephone interviews conducted among a representative sample of adults (those over age 18) within the 48 continental states of the U.S.

To ensure the greatest likelihood of actually making contact, those individuals who qualified for inclusion in the survey were called at various times of the day and night over

a period of at least five days. (This is a quality-control procedure that ensures that each individual in the sampling frame
has an equivalent probability of inclusion within the survey,
thereby increasing the survey reliability.)

All the interviews were conducted by experienced, trained
interviewers; the interviewers were supervised at all times;
and every interviewer was monitored using the Silent Mon-
itoring™ system employed by the Barna Research Group
(BRG) .

The survey was conducted using the CATI (Computer
Assisted Telephone Interviewing) system in place at the BRG
field center. This process ensures that the sequence of questions
is randomized and that survey data are recorded accurately.

Based upon U.S. Census data sources, regional and ethnic
quotas were designed to ensure that the final group of adults
interviewed reflected the distribution of adults nationwide
and adequately represented the three primary ethnic groups
within the U.S. (white, black, and Hispanic). The final survey
data were balanced according to gender.

NOTES

From Rules to Relationship
1. All information regarding the Andersonville National Historic Site was obtained during Rich Miller's personal visit.
2. Philip Yancey, *Soul Survivor* (New York: Doubleday, 2001), p. 1.
3. Yancey, pp. 4, 5.
4. Yancey, pp. 7-8.

Chapter 1—The Law Kills
1. Donald Kaufman, *The Dictionary of Religious Terms;* as cited in Greg Killian, "Legalism" (www.TCKillian.com/greg/legalism.HTML; accessed 8/29/02).
2. Charles R. Swindoll, *Grace Awakening* (Dallas, TX: Word Publishers, 1990), p. 81.
3. George Barna, *The State of the Church 2002* (Ventura, CA: Issachar Resources, 2002), p. 77.
4. Barna, p. 13.
5. Barna, p. 81.
6. Kevin A. Miller, "I Don't Feel Like a Very Good Christian," *Discipleship Journal,* Issue 47, 1988, p. 6.
7. Miller, p. 6.
8. Daniel Taylor, *The Myth of Certainty* (Downers Grove, IL: InterVarsity Press, 1992), p. 35.

Chapter 2—In the Grip of Guilt
1. Brennan Manning, *The Ragamuffin Gospel* (Sisters, OR: Multnomah Publishers, 2000), p. 18.

2. John MacArthur, *The Vanishing Conscience* (Dallas, TX: Word Publishers, 1994), p. 32.

3. Bruce Narramore and Bill Counts, *Guilt and Freedom* (Santa Ana, CA: Vision House Publishers, 1974), p. 34.

4. James Strong, *Strong's Exhaustive Concordance of the Bible,* "Greek Dictionary of the New Testament" (McLean, VA: MacDonald Publishing Company, nda), p. 29.

5. David Seamands, *Redeeming the Past* (Colorado Springs, CO: Victor, 2002), pp. 44-45. Emphasis is author's.

6. *Matthew Henry's Commentary on the Whole Bible,* vol. 6, "Acts to Revelation" (Old Tappan, NJ: Fleming H. Revell Company), p. 561.

7. Pat Springle, *Codependency* (Houston, TX: Rapha Publishing, 1989), p. 90.

Chapter 3—It's a Shame

1. Sandra Wilson, *Released from Shame* (Downers Grove, IL: InterVarsity Press, 1990), p. 10.

2. J.I. Rodale, *The Synonym Finder* (Emmaus, PA: Rodale Press, 1978), p. 1099.

3. Brennan Manning, *The Ragamuffin Gospel* (Sisters, OR: Multnomah Publishers, 2000), pp. 40-41.

4. Bipasha Ray, "Cardinal Law acknowledges 'terrible evil' of sexual abuse," *Asheville* (North Carolina) *Citizen-Times,* November 4, 2002, p. A7.

5. Manning, pp. 66-67. Excerpted from *The Ragamuffin Gospel* © 1990, 2000 by Brennan Manning. Used by permission of Multnomah Publishers, Inc.

Chapter 4—Fueling Fear

1. Author unknown.

2. For a comprehensive treatment of the subject of fear, including the fear of failure, see *Freedom from Fear* by Neil Anderson and Rich Miller (Harvest House Publishers, 1999).

3. Richard Walters, *Escape the Trap* (Grand Rapids, MI: Zondervan Publishing House, 1989), pp. 8-9.

4. "Perfectionism," *Gale Encyclopedia of Psychology* (as obtained through <www.findarticles.com>).

5. Les Parrott III, *The Control Freak* (Wheaton, IL: Tyndale House Publishers, 2000), p. 48.

6. Diana Loomans, "If I Had My Child To Raise All Over Again," from the book *100 Ways to Build Self-Esteem and Teach Values* (Tiburon, CA: HJ Kramer, Inc., 2003). © 1994, 2003 by Diana Loomans. Reprinted with permission of HJ Kramer/New World Library, Novato, CA, www.newworldlibrary.com.

Chapter 5—The Power of Pride
1. Adapted from Neil T. Anderson and Rich Miller, *Awesome God* (Eugene, OR: Harvest House Publishers, 1996), pp. 121-124.
2. Warren Wiersbe, *Real Worship* (Grand Rapids, MI: Baker Books, 2000), pp. 187-189.
3. Greg Morris, "Why Waddle When You Can Fly!" *Leadership Dynamics* e-mail newsletter (<www.leadershipdynamics@lb.bcentral.com>).
4. Morris.
5. A.W. Tozer, *Paths to Power;* as cited on the Web site of Christian Publications, Inc. (<www.christianpublications.com>).
6. Henri Nouwen, *The Return of the Prodigal Son* (New York: Doubleday, 1994), p. 71.

Chapter 6—Enemies of Freedom
1. As cited on cover of Cheryl Forbes, *The Religion of Power* (Grand Rapids, MI: Zondervan Publishing House, 1983).
2. Forbes, pp. 20-21.
3. Adam Clarke, *Clarke's Commentary,* vol. 5, "Matthew–Acts" (New York: Lane & Scott, 1850), p. 218. Emphasis in original.
4. David Johnson and Jeff VanVonderen, *The Subtle Power of Spiritual Abuse* (Minneapolis, MN: Bethany House Publishers, 1991), p. 117.
5. Forbes, p. 18.
6. Johnson and VanVonderen, p. 141.
7. Johnson and VanVonderen, pp. 141-142.
8. Richard Quebedeaux, *By What Authority?*; as cited in Forbes, p. 61.
9. Warren Wiersbe, *Be Loyal* (Wheaton, IL: Victor Books, 1986), p. 76.

Chapter 7—Grace to You!
1. Neil T. Anderson, "Living Under Grace" study help from *The Freedom in Christ Bible* (Grand Rapids, MI: Zondervan, 2002), p. 1286.
2. Sam Storms, *Pleasures Evermore* (Colorado Springs, CO: NavPress, 2000), p. 104.
3. Storms, p. 105. Emphasis in original.
4. Storms, p. 106.
5. Philip Yancey, *Soul Survivor* (New York: Doubleday, 2001), p. 55.

Chapter 8—The New You
1. John Eldredge, *The Journey of Desire* (Nashville, TN: Thomas Nelson Publishers, 2000), p. 37.

2. Brent Curtis and John Eldredge, *The Sacred Romance* (Nashville, TN: Thomas Nelson Publishers, 1997), pp. 96-97.

3. David Seamands, *Healing Your Heart of Painful Emotions* (Edison, NJ: Arrowhead Press, 1993), pp. 395-396.

Chapter 9—Living Like Jesus

1. Steve McVey, *Grace Walk* (Eugene, OR: Harvest House Publishers, 1995), p. 140-144.

2. Pauline Lamarre, "Asking for Guidance," as found on Christian Women Today Web site (<http://archive.christianwomentoday.com/reflection/guidance.html>). Despite their best efforts, the authors were unable to locate the copyright holder of this material.

Chapter 10—Bittersweet Pain

1. John Piper, *A Hunger for God* (Wheaton, IL: Crossway Books, 1997), p. 14.

2. Richard C. Halverson, "The Strength of Brokenness," *Perspective* newsletter, date unknown. Despite their best efforts, the authors were unable to locate the copyright holder of this material.

3. Excerpted from John Collinson, *Brokenness* (Regina, Saskatchewan: Canadian Revival Fellowship, nd). Italics in original. Used by permission.

4. Mark Gersmehl, "Breakdown," from the album *Awakening*. Words and Music by Mark Gersmehl. Copyright © 2002 Hill Spring Music. All rights controlled by Gaither Copyright Management. Used by permission.

Chapter 11—Breaking the Chains

1. M. Scott Peck, *The Road Less Traveled and Beyond* (New York: Touchstone, 1997), pp. 24,31-32.

Chapter 12—New-Kingdom Living

1. Taken from Nena Benigno, "Sharing the Freedom of Forgiveness," *People Reaching People* (a publication of Philippine Campus Crusade for Christ), September 1992, pp. 1,7. Used by permission.

2. Benigno, pp. 7, 9.

3. John Piper, *Desiring God* (Sisters, OR: Multnomah Books, 1996), pp. 248, 249.

4. Eugene Peterson, *The Message: The New Testament, Psalms and Proverbs* (Colorado Springs, CO: NavPress, 1995), p. 46.

5. Author unknown.